HAY HOUSE TITLES OF RELATED INTEREST

The Alchemist's Journey: An Old System for a New Age,
by Glennie Kindred

American Indian Prophecies: Conversations with Chasing Deer,
by Kurt Kaltreider, Ph.D.

*Animal Spirit Guides: An Easy-to-Use Handbook for Identifying and
Understanding Your Power Animals and Animal Spirit Helpers,*
by Steven D. Farmer, Ph.D.

The Divine Matrix: Bridging Time, Space, Miracles, and Belief,
by Gregg Braden

The Four Insights: Wisdom, Power, and Grace of the Earthkeepers,
by Alberto Villoldo, Ph.D.

7 Paths to God: The Ways of the Mystic, by Joan Borysenko, Ph.D.

Sixth Sense: Including the Secrets of the Etheric Subtle Body,
by Stuart Wilde

Visionseeker: Shared Wisdom from the Place of Refuge,
by Hank Wesselman, Ph.D.

OOO

All of the above are available at your local bookstore,
or may be ordered by visiting:

Hay House USA: **www.hayhouse.com®**
Hay House Australia: **www.hayhouse.com.au**
Hay House UK: **www.hayhouse.co.uk**
Hay House South Africa: **orders@psdprom.co.za**
Hay House India: **www.hayhouseindia.co.in**

SOUL ON FIRE

A TRANSFORMATIONAL JOURNEY FROM PRIEST TO SHAMAN

PETER CALHOUN

HAY HOUSE, INC.
Carlsbad, California
London • Sydney • Johannesburg
Vancouver • Hong Kong • New Delhi

Library of Congress Control Number: 2006932922

ISBN: 978-1-4019-1748-7

10 09 08 07   4 3 2 1
1st edition, June 2007

Printed in the United States of America

AUTHOR'S NOTE

While still a priest in the Episcopal Church, I embarked on a singular "quest." It was that archetypal "journey" against which everything in one's life is measured and by which everything becomes defined. I had a vision of what was possible and subsequently followed and lived it to the best of my ability. In following this vision, I came to challenge the existing paradigms of our time: those which the spokespeople of our religious and scientific communities so zealously defend, the current "consensus reality" of our world. In the end, after considerable struggle, I not only sought, but found, that Truth which sets one free.

OOO

Jesus said of the miracles that he performed,
"The works that I do shall ye do also;
and greater works than these shall ye do."[1]

I dedicate this book to
Astrid Ganz,
my earthly partner and twin flame.

No matter how many people you touch with your joy,
laughter, and healing hands, no one will ever be touched
more deeply than I. With all the miracles in my life, none
can compare with how you stepped out of my dreamtime
into my waking life to love and restore me.

CONTENTS

PRACTICAL GUIDELINES

INTRODUCTION

This book is a collection of stories that reflects more than three decades of my personal journey as a priest turned modern shaman. These titles reflect the changing moods, struggles, surprises, challenges, and multiple lessons that have accompanied my journey. They reflect the relinquishing of the belief system that I inherited from my culture and a 180-degree shift in my perspective of the world around me.

I am one of those many people today who was raised in a secular culture that for centuries deliberately destroyed all records of an ancient and timeless wisdom. Like many of my peers, I found that the societal offerings of our time failed to satisfy the deeper longings of my spirit.

As with many of my fellow seekers, I have been forced to rediscover, on my own, the priceless knowledge that should have been my birthright. My quest has often been met with raised eyebrows, ridicule, rejection, and even hostility—as so many before me have experienced. During the centuries of heresy trials, witch burnings, and inquisitions, we killed off all of our women and men of knowledge. These people were the wise ones, the shamans of their time, the village midwives and healers, herbalists and alchemists, that made up the lineages through which this wisdom had been passed down since the earliest times.

This assault on knowledge was not limited to people. Priceless records were destroyed with the burning and sacking of the places where these records were kept such as the great Library of Alexandria (Egypt) and the destruction of the Popol Vuh tablets of the ancient Mayans by the Jesuits. Such atrocities were tantamount to intellectual and spiritual genocide of an entire people. The price we as a civilization have paid for this is so enormous, that it can probably never be measured.

In time, I had to leave the church to find out what it had lost. Most people leave their vocation out of disenchantment or failure, but I was supremely happy in the life of service that I had chosen and was moving toward the peak of my power when I chose to leave the priesthood. When I finally discovered what was lost, I realized that it was not that any of the religions (including my own) were so wrong, but that they were incomplete. They were never meant to be ends in themselves, but rather, important stepping-stones into a larger ocean, unbounded and unfettered by belief systems and traditions. I saw that no matter what path we take, each one of us, in the end, must transcend all religions and belief systems.

I do not believe that any one religion or system of knowledge is superior to another, nor do I think that shamanism is better than Christianity. In its pure and undiluted form, the teachings of Christ are as high an expression of truth as has ever appeared in the world. But the teachings were tampered with very early on by the politicians of the Church of Rome who were manipulating the church councils.[2] The accounts of the life and teachings of Christ were edited over and over again by those in power to reflect their own special agendas.

My vows as a priest to uphold the doctrines of the church were superseded by my soul's mission to seek the truth. On this search, I discovered an ancient body of knowledge, sacred truths, that do not require the endorsement of a particular belief system and are provable, workable, and easily demonstrated in anyone's life—as described in the stories throughout this book.

○○○

A little more than three decades ago I began experiencing a spontaneous awakening of spiritual or paranormal abilities that I had always believed, if they actually existed, were exclusively reserved for native shamans or Eastern mystics. As a parish priest in the Episcopal Church, I was in no way prepared for what was happening to me. In fact, these bizarre changes had an unsettling effect on me, and I wondered if I were losing my grip on reality.

When people came into my office for counseling, I knew in advance what their problems were. I could even sense specific things about the lives of total strangers. I began anticipating people's statements and soon realized that I could read thoughts. All of these changes in me were but the tip of the iceberg. In the following years, I discovered that I could understand the thoughts of animals and plant spirits, and I was even able to communicate with and influence the elemental forces themselves.

During my initial period of awakening, I had a series of visions of what I was told were the probable futures of Earth and our human species. I realized that if these visions were accurate prophecies, then most people, including myself as a priest, were dealing with the wrong issues. I was told that we, as a species, were being poor caregivers of Earth, and that if such abuse and neglect continued, we would soon reap a bitter harvest. The implications were that our time is rapidly running out.

It was the awakening described above, combined with these disquieting visions, that caused me to make the reluctant decision to leave the parish ministry of the church at a time when I was moving toward the peak of my career to begin a personal quest that continues to this day. *Soul on Fire* is an account of actual experiences that reflect this quest. Each story I selected to share was chosen because it contains specific lessons that were important to me when they occurred and because the lessons also have a universal application.

During my quest, I began to realize that something even more profound than the awakening of latent powers or the learning of valuable life lessons was happening to me. Unknowingly, I had, all along, been on a path toward conscious and ecstatic union with

All That Is. I was told that it is the very path that we as a species have lost and must rediscover if we are to have any assurance of survival.

○○○

This path, the transformational journey, is the ultimate adventure. It is the singular quest by which one's entire life becomes defined. It surpasses in richness, depth, diversity, and drama any fictional account that could ever be concocted. It is a leap into the Unknown. It is the "path less traveled"—at once both the "fool's journey" and the "hero's journey." One is a fool in the eyes of the world to risk all for the pursuit of a vision. One is the hero in going forth on one's journey even in the face of adversarial, archetypal forces that threaten one's very being.

As will be apparent in the pages that follow, this journey can be heartwarming and heartwrenching, humorous and yet deeply serious. It can be profoundly challenging with confusion and fear as one's constant companions. There are bizarre moments, impossible scenarios, and absolutely ludicrous situations in which laughter becomes powerful medicine. The ability to poke fun at oneself and accepting one's humanness is a necessary protocol. There are times of discovery and breakthroughs; times when after much struggle doors open that one never knew existed. Then there are those "satoris" or portals that give one glimpses into the larger world beyond our own.

The journey brings epiphanies that leave us speechless with awe, after which we are never the same. As described in some of the stories in this book, there are times of great danger, life-threatening situations that challenge and test us to the very core. The transformational journey is not for cowards or the faint of heart. The least that can be said is that the transformational journey is not boring. Since embarking on my journey, I truly cannot remember a single day or even an hour of being bored.

Sometimes, during the periods in life when we are overwhelmed by the sheer magnitude of our challenges, we can only go forth on courage with trust in an inner radar to guide us through the fog. To choose the path of spiritual initiation is to walk the razor's edge. It is the sword of Damocles that always hangs over us by a thread. We cannot embark on the journey with a full cup. When our cup is full of expectations, agendas, or overflowing with self-importance, there is no room for anything new. It is best to take as little baggage as possible with us on our journey.

ooo

Years ago I was taken out of my body one evening and shown a book that I would someday write. I listened with rapt attention while a voice narrated experiences that had not yet come to pass, some of which, at the time, seemed unbelievable. The book was about the adventures, epiphanies, and challenges on my spiritual journey. It also included certain rites of passage that I would someday go through. It seemingly was to serve as an inspiration and guide for people embarking on their spiritual journey, as well as for those already committed to it. Amazingly, there were even sketches and photographs, along with captions on some of the pages depicting my journey. I was shown that in this life I would not have a teacher as such, but instead it would be my task to remember all that I had been in previous embodiments. As a Western teacher, I was to demonstrate many of the "siddhis" or spiritual powers as abilities that are latent in all people.

In the years that followed, knowing that I would someday write about my journey, I attempted to keep a journal. At first I balked at this practice, as I had neither the discipline nor the inclination of a journalist. On the other hand, as others have pointed out, I seemed to have an almost photographic memory for the events that unfolded on my journey. I can recall exact conversations as well as details of various landscapes.

I knew from the beginning, therefore, that the book would be presented as a collection of experiences and epiphanies, each of which would have its own special lessons or revelations. The archetype of the storyteller was beginning to emerge from the collective unconsciousness, and I recognized that storytelling would be the most powerful vehicle to convey the experiences related in these pages.

But there was another reason I felt that the book should be a collection of stories. This feeling was based on something that was once said to me years ago while I was still a student at the Virginia Theological Seminary in Alexandria. Some fellow students and I were sitting at the dinner table with an old Japanese priest who was a visiting lecturer. At one point he turned to me and said, "The reason that you westerners have had so much difficulty communicating the Gospel to those of us in the East is that you've all but lost the art of storytelling." I can still remember the impact those words had on me. It was as if the old priest sensed what I would someday have to do. I have never forgotten his words. Today, as in other ages, storytelling remains the most powerful and effective way to communicate the eternal truths.

ooo

Since the stories that follow reflect my spiritual journey, it might seem logical to arrange them chronologically. However, because consciousness, like the quantum universe itself, is expanding outwardly in all directions, I felt that to write a linear, time-based book would be limiting.

Instead, the stories of *Soul on Fire* are both topically and energetically arranged. Experiences can be energetically linked across time and space. For example, one experience that occurred in 1982 in the Teton Mountains of Wyoming can be energetically related to an experience that occurred ten years later across the country in the Great Smoky Mountains in Tennessee.

Soul on Fire reflects a wide array of experiences that occurred over several years and in a variety of places. Many of these experiences took place in some of the most awe-inspiring, natural settings on our continent, while others occurred in heavily populated, bustling urban areas. The stories in this first of two books span more than three decades of my life, including two partnerships, my daughter, and two sets of stepchildren, as well as residences in Atlanta, Taos, Santa Fe, Boulder, the North Carolina Blue Ridge Mountains, and, currently, the foothills of the Great Smoky Mountains of East Tennessee.

After four years of working on this manuscript, I was surprised that I had chronicled enough experiences for two volumes, and still a number of them remained untold. The stories in this first volume include most of my early experiences in the different areas of the spiritual landscape I traversed much of my adult life. The choices were obvious for me because nothing compares with the childlike wonder and elation I felt when those initial experiences began revealing to me a world that was more vast, awesome, and magical than the consensus worldview into which I had been born.

During the last four decades, I have worn many hats: that of priest, teacher, healer, seer, counselor, and writer. Yet, unbeknownst to me at first, I had actually been traveling the path of the ancient shaman and experiencing an awakening of knowledge and spiritual powers reminiscent of those mythic figures of antiquity.

Shamanism is not another religion or system of belief; it is a way of perceiving and relating to the wondrous world around us. It is the original source out of which all the religions and systems of knowledge evolved. I awoke to a way of knowledge and power that is rooted in the remote past.

Not everyone is cut out to be a shaman. In most traditions it is believed that one is born into this calling. Yet these timeless truths are applicable to all people of any culture or age. The knowledge of this ancient system can complement and enhance all paths, both ancient and contemporary. This body of knowledge, however, must be redefined and restated in every age and served in the vessels of the existing culture.

There is nothing more mainstream and Eurocentric than my background—an Episcopal priest born into an established, well-known, Caucasian Atlanta family. It would seem that I am the most unlikely person to write a book of this type. Yet, just the opposite may be true, because a world that is in danger of committing ecocide and torn by division of every kind needs voices that can address the mainstream culture and a methodology that can heal our separation from Earth and from life around us.

Today the archetype of the shaman is emerging out of the shadowy past and from the murky depths of the collective unconscious into the clear light of conscious awareness. Shamanism is the most Earth-friendly system in existence and, therefore, it may be the most relevant path for our age. It is by far the most practical since it evolved out of the survival needs of our species from its earliest times. It may once again hold the keys to our survival as a species.

It is my fervent hope that you, the reader, will not only find wisdom in these stories, but also will enjoy them simply as a "good read."

— **Peter Calhoun**

❁ ❁ ✺ ❁ ❁

CHAPTER 1
SACRED WILDERNESS JOURNEYS

*O*ver the years I have made numerous personal treks into wilderness areas as well as having accompanied groups of adults and young people on vision quests and other sacred wilderness journeys.

A vision quest is an ancient rite of passage that finds its expression in many cultures throughout the world. Vision quests have been practiced by the native peoples of the Americas for thousands of years, and today, modern seekers of many different spiritual traditions engage in them.

A vision quest is a time for a person seeking direction in his or her life to withdraw from the routines and pressures of modern living into the solitude and silence of the wilderness. It is also a symbolic journey into the wilderness of the mind and spirit. Direction usually comes in the form of visions, powerful synchronicities, *lucid dreams, spontaneous revelations, and/or magical experiences with the natural world.*

I have led hundreds of seekers on vision quests and other sacred wilderness journeys. In my opinion, it is the single most transformative experience a person can have. I have witnessed numerous lives, including my own, changed as a result. In contrast to workshop "highs" that all too often wear off with the passage of time, a vision quest always seems to effect permanent changes in a person's life.

OOO

FIRE IN THE DESERT

Canyonlands Base Camp, Utah:
Late April and Early September
(15 years after my farewell sermon)

As I was crossing the Rockies from Boulder to central Utah, the contrast of warm sunshine and the newly fallen snow from a late spring storm had rejuvenated my spirits. I turned off Interstate 70 onto Utah State Road 191 and viewed the awe-inspiring red-rock formations for which Arches and Canyonlands National Parks are known. I knew that I had come home again.

For me, those canyons were like nowhere else on Earth. The huge rock formations felt alive, their presence pervading the landscape. It seemed to me that anyone who had spent time in the interior of this region could not help but be changed in some profound way.

Soon we were making the final leg of the journey to our base camp. The last seven miles took us down a rough forest service road, which included a creek crossing that challenged even our four-wheel-drive vehicle because the creek's banks were flooded with snow runoff.

At last we arrived and the trip was well worth it. A huge stand of old-growth cottonwoods lined both sides of a stream that flowed through a wide canyon of towering rock walls. By the time we had unloaded and set up camp, we were exhausted, and the late April sun was already beginning to set over the western rim of the canyon.

That night we gathered with our travel-weary students around

3

a council fire for introductions and an orientation. Most of the students had already been apprenticing with my former partner Marilynn and me for a year or more. They were all in this program for the long haul, and I had become quite attached to many of them.

After retiring for the evening, I remained awake under the bright moon for some time. Night holds its own counsel in these canyons. The interrogatory call of the owl was soon answered by the haunting soprano voices of a family of coyotes.

Before falling asleep, my thoughts turned to the many shared experiences we have had with our groups in these wilderness areas. Like Elijah and Moses, Jesus Christ, John the Baptist, and St. Francis, we had journeyed into the pristine wilderness. What happened on our wilderness journeys was not an educational program, because spiritual knowledge can never be taught. It must be experienced. Instead it had been a dance that was at once exquisite, healing, empowering, and self-validating.

For some there was an incomprehensible yet transformative encounter with the Unknown. We each brought to the group our own special energy that, when combined, created greater possibilities for personal transformation than our individual abilities alone. Each of us, in our own way, had been seeking to understand the Great Mystery.

The majority of us had come from urban areas around the country and had, until recently, little experience of the wilderness. How different it all was out in the midst of such vastness, remoteness, and deep silence, in this place defined by the steep sandstone walls of the broad red-rock canyon, towering over us like gigantic ramparts.

It is our condition as humans in this modern world to be caught in the tangled webs of self-absorption, trivia, and distractions. But out here, it was different. No one seemed preoccupied with personal agendas. There was a pervading consciousness of being a part of something greater than ourselves, greater even than the summation of what we were. Our spirits needed this as much as our bodies required food and drink. We needed endeavors that would take us out of ourselves and beyond the vicissitudes of our mundane lives.

Grandmother Moon had almost completed her nightly journey across the sky when I slipped into dreamless sleep. The next morning, following a sunrise meditation, we began preparing an area for a sweat-lodge ceremony to be held that evening. This traditional native ceremony of purification involved the release of not only our physical toxins, but also the mental and emotional pollution that we all brought with us as an inevitable result of the impact of daily life in the modern world. Through this ceremony, we would be more open and receptive to the higher spiritual energies that we were seeking in this wilderness retreat. In addition, each of us had our own methods of individual preparation.

For our fire, we dug a shallow pit in the sandy desert floor and carefully laid a number of sticks within it, pyramid-style, in alignment with the Four Sacred Directions. As with all of our ceremonial fires, we used no paper or chemicals. I felt the calming effect this preparation had on us. It provided the spiritual foundation for our sacred ceremony that would follow in the evening. This inner silence was an essential prelude to what would happen next.

In my wildest fantasy I could not have anticipated the sequence of events that followed. It was dreamlike. I remember my gaze being drawn to a certain spot on the pyramid of sticks that were carefully placed in correct alignment with the Four Directions by our fire-builders, Mark and Lynn. I was aware of the piercing whistle of a red-tail hawk soaring somewhere over the western rim of the canyon. Perhaps my ally was alerting me to what was about to unfold. There was no other warning! Other than the hawk's cry, there were no signs, synchronicities, or premonitions to alert us. One moment we were in that ordinary time and space. The next moment we were in that magical time in which the normal laws of our third-dimensional world no longer apply.

Suddenly, without even a trace of smoke as a warning, the sticks we had just laid for our fire mysteriously burst into flames. We looked on in disbelief. I realized at that moment that since arriving at our base camp I'd been expecting something to happen, yet I never could have envisioned this. Before us, reality had been stretched, bent, and folded onto itself to precipitate an inconceivable spontaneous combustion. The awesome mystery silenced us all. Time stood still.

A hush fell upon all of us as we gathered before the fire. The sky had become pink and gold, and the late morning sun illuminated the pastel colors of the upper canyon walls. The ineffable splendor of the brightly burning fire against the desert landscape shifted me into heightened consciousness.

Then the Inner Voice that often accompanied my visions said, "There is a spiritual force within all fire, and this is what has been spoken of as the elemental force of fire. As a group, you have inadvertently entered a state of magical consciousness and in the power of that awareness you have brought forth the element fire itself." For a brief span on the desert, we had altered the very fabric of reality. It was truly a sacred moment.

I was told that this sacred fire burns within each one of us as well. It is the very same fire that is found within the stars themselves. When this fire within is activated, then we, ourselves, burn like miniature supernovas. In the scriptures, fire is frequently associated with the manifestation of a deity. Moses heard the voice of God in the burning bush, and the children of Israel followed a "cloud by day" and a "fire by night"[3] in their wilderness wanderings. Elijah was taken up in a fiery wheel. The Holy Spirit descended on the disciples gathered in the upper room on the day of Pentecost as the "rushing of a mighty wind" and in "tongues as of fire."[4]

Similarly in Christian mysticism, fire is experienced as a manifestation of divinity. Blaise Pascal described his encounter with divine fire in this ecstatic utterance: "Fire! God of Abraham, God of Isaac, God of Jacob. Not the god of the philosophers and scholars. Absolute certainty! . . . Joy! Joy! Joy! Tears of Joy!"[5]

The inner guidance I received, however, only served to deepen the mystery for me, because what had just been shared among us in the desert was beyond syntax and could not truly be explained. From a traditional religious point of view, what happened to us was miraculous. But miracles are not an intervention in the divine order, but a calling into play of laws beyond our present understanding. It has been said that the miracles of today are the science of tomorrow. An automobile, a television, even the lighting of a match would have been a miracle to those of Jesus's time.

The story of our experience with the sacred fire did not end there. If that had been the case, perhaps it could have been passed off as an anomaly of nature, or even one of those random events in a universe of infinite possibilities about which quantum theorists love to postulate. Fast-forward just over three years, to early fall, and this time we were with a new group of people in the same location.

On the second day of our gathering, while I was teaching I was struck with the realization that I could manifest fire once again with conscious intent. I shared the story of our experience three years earlier. Our ceremonial fire for a Native American sweat lodge had been laid on the sandy desert floor waiting to be lit the next day, and I stated my intent.

The following afternoon, as our large group of vision questers waited for the tender to light the fire, it happened again. Suddenly and mysteriously the sticks ignited! This time, unlike the episode three years ago, I had set my intent in the presence of our vision questers. I'd had the audacity to ask my teachers from the spiritual realms to honor us with another spontaneous combustion. Not only had the wondrous fire elementals responded to my petition, but they also simultaneously honored us with a second and third combustion in two separate piles of wood that were resting 20 feet away. Amazingly, not a trace of smoke alerted us—just unexpectedly, out of nowhere . . . *fire!*

No one uttered a word. We simply gazed awestruck at the three rapidly growing flames. I could sense the mounting elation in the hearts of those around me. It was an ecstatic moment! It was another *epiphany!*

ooo

Years ago while still a priest in the Episcopal Church, I had concurred with the general consensus that the age of miracles was over. I could no longer say that now. I had witnessed too many inexplicable things. Jesus said of the miracles that he performed, "The works that I do shall ye do also; and greater works than these shall ye do."[6] This is an enormous statement! I wonder why we have not claimed this promise after 2,000 years. My great audacity is that I took the words of Christ seriously and dared to lay claim to his promise!

In contrast, biblical scholars and theologians have warned us that such claims are blasphemous. Unfortunately, these people are no more than modern-day "pharasees." If our religious spokespersons have taken the position of blasphemy, then the scientific community has disempowered us just as much by maintaining that they are scientifically impossible. It is time we began questioning these negative and limiting ideas. We need to realize how much we have given up our power to these cherished belief systems and institutions.

In my journey into the vast reaches of cross-cultural shamanism, I had begun to feel like a bloodhound on a strong scent. I felt that I was hot on the trail of something of enormous proportions. I realized that this trail was leading me not only to the amazing answers to my questions, but also into a whole new world about which I had only dared to dream. My questions and my quest had become one and the same. I discovered that many of these abilities that Christ said were inherent in each of us have always been recognized and described in story and myth and demonstrated by the holy men and holy women of various tribal traditions.

Sadly, most of the accounts from our European traditions describing these abilities were purged from our records and collective memory beginning with the politically motivated church councils and continuing through the long centuries of persecutions, inquisitions, and heresy trials. I think we are justified to react to these revelations with enormous righteous indignation accompanied by an ardent desire to rectify the mistakes of the past. I have discovered that this "lost" knowledge can be rediscovered by anyone who is willing to search.

Organized religion has produced followers who often have great zeal, but who remain spiritual adolescents, because of having bought into an artificial belief system. It is time that we begin questioning the consensus view of our world, which organized religion and empirical science have defended with such fervor. Such questioning is a key to the liberation and empowerment of our spirits.

I'd had to leave the church to discover what the church has lost. I was saddened that such priceless treasures had been lost through man's arrogance and ignorance. Within Christianity is the "pearl of great price," but it has been all but concealed by the trappings of ritual observance and correct creed of dogmas and definition. I wanted to say to my sisters and brothers in the churches, and other forms of organized institutional religion, that miracles are alive and well today. That which has been lost can be recovered. For all that I had witnessed, all that I had experienced since making my leap of faith, only bore witness to the literal truths behind the miracles recorded in the sacred scriptures of all faiths.

As I gazed into the flames of the fire that had miraculously started, I thought of a verse from the Hindu scripture, *Sh'vet Upanishad*, II,17:

To the God Who is in the fire and in the waters,
To the God Who has suffused Himself through all the World
To the God Who is in summer plants and the lords of the forest,
To that God be adoration, adoration.

These episodes, among many others, have led me to believe that we live in a very magical world and that humans are by nature magical beings. Even with this growing realization, I was haunted by certain questions: If this were true, what happened to our magical nature? Where had it gone? And if a magical nature was something that is an essential part of each of us, why are so few people able to access it?

These questions had become central in my spiritual quest. In fact, answers about the elusive phenomenon of magical consciousness had become the Holy Grail I sought. I knew in my heart that until I discovered it, my quest would not end.

ooo

IN THE SHADOW OF THE TETONS

Wilderness Retreat, Gros Ventre Base Camp,
Western Wyoming: Mid-July

Late one afternoon my former partner, Marilynn, and I were approaching the east entrance of the Grand Teton National Park, home of the most photographed mountains in the world. Before the majestic mountains came into view, I sensed that something was wrong. It was as if the natural rhythm and flow of the land had been interrupted.

This was not the first time I'd had such an experience. Whenever I developed a spiritual link to a place, I'd not only been able to draw on the energies of the place, but also could always sense when something was amiss. I had learned to merge with the essence of these mountains. I knew the spirit of their lofty peaks, their changing moods and faces, their rocky canyons and verdant valleys.

Once, when I was alone with the Shoshone medicine man, Rolling Thunder, he said to me, "You must always know the spirits of a place." In the years that followed, I came to realize how valuable this advice from the old shaman was.

It was not until we had crossed a low pass and descended into the valley known as Jackson Hole, which stretched for ten miles to the base of the mountain range, that we suspected the cause.

The land was parched and dusty; the temperature unnaturally hot, even for midsummer. The usual lush green vegetation of mid-July was already as brown as one would expect it to be in early fall. Conspicuously missing were the endless fields of paintbrush, lupine, columbine, fireweed, geranium, and wild rose.

At the visitor's center for the Park, Marilynn and I learned that western Wyoming was in the throes of a drought that had begun in early spring. Since April, only a single thunderstorm had graced the area. For the last month, the drought had been compounded by a severe heat wave, with temperatures hovering in the 90s. I wished I could have just waved a magical wand to heal the area. Little did I know that that was exactly what would soon be asked of us.

We took take care of business in town as quickly as possible and then drove to a secluded area near the Gros Ventre River, which had been our base camp the last few summers. This base camp is special, known only to locals, and free of tourists. Our encampment was close to the river, near a spring-fed pond that provided fresh drinking water and a wonderful place to swim and bathe.

As soon as we had set up our camp, we were attacked by every known biting insect—ants, mosquitoes, deerflies, horseflies, and creatures we couldn't even begin to identify. I sensed that the extreme dryness and unnatural heat wave had brought about atypical aggression among these little ones. We did not know what, if anything, could be done. We were quite miserable, for even commercial repellents seemed to agitate the insects rather than repel them. It would be a long two weeks if nothing changed.

For the next two and a half days the assault continued without reprieve. Then on the afternoon of the third day, the last day before our students were to arrive, we received unexpected guidance. We were asked by the Spirit of the Land to go to a particular power place and, in the tradition of the ancient shamans, perform a ceremony for rain and cooler weather. We were told to conduct the ceremony in the late afternoon, which, in shamanic cultures, is the time of the West, the sacred direction for the healing rains. Never before had we attempted such a ceremony. Personally, I had my doubts. Yet, I had learned through the years not to question any kind of directive that comes from the spirit world.

Such practices have always been part of shamanic traditions

across cultures. However, our modern culture had no precedent for what we were about to attempt. Nevertheless we both felt a mandate to perform such a ceremony.

Weather reflects the mood of the Earth Spirit. Thunderstorms recharge the electromagnetic field, clearing the negativity from the subtle landscape. The reason people feel so good after a storm is that the earth has been cleansed, regenerated, and restored to its natural rhythms and cycles.

For several hours we made preparations for our ceremony. We gathered sage and sweetgrass to cleanse and burn as offerings. Our destination was an hour and a half away, and the final half-mile walk was along an eroded horse trail.

As we continued, I began to experience the usual quieting of the mind accompanied by subtle shifts in consciousness. This required no special techniques or extraordinary effort. The attitude as one prepares for a sacred ceremony is just as important as that of the ceremony itself. The preparation sets the stage, drawing one into heightened awareness in which one exists simultaneously in both ordinary and alternate realities. As this occurs, there is often the sense of being part of two worlds that are separate and yet interpenetrate each other.

In silence we completed the half-mile meandering trek through the pine forest, passing a small herd of mule deer that seemed more curious about us than afraid. Conversation at such times is always distracting and draining.

Finally, we entered a small meadow at the foot of a stream flowing off the Grand Teton. I could feel the natural magnetism of the place and knew it to be an ideal site for our ceremony.

As we stood in the shadow of the Grand Teton itself, the sun was about to set behind its peak. The mountain loomed over us, rising more than 13,000 feet above the forest floor. In spite of the current heat wave, patches of snow still lingered in the ever-shadowed depressions near the summit. Higher up, the stream appeared as a narrow silver thread bisecting the eastern slope that faced us. It made the sound of distant thunder in its descent from the alpine country far above. I could feel a tremendous confluence of power extending from the peak to the valley floor.

A mile to our north was a picturesque glacier lake. A hundred yards behind us lay a moose pond. To our south and east flowed the wild scenic Snake River, cutting its serpentine path through the broad valley. In front of us, in the west, were the Grand Tetons themselves.

It was the time of the west, the sacred direction for the great storm devas, the "Thunder Beings" of Native American tradition. I could feel an electric tension in the ethers as if some power was poised to come into being. The moment had come to unite with these powers of the angelic beings who work with the nature kingdoms and invoke their assistance.

Standing in the shadow of the mountain while facing west, we burned sage and sweetgrass, and made tobacco and cornmeal offerings to the storm devas, the spirit of the mountain, and to the One Infinite Spirit. With strong voices we stated our purpose while recommitting ourselves to the healing of Mother Earth and to the greater work of Creation. We called upon the powers responsible for the tenuous balance between earth and sky, expressing our concern for the current suffering of both plant and animal life, and for humans.

Last, we remained in silence for a few minutes. Just as we began to leave this sacred space we experienced such a noticeable atmospheric change that it stopped us in our tracks. A cool breeze had begun blowing down from the mountain. Within only minutes the temperature had dropped 15 degrees. Feeling a deep sense of gratitude, we departed, and reached our jeep at the trailhead minutes later.

The following morning we awoke to considerably cooler weather. We put on our wool sweaters as we crept out of our sleeping bags. At least the heat wave was gone.

Late that afternoon, after most of our group of apprentices arrived, the first thunderstorm rolled in with great fanfare over the western mountain peaks. We could feel the power of the storm, which had seemingly moved in from nowhere, as meteorologists had not predicted rain. We had little doubt that the rain would continue. Over the next nine days storms rolled in, usually in the afternoon. On the tenth and eleventh days, the earth received a soft, gentle rain. Our resilient Mother Earth had healed Herself.

An Encore in Idaho

When our ten-day wilderness retreat ended, Marilynn and I spent two days and two nights in our tent while the rains continued. Before we left, we performed a farewell ritual. We had hoped to have those two days for hiking, but as the saying goes, "You can't have your cake and eat it, too." Finally we packed up and made the six-hour drive to Sun Valley, Idaho, where we were scheduled to do seminars and consultations.

We learned that Idaho was still suffering from drought, having received none of the rains that fell on western Wyoming that week. This time there was no need for deliberation. We knew that we must perform another rain ceremony.

We asked Mark, one of our senior apprentices in town, to join us in the ceremony. We also asked that he bring a fourth person so that we would have each of the Four Directions represented. Mark asked a friend who taught yoga to join us; he felt that this teacher would be "tuned in" to what we wished to do.

When we came together the next morning, Mark led us to a secluded area in the adjoining national forest, where we sought spiritual intervention in the weather conditions. Once again it seemed as if we were carrying out a directive from the invisible world.

We awoke the following morning to another of what the Navajo call a "soft female rain" that continued throughout the day and following night. We learned later, to our amusement, that the yoga teacher had complained about the rainy weather because he had planned an outing with some friends.

When we saw the yoga teacher that afternoon, we reminded him about what we all had asked for in the ceremony. He seemed shocked at first. Did he really not believe the rain would come, or had he simply forgotten the ceremony he had participated in the day before? He began to smile and then quickly joined us in laughter.

OOO

BY THE RIVER OF NO RETURN

Vision Quest at Salmon River Base Camp, Idaho: Spring

For the last hour I had been navigating a narrow forest service road, which follows what is known as the North Fork of the Salmon River. The North Fork and Middle Fork are internationally renowned for their scenery and whitewater rafting. The remoteness of the rugged canyon, along with the warm sunshine and the lush new vegetation of early spring, took me away from my everyday concerns.

This was the first trip for Marilynn and me into the northern tip of Idaho, home of the largest wilderness area in the lower 48 states. Its popular name is the River of No Return, so named because once having entered at the base of the river, there is no way out apart from a dangerous journey through the wild waters of the canyon. A popular movie of the 1950s, named after the river, was made there. The scenic river flows through steep canyon walls, making frequent turns, and occasionally surging past hidden side canyons.

With no pressing agenda until the next day, when a group was to arrive for their first vision quest, the drive down the forest service road became an excellent "non-doing." At the point where one of the side canyons converged with the main canyon, we spotted a family of bighorn sheep, who blended in so closely with the canyon's rock walls that we could have easily missed them. The bighorns stood like frozen sculpture, eyeing us warily. I knew that even the least sign of aggressive intent would send them bolting back up the impossibly steep and narrow trail to the canyon rim.

Without speaking, we parked about a hundred feet away and began climbing out of our vehicle, being careful not to make any sudden movements. I felt a surge of adrenaline from being so close to them, knowing the reputation these wary creatures have for being unapproachable.

It was a half hour before dusk. We'd been told that we would have to pull ourselves across the river in an old mining cable cart to get to the homestead property that would serve as our base camp for a week. I certainly didn't relish doing this in the dark. Yet the sheep took precedence. On some mysterious primal level, I felt a powerful bond with these lovely creatures.

Once out of our jeep, as if by tacit consent, we dropped to our hands and knees. On all fours, we began imitating grazing animals and put the chatter of our conscious minds to rest in the hopes of being able to get closer to the sheep.

Through past experiences in the wilderness, I had concluded that our process of thinking contributes to the instinctive fear that wild animals have of us. Perhaps they see disturbing configurations in our surrounding light field or sense a distortion in our vibrations, or maybe our smell changes when our conscious mind is active. I knew that the surest way to frighten a wild animal was to have your mind racing.

What happened next unfolded as if in a dream. Inadvertently we had stepped into the shoes of those ancient shamans who had reputedly been able to accomplish prodigious feats of awareness that grew out of their intimate relationship with All of Creation. We approached the herd slowly and obliquely, being careful not to look directly at any animal. My breathing was shallow, and my heart seemed to skip a beat as we drew near.

I continued to remain in a state of quiet detachment, allowing my consciousness to expand outward, becoming an equal part of all things in the world surrounding me. Then, almost without realizing it, we had worked our way into the very midst of the herd.

It was not until later that I allowed myself the luxury of wondering if anyone had ever succeeded in approaching such wary and skittish creatures, getting so close as to be able to touch them or speak to them. I resisted the temptation to reach out and touch them, for they had demonstrated their trust in us, and I did not want to break it.

So empowering was this acceptance into the family of wild sheep, that I wondered if we could invite them to visit us at our base camp a few more miles up the forest service road. The idea was not as far-fetched as it seemed because animals are very telepathic, and we had already experienced success in this kind of communication.

In a soothing voice, I invited them to visit our group. As if these creatures understood human speech, my partner explained that we considered this encounter with their herd a sign that they were the designated allies for our group. An ally is a representative from the nature kingdom, a mammal or bird, for example, to which one has a natural affinity and energetic connection. An ally is a teacher for us in the reflection we see of ourselves in them, and they may even provide us with particular empowerment.

These bighorn sheep, which are capable of such sure-footedness and single-mindedness in their ascent to the mountaintops, would be appropriate symbols for those of us seeking to ascend spiritual heights. Their ability to traverse difficult passages and narrow, winding trails embodies many of the qualities so essential in the spiritual journey.

I was amazed that our human voices instilled no fear in the animals. However, since darkness was only minutes away, we reluctantly retreated back to the jeep, our hearts pounding rapidly. Amazingly, this whole endeavor had taken no more than 20 minutes. Yet, the encounter was utterly timeless. In some strange way, it felt like the most natural process in the world. It was as if the experience of being accepted into the herd of bighorn sheep and our communication with them was an intrinsic part of who I was.

The following day, the vision questers arrived: a curious cross-section of individuals who included a stockbroker, an investment counselor, director of a hospice, a waitress, an Olympic skier, a socialite who owned a classy boutique in a resort community, a physical therapist, a manager of a small-town retail store, and incognito, of course, a drug dealer from Florida (who turned out to be the most naturally gifted individual present). My gut-level feeling was that they were going to be an interesting group.

I could not imagine these same individuals coming together to share such intensely personal experiences in any other venture. It is common to draw from many classes, backgrounds, and vocations in all our wilderness retreats. This type of spiritual commitment cuts across all artificial divisions created by society.

Once everyone in our group had crossed the river in the old mining cable cart, no one in our group could leave on their own. If someone did leave without an assistant, the cart would be on the wrong side of the river for the rest of us. We were all in this together, and no one could bail out without leaving the rest of us stranded. The river itself was still icy from snow runoff and too swift and cold to swim in. I was certain that this precarious crossing over the water, and its finality, was going to help give us a sense of solidarity in the days ahead.

Although the vision quest itself is solitary, we spend three days together preparing for the experience. Through all that is shared and felt and experienced, the group bonds together, and a powerful group spirit emerges. This makes it possible for each person to conduct his or her personal sojourn alone, and yet to be connected to the consciousness of the whole, drawing strength and comfort from the many.

That night after base camp had been prepared, we gathered around a fire built on a sandy beach along the river. The water here made a low murmuring, speaking to us in muted tones that intermingled with occasional night sounds. The crescent moon, still low in the sky, illuminated portions of the shadowed cliffs of the canyon, reflecting off the river itself.

The setting acted as a calming agent for the many fears and anxieties everyone had brought with them to this experience. An undercurrent of excitement transcended our natural fatigue. I felt that this positive response boded well for the week ahead.

We opened the vision quest with the usual announcements about logistics, and introductory remarks on the nature and purpose of the quest. Everyone was given the opportunity to share something about him- or herself.

When my turn came, I shared our extraordinary experience of mingling with the bighorn sheep. A few laughed when I mentioned that we'd invited the wild sheep to join our group here on the homestead property. Even though most in the group believed I was joking, this magical encounter with the sheep captured the imagination of everyone, heightening our excitement and anticipation.

Fatigue, however, had set in with our group of weary travelers. We closed the council fire so that everyone could retire to their own pitched tents somewhere along the grassy meadow stretching between the river and the steep slope of the mountain.

I awoke at first light. Through the soft light of dawn I could see the early-morning mist rising off the river, drifting slowly across the meadow where we were camped. The plaintive calls of mourning doves hidden in the grass and sage were soon joined by the noisy ravens and western jays. A lone coyote called out for its mate from somewhere up the river. Soon the sun would strike the upper canyon walls, turning them brilliant gold and amber. Through the door of the tent I watched a pair of eagles riding the thermals above the canyon.

My reverie was broken by the sound of one of our students approaching our tent. I recognized the voice of Gail, the stockbroker from New York, who whispered that the wild sheep had crossed the river and had moved up to our homestead property. They were grazing under the cottonwoods by the river, unperturbed by our presence.

"I've read somewhere," she continued, "that these are such reclusive animals that few people ever see them, especially close-up. What on earth did you guys do? I want to know how to do this!"

Gail noted that there were 13 sheep in the herd which, with synchronicity, was the same as the total number of students and instructors in our group. It was as if they, as symbolic teachers and totem animals for our quest, had come to pay their respects and wish us well. The bighorn herd remained with us throughout the day, intermittently grazing and napping beneath the trees, unconcerned with our movements. We went about our way, respectful of their space. I sensed that they were as aware of us as we were of them and felt a powerful kinship.

The following sunrise revealed a slightly different landscape: Our visitors from the day before had moved on to other grazing sites. I sensed that after honoring our request, they would not return.

Epilogue

When our week together had ended and everyone had departed, Marilynn and I reluctantly made the cable crossing to our car and drove away. When we finally came to the end of the forest-service road where we had to part from the river, we pulled over and got out of our car. There were two large cottonwoods at this spot that provided a good shaded area. The shallow river several dozen feet below made a hissing sound as it glided over black basalt worn smooth by eons of water sculpting. Across from us was an orchard on one of the homesteads that dot this long stretch of narrow road that follows the North Fork River.

These small tracts of land that would eventually become part of the national wildlife preserve were tiny islands in a vast area, protected by the sheer ruggedness of the surrounding terrain. An unfamiliar aroma of fruit drifted across the waters; I knew it couldn't be the apple or cherry trees, as it was too soon in the season—even in this more temperate zone of the Northern Rockies.

The river looked inviting, but I remembered that it was icy from the snowmelt and still too swift to swim. The "real" whitewater river, the Middle Fork, converges only a mile or two above where we were camping.

It was time to perform our farewell ritual to the Spirit of the Land to which we had become bonded. A ritualistic farewell is found in many ancient traditions. It's important to release the energetic connection to places where there are powerful memories so that later we're not pulled out of the present moment into the past again and again. This is related to the discipline of being free of all attachments.

Marilynn lit a bundle of braided sweetgrass, offering our silent good-byes to the Spirit of the River and the vast wilderness surrounding it. I repeated some verses from one of my favorite poems by T. S. Eliot:

> Teach us to care and not to care
> Teach us to sit still
> Even among these rocks,
> Our peace in His will . . .
> Sister, mother
> And spirit of the river, spirit of the sea
> Suffer me not to be separated
> And let my cry come unto Thee.[7]

I knew that I was no longer the same person who had entered this wilderness a week ago. The magical experiences of that quest were immeasurable. In the tradition of the vision quest, I had undergone transformation and rebirth. I prayed that the gifts I had received from this place would not be lost and the seeds of new insights and experiences we had would not fall on fallow soil.

I didn't know whether or not I would return to this place, and it didn't matter. These experiences would be indelibly imprinted in my heart for the duration of my life.

This was one of my first attempts to communicate with animals in the wild. Like so many experiences that followed, I felt an ecstatic joy over the sense of unity with the world around me. I sensed that both my partner and I must have achieved some level of unity with the Creation. The entire experience was a little like remembering something that I had known long ago and had since forgotten. As always, one part of me—the "doubting Thomas," the Westernized man—was surprised by the experience and sought a logical explanation. But another, older, more mature part of me expected this to happen and recognized its significance.

It is not to the ego-based, younger part of us that always feels the need to defend its position behind cathedrals of logic and a mote of belief systems to which I appeal. It is to the older, wiser part of each one of us that I make my case.

Although this experience was magical, I was haunted by the questions, "What have we lost as a people? Is it not that wild, primal part of us that has been all but eclipsed by the 'civilizing' influences of the modern era?"

ooo

THE WIND'S WARNING

Near Canyonlands National Park, Utah: Late Spring

From the moment I drove into the canyon, I knew that this vision quest would be different. I had been on numerous quests before, and each one had its own special energy. The experiences were as varied as life itself, the lessons as unique as each individual.

I sensed nothing foreboding, and I certainly would not have dreamed that I could have been stepping into a life-threatening situation. If I had any such premonitions, I would have postponed my trip without hesitation. I realized later that, because I did not receive an adverse warning sign in advance, I was supposed to take this quest and face the challenge that awaited me. It would prove to be an important step in my growth.

What you bring to a vision quest helps to determine its nature. Although one's current unresolved issues, past experiences, and aspirations are paramount, there are unseen factors that combine to create Spirit's hidden agenda. All of these factors make it impossible to anticipate what lies ahead in a quest. It is best, therefore, to enter a vision quest without expectations.

I had chosen as the location for my sole quest site our former base camp outside of Canyonlands National Park. This sacred site is the center of a powerful vortex of energy. In addition, during our years of bringing in groups, so much spiritual work had been done there that the land had been blessed and charged with powerful positive energies. This alone is enough to make a place sacred and blessed because the land itself, like a huge magnet, holds spiritual energy.

The exact quest site I chose was surrounded almost entirely by foliage, which blocked out the magnificent panorama of the canyon. This choice was intentional. Contrary to what is commonly believed, the best site for a vision quest is not a lofty mountaintop where one can look out over a vast landscape. There is too much to see, too much to distract you. Instead, a contained space where the mind is easily bored is best for a quest, as it allows the mind to become empty of all distracting thoughts and feelings.

My bed was beneath a huge old cottonwood that leaned over nearly 45 degrees. Little did I know that the cozy location I chose would play such an important role in the unforeseen events that followed.

It was high noon on my fourth day of vision questing. So far things had gone smoothly . . . too much so. This quest was going much too easily. Usually a quest involves an initial struggle with unresolved issues and the difficult adjustment to being alone for an extended period of time. A vision quest is a time for one to face his or her personal demons. Confrontation with the aberrations of oneself and incongruities in one's life makes spiritual breakthroughs possible.

My demons must have been on vacation, because none had arisen. Things were strangely quiet for me, but not in the sense of the Sacred Silence. Instead, it was more like the proverbial calm before the storm. It was as if I were waiting for something to happen and could not fully relax until it came to pass.

The day was quite still, free of even the faintest hint of a breeze, and the temperature of the dry desert air remained moderate. Then, around midday, I felt a brief, almost unnoticeable stirring of the air. A gentle breeze had come in, throwing up a small dust cloud. I could see the surrounding foliage and grasses waving momentarily as if an invisible giant hand had brushed across the landscape. The grasses ceased swaying, leaving everything as before with one exception: The desert birds had grown inexplicably quiet. It was as if they were disturbed by something riding on the wind.

I, too, felt something. There had been a subtle voice in the wind that set off alarm signals deep inside me. I wasn't certain whether I'd actually heard the message or felt it, but its content was unmistakable. It was a warning: That night there would be high winds, and the place where I was sleeping would not be safe. I needed to move my sleeping bag to an open area.

Perhaps at an earlier period in my life I would have disregarded this warning, explaining it away as a figment of my imagination, a surfacing of my own hidden fears. After all, the surfacing of hidden fears is often what happens during the solitude of a vision quest, which is why it can be so powerful.

Changing sites in the middle of a quest is extremely disruptive because one has already become acclimated to the place and attuned to its subtle rhythms. That day, however, there was no wavering. I felt I had no choice but to follow the subtle directive from the invisible world.

The wind is my ally, and this was not the first time it had given me information about future events. I had come to trust it as I would a good friend and mentor. I packed up my few belongings and began walking toward the open canyon, where I could be safe from the effects of the storm. In doing so, I wondered if I would then lose the spiritual momentum of my quest, and I feared the worst.

Late in the night, just as foretold, the wind blew in with sudden violence, whistling and sweeping up great clouds of dust in its path. There was no buildup in its intensity. The gale-force winds appeared suddenly, without warning. Nor was there the expected lightning, thunder, or rain. Instead, it was a hot, dry wind blowing in from the southern deserts—the kind that makes animals restless and puts people on edge. And even out in the open, I was frightened. Sleep was impossible.

The winds raged far into the night. Ordinarily, I love storms— the wilder, the better. To be out in the open, in the midst of a storm, is an ultimately insane ecstasy, but this storm was very different. I felt vulnerable and scared even though my common sense was telling me that I was safe. This was a "bad medicine" wind that had stirred up some kind of primal fear in me. I wanted it to end.

Shortly before dawn the wind subsided, and the land was calm once more. I fell asleep, exhausted, not waking until the sun was high in the sky. As I awoke, I had but one thing on my mind: to return at once to my quest site and continue my meditation and spiritual practices. I felt out of sync, and I had hoped I could get back into the right frame of mind. As I began walking back to my quest site, I wondered what I might find. Had I merely given into my own unconscious fears? The message I received the day before seemed more unreal than ever. And yet, the high winds had come.

Entering the huge cottonwood grove, I was struck by the unusual sight of the canyon floor completely covered with the litter of fallen leaves and branches. However, I found no evidence of any large branches that were blown down. Regardless, I breathed a sigh of relief that I hadn't spent the night there.

My actual quest site was a different story. A huge limb with a diameter the size of my torso had fallen butt-end first on the exact spot where I had been sleeping. In the entire area, it was the only large branch to have fallen. A chill swept through me as I looked on in disbelief. I stood there, trembling and weak-kneed. I knew that before me was the scene of my death along the road I had chosen not to take. I realized that only 24 hours ago I was given the opportunity to change my future and could have so easily misinterpreted that opportunity.

In a strange way, I wasn't surprised. Perhaps I knew deep down that I would find something like this before me. I did the only thing I knew to do. I gave thanks and made an offering to the wind spirits who had been wonderful teachers over the years, and this time had saved me from certain death. Most of all, I gave thanks to the One Infinite Spirit.

In spite of my close call with death, or perhaps because of it, I was unable to return to the bliss of my first three days on the quest. The spiritual momentum had been lost. Even the place itself seemed to have lost its power. I felt restless and depressed, and was angry with myself for being too weak and undisciplined to overcome these feelings.

Only when I gave up trying was I struck with several stunning revelations. Spiritual quests are not about feeling good, but about growth, which can sometimes come through negative catalysts. Instead of my quest being interrupted, the interruption was itself my quest experience. My great lesson and achievement was about listening to the subtle warning that came on the wings of the wind and following its message.

Why is it, I asked myself, that when I'm in the greatest danger I almost never feel threatened or fearful? Instead, in these times the danger shows itself so fleetingly, so subtly, as to easily go almost unnoticed. The only indication of peril might be a nuance or a dream, an invisible wall on a ridge top, or a whisper heard in the gentle stirrings of the wind. Fortunately, so far, I've acted on these silent alarms. Yet even as I acted, I had no visceral feeling that I was avoiding plunging into the abyss. How fragile and precarious our lives really are.

It is said that this is the path of initiation. It is the razor's edge. Under the sword of Damocles, life hangs by a thread. The very wind that had been my benefactor, and had just saved my life, has another face. It has a darker side—one that is highly dangerous and indifferent to my well-being.

That was my final lesson in the canyon, and I knew that it was time to leave. Indeed, I felt I had now overstayed my welcome. The place I had loved so much had begun to feel malevolent, as if I were being pushed away. The "bad medicine" wind had left bad medicine in this place.

I quickly broke camp and departed with the utmost haste. A few miles down the road I passed through an invisible boundary, and everything was once more peaceful and balanced like the Canyonlands I knew. All this came as no surprise. I was learning that this is how the world works.

○○○

Had I only heard the soft whisper in the wind on this halcyon day in the red-rock canyons of the American Southwest, I might have passed off what I heard as my imagination. There was, however, a palpable feeling of fear that remained after the wind had gone, along with the mysterious silence of the birds. The threshold between the inner and outer world can be very thin when signs are given. When a message is accompanied by an emotion, it does not need to be subjected to various interpretations such as "Could I have imagined this?" or "Am I really getting a sign?" In the story "The Wind's Warning" and also in "An Airliner Crashes," the prevailing emotion that accompanied the signs I received was fear—and rightfully so since without intervention I was heading toward certain death in each instance. In a similar way, when I was stopped from continuing on a hiking trail by an invisible force on a mountain ridge with a group of apprentices (told in the next story "Escape from the Mountain"), we didn't know that our lives were in danger, but the message of the fear we felt was unmistakable.

The experience of interpreting signs was nothing new to me; the scriptures are full of signs. Yet, in all of my training as a priest, nothing was said about the present-day signs we receive from Creation and how to recognize and interpret them.

OOO

ESCAPE FROM THE MOUNTAIN

*Wilderness Journey, Nantahala Forest,
North Carolina: July*

It had been an easy climb to the long ridge of Selu Mountain from where we had parked at the trailhead. The fragrance of azaleas, mountain laurel, and rhododendron permeated the summer air. The latter two were in full bloom, while the earlier flowering wild azaleas still lingered in shaded areas in brilliant batches of orange and flame.

Our small group of ten adults was captivated by the numerous mountain ranges to the west with their chalk cliffs and bold granite faces. To the east, a soft mist stretched along the horizon as far as one could see.

My Native American friend, Ken, once told me that *Selu* is a Cherokee word meaning "grandmother." Feeling the power of the mountain beneath me, I realized that the native peoples were right: This truly was the grandmother—the wisdom, the gentle power of the ancient land.

We were walking along an almost level two-mile-long ridge, and no one was in a hurry. After all, when you have all of this before you, where is there to go?

Periodically we passed rocky faces on the eastern slope where we got varying perspectives of numerous mist-enshrouded mountain ranges. I had not always been so lucky! On my past several trips up the mountain, the ridge top had been enveloped by an ever-present fog. Although the ridge to our right made a sharp descent down the western slope, we were blindsided by a dense growth of rhododendron and mountain laurel, as well as scrub oak and yellow pine.

It was not until later that I realized we were about to be given a choice. As we strolled in our meditative ridgetop walk, there came a subtle change in wind direction and the faint hint of moisture that accompanied that change. No one thought to wonder why the vociferous vireos and yellow-throated warblers or the chattering gray squirrels had suddenly grown silent. No doubt, if we had been paying more attention, someone would have noticed distant rumblings of thunder that surely must have accompanied the approaching storm.

As fate would have it, we were about to experience another side of Selu. It was not the gentle beauty that enthralled us but her wild and savage fury. We had not missed the fact that all along the veiled side of the ridge were a number of lightning-struck trees.

In both Celtic and Native American traditions it is believed that such trees hold locked within them the power of the thunder and lightning that brought about their demise. There is a trade-off, it seems—the storm takes the life of the tree but in exchange leaves within its skeleton a bit of its own life—the power of the storm. Thus, lightning wood, especially if found in places of power, is coveted by some. At the insistence of several members of our group, we stopped to allow time for some to cut a few choice pieces of this wood for ceremonial use.

I noted these trees without perceiving them as omens. A sign from the natural world can be an extraordinary phenomenon or an ordinary one that somehow grabs one's attention for no accountable reason.

Why, with all the natural beauty, with so much life around us, had our group just become obsessed with something once destroyed so violently? I sensed there was a deeper meaning here, but it eluded me.

Finally, I called our group together, pulling them away from the dead trees they'd been examining. I wanted us to reach a special power spot where we could meditate.

Later I grasped the irony of my plan. There are times when we are striving so hard to hear the soft whisper of truth that we do not realize it is being broadcast from the heavens. This was such a time.

As we struggled up the mountain, I was stopped abruptly on the narrow trail, which had forced us into single-file procession. I had run into an invisible barrier that felt just as impenetrable as if it were made of concrete. *What is so terribly wrong?* I wondered.

Looking back, I saw fear on the faces of several in our group. These were the sensitive ones, I realized. The invisible barrier had a foreboding feeling about it. It was not malevolent. This I knew. I realized that the energy here was not evil, but psychically impenetrable. I wanted to continue our hike but could not. We were like a team of plow horses, suddenly and mysteriously frozen in place, unable to move forward.

In old homes and buildings, as well as in the natural world, I have encountered situations many times where the dwelling place was polluted or the landscape scarred from the tragic affairs or violent acts of humans. Usually I have found lingering sadness, anger, or fear in such places. These sites tend to become magnets for troubled or negative spirits.

Sometimes, often with the help of others, I have been successful in healing and restoring balance in such places. But there have been times when the negativity was so overpowering that it was like trying to hold back the ocean to dispel it. Whatever gains there would be from healing and depossession were soon lost in the tidal forces of negativity that inexorably rolled back in.

There were other times when the land had turned me away because my human vibrations were incompatible with the energies of the land. There were also times when the land itself had rejected me—not because it was negative, but for my own protection. It was this last scenario that our group of students and I faced that summer afternoon on the Selu Mountain.

I knew we should go back, yet still I hesitated. This was not how I usually react when confronted with such powerful omens. I felt that I was missing something extremely important about the invisible landscape around us . . . I so wanted the group to experience the sacred place ahead. I suggested a brief healing ceremony to clear the energy. An offering of cornmeal was made. As a last attempt to appease the nature elementals, a flute melody was played. Still nothing changed. My mind was confused, uncertain as how to resolve the impasse.

My body, however, had known exactly what to do from the moment we met the barrier—to get the hell out of this place. The very sense of danger that my mind wanted to reject, my body accepted completely. This kind of dichotomy between body and mind is not good because one's body is incapable of deceit. When I announced my decision to turn around, an almost visible wave of relief flowed through our group members.

The first clap of thunder caught us all off guard. We had walked only a few steps back the way we had come when it happened. We had just wasted nearly 20 minutes in our pause to try and clear the heavy energy, the time it would have taken us to get off that ridge if we were moving at a fast clip. Within seconds it seemed that the sky, which had been clear, suddenly became dark and threatening. The thunderclouds moved in from the west, propelled by the strong wind that had suddenly arisen.

The second bolt of lightning occurred simultaneously with a loud clap of thunder, striking a tree less than a hundred yards ahead of us. When we rounded the next bend in the trail and saw that first charred, smoking tree, there was no more mystery, just fear.

Within minutes we passed another burning tree, then another, and another, with the lightning continuing to strike all around us. We were in the midst of a ferocious bombardment of nature's artillery, and we would be lucky to escape unscathed.

The wind had begun blowing furiously, and when the hard rain came, no one minded getting drenched. We just didn't want to end up scorched like those trees.

Later, when I tried to count, I could remember seeing four trees that had just been hit. How many more were there that we hadn't seen?

Now I knew why we had seen so many lightning-struck trees

on our trip in. This ridge was a veritable lightning zone. I had heard of such places before but was not sure they actually existed. But here, judging by the present bombardment and the legacy of previous storms, we probably were in the midst of a magnetic anomaly, a lightning rod of nature.

Obviously we needed to get off the mountain as quickly as possible. Striking out down the eastern slope would have taken us to treacherous rocky faces, which would have been slippery and steep, and would have further exposed us to the lightning. The western slope was blocked by almost impenetrable stands of rhododendron. We were left with no choice but to go back the way we came.

The retreat off the mountain was dreamlike. We double-timed our steps, impelled by the crashing thunder and rapid lightning bursts. Several times it was as if the atmosphere simply exploded in a cacophony of deafening sound and blinding light. The sky had grown very dark, and the intense driving rain had greatly affected visibility. The trees and shrubs appeared as ghosts in the storm. The path had become extremely slippery. I watched for the spot where the trail was washed out by a spring. When we finally reached it, there was such a torrent that we held hands to pass through it.

By failing to correctly read the signs, I felt I had let the group down. It's one thing to endanger one's own life through stupidity, quite another to endanger the lives of nine others.

By now everything moved in such an accelerated fashion: the storm, our escape, and the shifting levels of awareness. It was as if there was within our consciousness both an interplay and struggle for dominance of the different ways of perceiving what was happening to us, just as there was a struggle for dominance of the elements of the storm: wind, water, lightning, and thunder. Our inner storm reflected this natural phenomenon, which arrived with such suddenness.

Then . . . all was settled. The opposing forces within suddenly were balanced and harmonious. I was no longer fleeing from the storm, but had become one with it. Looking at the group, I noticed that the terrified, panicked faces had been replaced by beatific expressions.

I knew then that we all had surrendered to the situation. The enormous power of the storm and the threat of death forced a heightened group consciousness. I also understood that the shift took place with all of us at the same time. It was like the school of minnows I once watched at the lake near my home, which would turn, surface, or dive simultaneously as one organism. When we became one mind, when we were forced off the island of our egos, the storm within was calmed, and in some inexplicable way we sensed that we would not be harmed.

I did not see the fork I had been looking for and, though the lightning was still terrifyingly close, nothing mattered anymore. We had achieved an ancient union with the elemental forces in one of their most violent yet powerful expressions. At the moment when our own spirits fused, there was fusion with the storm itself. It was not that we felt insulated and protected from the raging natural forces, but that we had become one with them.

Another 15 minutes and we were out of the storm, our drenched clothes quickly drying under the blazing July sun. Soon it was as if the experience had never really happened. Perhaps it was too removed from our ordinary lives to seem real. In no time our clothes were dry and, unbelievably, conversation had become mundane.

How unpredictable we humans can be. Was our encounter with the storm that alien to us, or were we just experiencing a necessary defense mechanism of the mind? Certainly no one can remain for long in that kind of intensity without a reprieve. Finally, we saw our cars at the trailhead where we'd left them.

Our morale was very high from the safe passage through the storm and the adrenaline pump we'd all experienced. It seemed as if everyone was almost sorry that the adventure was over so quickly. Needless to say, feelings would have been very different had we not made such a successful escape off the mountain.

OOO

What had once appeared as the wrath of Zeus now seemed like an ordinary summer storm. How narrow sometimes is the threshold between excitement and fear, adventure and danger, life and death. How quickly and drastically our perspective can shift.

As a group we were left with an assortment of conflicting emotions. We strongly felt the vulnerability, the fragility, and the impermanence of our lives. On the other hand, the experience was empowering for all. It had given us a deeper sense of the mystery of our connection to the primal forces of nature.

For me, personally, awareness this time had nothing to do with pristine beauty or the meditative silence of a mountaintop. It was all about the invisible impasse and those charred trees, the legacy of forgotten storms.

I hesitated when I shouldn't have. When one is blocked on any path through life, there isn't always the luxury available to take one's time, questioning the reasons why. Sometimes we have to simply take the signs and omens at face value, acting unhesitatingly to move with quiet deliberation in the direction toward which they point. Then, if we're lucky, understanding will follow at a later time.

Still, there is a lingering question: Were our lives in as great a danger as it appeared on the ridge of Selu Mountain, or was this just another ordinary summer storm?

❂ ❂ ❂ ❂ ❂

CHAPTER 2
ANIMAL MAGIC

W^{*hen*} *I discovered that it was possible to directly communicate with virtually any species of animal, a whole new world opened up for me. I discovered that animals in the wild know our intent and the degree to which we are in harmony with our surroundings. When our minds are still and we are at peace with ourselves, wild animals will often allow us to approach them. Sometimes they will even come to us.*

Our pets know virtually everything about us. They not only read our thoughts, but also understand them. Some pets are capable of grasping complex ideas. Animals (try to) communicate with us in the form of pictures and feelings. I sense the deep frustration our animal friends feel that we do not understand or respond to their communications. Learning all of this came as a shock for me.

SIGN OF THE DOE

Northern Rockies: Early Fall

For nearly an hour, my friend Robert and I had been hiking along a trail that wound through a mixed fir-and-hardwood forest. To our left, we caught glimpses of a large lake whose mirrored waters reflected the steep mountain rising sharply beyond.

I always enjoyed my friend's company in such places because he was not prone to mindless chatter. He understood the importance of silence when in the temple of Creation. At one point when the trail opened into a small meadow, we spotted a doe grazing with her fawn close by.

I've always been deeply touched by scenes such as this when I'm in the wilderness. The beauty and innocence of such creatures brings me closer to the Spirit which is within all life. The scene captured my imagination, and I was inspired to attempt something I had not tried in years. I whispered to Robert, "This is a time for acting without thinking. Why don't we become like deer ourselves and join them?"

Once I had shared with him the time when a partner and I had been accepted into a herd of bighorn sheep in northern Idaho. He had been intrigued by this story but had difficulty understanding how such a feat was possible for us here. I explained to him that for us to approach these lovely creatures we would have to go deeply into our inner silence. In addition, it would help if we imitated grazing animals by approaching them on our hands and knees. I also urged him to let go of the idea of separateness.

"If we truly are all things, then surely we must be part of this doe and her little one," I said.

Robert, who was a former student, said, "I can't possibly do these things!"

I assured him that he could.

This seemed to satisfy him, because soon we were moving on all fours across the tiny clearing toward the deer.

By this time I had become connected to the cadence and flow of the forest. It's a good feeling, a familiar one, and nowhere in the world of humans do I feel so alive. The ambient light of the late afternoon forest made the doe and fawn almost invisible.

While we were approaching the deer, I warned, "Don't look them in the eye. If you do, they'll be out of here in a flash. Focus farther back on the body and try not to allow any emotion to well up within you."

We emerged into the small clearing, and I noted that there was not even a ripple in the mother and baby. I was in awe of their apparent acceptance of us.

All this came to me, not in thoughts, but simply as awareness, for my mind was still empty. I sensed the essence, the "deer-ness" of these creatures, and I knew that the same essence was within the two of us. Otherwise, this would not be happening.

When I brushed a shoulder against the mother, she took only a step away. During this time she postured herself between us and her fawn. She was cautious but unafraid.

I asked Robert to reach over and touch the doe. When he did, the doe jumped away from him, as if she had noticed us for the first time. Her continuing presence told me she accepted us as a nonthreatening part of her environment. Like my experience among the bighorn sheep, I was deeply moved by what we had accomplished. I knew that this experience could never diminish in its luminosity. Robert had become speechless. I saw the tears in his eyes and suddenly my eyes were watery, too, because I felt the magic of this encounter with these creatures.

While we were next to the doe and her fawn, I invited them

to visit us at our campsite, just as we had done with the bighorn sheep on the North Fork River in northern Idaho.

I wanted to know if this phenomenon could be repeated. Certainly, I had never perceived it as a random event, but was it possible to achieve the same kind of rendezvous with other species anywhere and with other people involved? If so, it certainly would suggest the possibility of a far deeper and more complex kind of relationship with our wild kin than most have dared to dream.

Since we were in a primitive camping area a few miles away, which we shared with about 40 other groups, I felt that it was unlikely they would come this close to so many humans.

We awoke the next morning at first light. No one in the campground had arisen. As my thoughts turned to the experience of the day before, I felt certain that I detected movement beyond the opening of the tent, somewhere out in the diffused light of early morning. My heart skipped a beat. I saw a doe moving stealthily through the trees. I sensed that it was the same one. I was positive. Robert, who awoke at the same time as I, saw her, too. We scarcely dared to breathe. The fawn followed her mother. He whispered to me that the markings were the same. We watched with rapt attention.

As if to remind us that they had accepted my invitation, they remained grazing near our tent for about five minutes before moving on.

ooo

This encounter with a doe and her fawn that paralleled my experience with bighorn sheep five years earlier illuminated for me the unknown possibilities for us humans to interact with creatures of the wild. Animals have a deep intelligence that has gone unrecognized by most of us because we have not been aware of their telepathic abilities. Very real possibilities exist for us to be able to approach animals in the wild without their responding with fear, to be accepted into a herd or animal family, and to set up a rendezvous for a later time and different location. Although these are inconceivable feats to most people, through a shift in consciousness, these "feats" are within everyone's ability.

The creation myth of the Garden of Eden is actually the story of a state of consciousness we had at one time and lost, probably with the development of the rational mind. This loss of Edenic consciousness is what accounts for the loneliness and sense of separation from life around us. We may never find a lost Eden in any geographical location, but it does exist in the roots of consciousness in every one of us. When we, as a species, discover this original harmony with life, it will transform our lives. The "fiery sword" that barred our return to Eden will vanish in the twinkling of an eye, and our bond with Creation will be restored.

Perhaps, someday, future generations will read about our current state of separation from all life on this planet and find today's time as incomprehensible then as we do now when we imagine the mythic "garden" in which we lived in complete harmony with life around us.

○○○

SNOW EAGLE

Sangre de Cristo Mountains, New Mexico: Late Spring

The pre-dawn hour is the most common period for lucid dreaming, the time this dream occurred.

I'm walking through the Carson National Forest in the mountains outside Taos where we're living when I come to a small clearing with a brook running through it. A light covering of snow is on the ground. I remark how strange it is that there's snow in mid-July. Then I see a large white eagle drinking from a stream that crosses the clearing. A voice says, "Your name is 'Snow Eagle.'"

I awoke filled with a sense that something important had just occurred in my dreamtime. When I shared the dream with Marilynn, she suggested that my soul name had been revealed to me. I was familiar with the esoteric concept that each of us has a soul name, the revelation of which is considered a great blessing. However, I needed further clarification.

Several days later we were exploring some of the national forest above the log cabin that would be our home for the next year. I felt energized by the midsummer warmth of these mountains.

At one point, we came to a small opening in the fir forest. Although I knew that I had never been there, the scene seemed strangely familiar to me. Then simultaneously we both saw it. On the ground in front of us, a golden eagle was drinking from a tiny stream. The sunlight reflecting off the stream and the eagle itself caused it to appear, at first glance, purely white. Immediately, we both remembered my snow-eagle dream. Upon detecting our presence, instead of flying away, the eagle just flapped its wings and landed on a nearby branch only ten feet away from us.

From that vantage point, it observed us with those piercing eyes that are characteristic of its species. At once, I felt as if an ancient bond had been reestablished, and I knew that I was a brother to all eagles.

I realized that this was a natural-world confirmation of my dream. It was also my first experience of a mysterious phenomenon in which I would have certain lucid dreams that would be reenacted on the physical plane exactly as I had dreamed them.

Not only had I met an ally, but also a soul name had been revealed to me and confirmed. I felt doubly blessed. Not fully comprehending the meaning of this experience, I resolved to understand more.

In the years that followed, I had frequent encounters with eagles, not only in the west, but also in the eastern United States where they are less abundant. The eagles would usually be circling overhead, but sometimes they were perched atop a tall pine or even on the ground. Significantly, prior to my encounter in the Sangre de Cristos Mountains, I'd never once seen an eagle in the wild.

The most auspicious appearances were on our wilderness retreats. At first I thought it was coincidental, but then I began to realize that a powerful synchronicity was involved. For example, whenever we began a class or ceremony in one of our magnificent outdoor classrooms, a lone eagle or a pair would soon be circling overhead. It got to be a contest with us to see who could guess when an eagle would make its appearance, and from what direction.

To a traditional Native American, such an experience would come as no surprise. Indeed, a Native shaman's totem animals would be expected to appear if he or she had any power at all.

In time, my connection with eagles deepened.

One afternoon while walking through the large field near my home, I began to have a peculiar sensation of flying. I received a visual image of the earth as seen from above. At the same time I was aware of the opposite feeling of being supported by the ground beneath me. Instinctively I looked up and saw that an eagle was circling directly over head. I had the odd sensation of being in two places simultaneously. The eagle remained in the vicinity of my home and began making regular appearances following this experience.

In the months ahead, I often felt the eagle's presence before actually sighting it. For me, it signified a deepening connection to my ally. Of all the encounters I've had with eagles over the years, the most remarkable took place when I got caught in a blinding snowstorm on a back road in the northern Rockies. To my consternation, the road disappeared entirely under the snow, and I was no longer able to find the edges of the pavement. Afraid of going off the road, I decided to stop driving.

The snow filled the air, and visibility was almost zero. It soon occurred to me that I would get stranded on this seldom-traveled road, and my anxiety mounted. It was late afternoon, and I only had enough gas to keep the car heater on for another hour. After that, the interior of the vehicle would be as cold as the outside. I also realized that since no cars had passed me for a while, the road had probably been closed and there would be no one coming along to assist me.

While these anxious thoughts were going through my head, a large bundle of feathers hit the window on the driver's side with a thump and disappeared. Moments later the visibility improved and I could see a large golden eagle and its mate flying off in front of my car. I realized that they were hunting together, following what once had been the road. I took this as an omen that I should move forward. For a time it seemed as if the eagles were piloting my car. I had the distinct feeling that they actually understood my plight and were trying to help.

Five minutes later, I emerged from the worst of the storm and could see patches of pavement. I would be safe, and I felt extremely grateful to have such wonderful protection and support system from my allies in the nature kingdom.

OOO

Six months after my soul name was revealed to me and I met my totem animal, I received an amazing confirmation of this information. As part of a lecture I was giving in Austin, Texas, I shared the story of "snow eagle." While I was describing the events that unfolded, I noticed a well-dressed man in a dark pinstriped suit growing more and more uncomfortable. As I neared the end of the story, he stood up and, interrupting me, asked permission to say something. I was taken aback by this unusual turn of events and nodded for him to speak.

"This evening," he said, "I came to prove that you were a fake. You see, I am a Methodist minister. But the story you just told affected me deeply. Last night I had a vivid dream that a white eagle came to me and said, 'I am Snow Eagle. I'm here to help you.'"

I could see tears welling up in his eyes. He had obviously been moved by my story. But his next statement caught me by surprise.

"Father," he said, "will you please bless me?"

Before I had a chance to answer, he was walking up to the front of the lecture hall and knelt down in front of me. I then did the only thing I could do. I said a blessing for this courageous man of the cloth and told him that I loved him.

Since this time, I have received similar confirmations by others of my soul name, Snow Eagle, but none of them were as dramatic and emotionally charged as the first.

OOO

BEAR MEDICINE

Sangre de Cristo Mountains, New Mexico;
Grand Teton National Park; East Tennessee

The day marked the close of the final holistic health confer-
ence for the summer, and those attending headed for their homes
in various parts of the country. My initiative had helped bring
together a dozen investors to purchase a guest ranch in the Carson National Forest outside Taos. I had been deeply involved in
promotion, program planning, and recruiting ten staff members
as teachers and cooks. The program was a huge success for those
attending, but as the summer progressed, it became increasingly
evident that it would not be financially feasible to continue. I personally had come to a major turning point in my life because it
was the first time I'd ever failed in an undertaking.

Where had we gone wrong? For weeks I had been torturing
myself. Had the guest ranch been too remote? At 85,000 feet, was
the season too short? Did we do too little advertising?

That morning I realized how much of my own personal power
I had given up to this project. I had become so attached to its
ultimate success that little else seemed to matter. I also realized
that management, promotion, and recruiting are not my areas of
expertise. In a deeper sense, I realized that I had deviated from my
personal path. My bliss had been teaching spiritual philosophy
and helping people learn how to reestablish their ancient union
with the natural world. In the past, whenever I focused on this,
many other things in my life fell into place.

I had become spiritually and emotionally depleted. I wondered if I would ever regain my enthusiasm or be able to act with any real power again.

Inexplicably, while having these thoughts, I had been receiving a clear image of a bear in an aspen grove. What did this mean, I wondered? Finally I felt compelled to tell some staff members that I was going for a walk in the national forest where I would meet my Bear ally who would help me reclaim my power. Everyone laughed with me. I wondered if I really meant this.

Minutes later I was hiking on the main horse trail behind the guest ranch, the image of the bear still clearly imprinted in my mind. I soon discovered a narrow animal trail bearing to the right and wondered why I hadn't noticed it before.

I proceeded no more than a hundred yards down the new path when I heard a crashing sound in the woods ahead of me. It was too loud to have been made by a deer or elk—maybe it was a bear. Rounding a bend in the trail, just as I had suspected, I spotted a cinnamon-colored bear moving up a hill. It was only then that I noticed the aspen grove.

The bear, apparently having caught my scent, was anxious to get away. Suddenly, however, he stopped in his tracks, turned his head back, and gazed at me. I'll never forget what happened to me at that moment. When our eyes met, something was exchanged. I could feel his strength and courage pouring into me, and I began to feel large and formidable. In that moment, I knew that this rendezvous had been set up on another level. With the bear encounter, I realized I had bonded with the spirit of this species and could draw on its powers to overcome the fears and self-doubts that had plagued me. I knew the spiritual connection I made with the bear would always be available to me.

A subtle shift had taken place, but I had no idea what it would bring. Then several days later, I received invitations to teach in several major cities. I knew at the time that the direction of my life was set, at least for the immediate future. I was to be on the lecture circuit. If people could not come to me, then I would go to them. Already, I was thankful for my bear medicine. There was just one thing I had not yet realized—I would always know where and when I would see a bear while I am in the wilderness.

My next two encounters with bears paralleled the first. They both took place in Grand Teton National Park. In both instances, I was shown a mental image of a bear and its surroundings before I ventured out into the park, and I intuitively knew the approximate time and place they could be seen.

The first of these encounters took place several years after meeting my Bear ally. My former partner, Marilynn, and I had been camping for a week by Jenny Lake, which is at the base of the Grand Teton itself. We had planned to listen to a ranger talk in the early evening, but by midday I knew I would have the opportunity to see a bear at a certain spot near one of our favorite trails. I also knew that the bear would be there about an hour before dusk.

That evening while there was still plenty of daylight left, I made the 20 minute walk along Cottonwood Creek to the spot where I had seen the bear in my vision. From there, I could look out over a large meadow through which the stream meandered and thick stands of willows were scattered throughout the meadow. While I was looking at the area, I was startled to see a huge bull moose emerge from a willow stand no more than 50 feet away. I froze on the spot, aware that these males are unpredictable and can sometimes be aggressive and territorial. At the same time I spotted his mate.

I laughed to myself, thinking it must have been a moose rather than a bear that I saw in my vision. No sooner had this thought come to my mind than a dark shape emerged from the woods and headed directly for the female moose.

I could scarcely believe what I was seeing! A bear was actually charging a moose! I had never imagined that a bear would attempt to kill a healthy full-grown moose, especially in July when food was abundant. I later realized that the bear might have just been feeling territorial.

The female bolted, and then stopped about a hundred feet from where she had been. To my surprise, the bear made another charge toward the moose, which this time ran over to join her mate. The bear quickly gave up the chase at this point, apparently having no interest in tangling with the much larger male who may have weighed close to 1,600 pounds.

My second encounter with a bear occurred several years later in the exact same place. I'd been camping outside the park with a group of adults who were joining me on a wilderness retreat. I had received a vision of a bear on our last day together, and I asked three of my students if they would like to go observe a bear from a close vantage point. Curious and slightly skeptical, they elected to go. We hiked at the same approximate time and on the same trailhead as I had been shown in my vision.

As before, there was no bear in immediate sight. Instead, across the meadow at the edge of the woods, I could see a herd of about 30 elk, consisting of mothers and calves. Although we were concealed and downwind from the elk, I noticed how nervous the mothers were. They appeared to be looking in our direction. Two of the females, apparently the matriarchs, took the responsibility to corral the calves that had ventured into the clearing away from the herd.

I became captivated by this wilderness drama of the two matriarchs attempting to control so many rambunctious calves. But after a while I began to have the growing feeling that they were not concerned by our presence, but by *something else* in our vicinity. I could feel the hair standing up on my head.

All at once I heard a large limb snapping near me. As I now suspected, a bear was foraging less than a hundred yards away. It was a bit too close for comfort, and I decided that it was time to make a hasty retreat back to the trailhead.

In the years that followed, I had additional premonitions of bears while I was in wilderness areas. One of these, however, occurred not in a wilderness area, but in front of my home outside of Knoxville, Tennessee, where my wife, Astrid, and I were living at the time.

It happened in 2002 when I had begun writing this very story. Throughout the day I had attempted to write about the above experiences, but the words were simply not coming together.

Consequently, I decided to leave these accounts out of this book. After all, I had more than enough animal stories for my "Animal Magic" chapter.

That night I had a lucid dream about a bear and awoke wondering what it meant this time. I did not have to wonder for long. When Astrid and I went out on our front porch the next morning, our eyes fell to the ground, and we were looking at something we had seen numerous times in wilderness areas. It appeared to be a huge pile of bear scat—larger than any I had ever seen even in the western states. Closer examination revealed the partially digested nuts and berries in the feces such as I have seen so many times in the wilds. But how could a large bear wonder into our yard a few miles from Knoxville? There could only be one answer. My Bear ally, or perhaps the Spirit of all Bears, wanted this story told!

ooo

A year later we moved out of the house, and an apprentice of mine moved in. She had already established a spirit connection with several animal allies, and many of them visited her nearly every day for a week after she moved in to welcome her. Just before dawn on one of those days, she awoke to the sound of her two cats running like crazy from window to window to look out at the porch. She had not gotten up to see what startled them, and later that morning, she was quite surprised to see a huge pile of bear scat on her porch. Having heard me tell about my experience with bears, particularly outside the same house, she shared her story with me.

"Your power and abilities are increasing," I told her. "And the land is honoring the spiritual work you are doing."

She had felt that she now had a Bear ally, and I was able to confirm this. "The bear came to welcome you," I added. The Spirit of all Bears was persistent with her, too, and that night a bear appeared to her in a lucid dream—this time without leaving partially digested nuts and berries.

ooo

WOOD BEES AND HONEYBEES

Middle Tennessee: Late Spring

It was late spring. I had recently moved to Middle Tennessee to be close to Astrid, who began doing promotional work for me not long after we met.

One day a few months after my move, Astrid asked me if I could persuade some wood bees to leave her home. The bees had appeared a few months earlier and were causing damage to her renovated log house. She had heard me speak at a lecture about the successful deal I once made with some yellow jackets, which had made hives in some railroad ties I needed to use.

In addition to the problem with the wood bees, a number of honeybees had made hives in the eaves of her home and roof. Somehow the honeybees had managed to work their way into her house in increasing numbers. As a consequence, she had been spending more and more time each day catching and releasing them. She wished no harm to come to the bees, but at the same time, she knew that she needed to protect her home and children.

I learned that, though she had spent much of her life in the woods and working in her garden, she had not been stung since she was eight and had always felt that her protection came from her strong desire to never cause harm to any creature. She believed that the bees didn't attack her because they had always sensed that she was harmless.

Her theory intrigued me, and I thought we must share a common sensitivity. I readily agreed to help, although it had been a while since I had done this sort of thing. I wondered if I would be successful in establishing communication and negotiating a solution.

Walking through her home, I saw where the wood bees had created a number of piles of sawdust beneath the natural wood beams of the ceiling. I surveyed the damage. They continued their work with a sense of purpose.

Within a few minutes, I was ready to begin attuning to the little creatures, hoping for some kind of mutual understanding. With my awareness I "touched" the awareness of the bee. I felt their little bodies buzzing and felt almost what it was like to be them. Once I had attuned to their vibration, I played images in my mind of their peacefully leaving the place. I also talked to them, knowing that all creatures are telepathic to some degree and can often discern our thoughts if not our words.

After spending a short time with the wood bees, I sought to work out a deal with the honeybees. As always, I promised that no harm would come to these little ones but sought to communicate the idea that they were in the wrong place. After I finished, I had my usual doubts as to whether I had gotten through to them.

As it turned out, I need not have been concerned. Within an hour the wood bees had permanently left; the honeybees, too, had vacated their hives and flown to places unknown. I had never seen such a quick response in my negotiations with the animal kingdom. Perhaps like wine, I had become better with age.

I could hear the amazement in Astrid's voice as she continued to go over this whole episode with me again and again. Truthfully, I too was astonished that such contractual agreements are so effective with those with whom we share our planet. A "deal" with our wild brothers and sisters should never be a veiled threat, but rather an invitation to God's creatures to participate in a win-win situation. We humans nearly always underestimate the acute sensitivity of other life forms and tend to assume that we have an exclusive market on awareness.

While I had conducted negotiations with the bees, Astrid and her son, Aidan, who was five years old at the time, had gone up to their garden. Upon returning, he was relieved to see that the creatures that had once frightened him were gone. After this, he frequently brought up the subject with his mom, requesting that she tell him the story over and over again.

Finally, he asked his mother the tantalizing question that must have been on his mind all along. "When Peter talks to the bees, do they all fly around his head and listen to him?" She invited him to ask me himself. He did, and I told him he was pretty smart to have figured it out. I also told him that although they may not always understand our words, they can see the pictures in our minds and sense our intent.

I sensed that Aidan was a very special young boy and felt fortunate to share an experience with him that undoubtedly would make an indelible impression. His perception of wild creatures, with whom we share this world, would never be the same.

ooo

I am convinced that we must find a new way of relating to the natural world. What I did grew out of a certain attitude I have long held toward all life on this planet. We humans have the sad history of violently seeking to exterminate any creature that gets in our way. Too often our responses have been those of retribution and the use of excessive force, rather than considering that these lovely beings with whom we share this world might simply not know that they are in the wrong place. Even more tragically, they might have been driven into our habitat because our human development altered what once had been their natural territory.

Experiences like these led me to the growing conviction that it is possible to live in harmony with all life on this planet and to be in relationship with it in ways that only a few years ago would have seemed inconceivable to me.

ooo

LITTLE DOVE

Foothills of the Great Smoky Mountains, Tennessee: Late Summer

Although we had known each other for several years and had recently been married, Astrid and I were still caught up in the euphoria of sharing time together in the natural world that we so deeply loved and revered. We left early one morning for a trip to the nearby Smoky Mountains. We took about 20 single-gallon plastic jugs to fill with water from a natural spring used by local people for drinking water.

It was one of those halcyon days in the foothills; the calm late August day had a hint of fall in the air. The serenity of the place was conducive to a sense of lightheartedness and abandon. I was remembering an extraordinary experience I had ten years ago with a dove. While driving down a country road one day, a dove had flown into my windshield. Feeling sick with grief, I pulled over and said a prayer for the spirit of this dove. I asked that it be healed of the trauma of its death and be guided on its return to its source. I blessed it, sending my love to this being whose life I had unintentionally taken.

Then a most unexpected thing happened. An ocean of love that rolled in like an invisible tide enveloped me. I had no idea where this love had come from, but I knew that the love I had sent out had been reciprocated. Throughout the day, I basked in the wonderful energy. The dove I thought I had lost had become more alive to me than ever in this tidal force of unconditional love that understandably had come from the Spirit of all Doves.

This morning was the first time in years I had thought of that experience. At the time I failed to see that it was a premonition of another remarkable encounter with a dove. Once our jugs were filled, Astrid and I waded out to the middle of the shallow river, whose crystal-clear waters flow out of the Great Smoky Mountains less than ten miles away.

Wading in a cold mountain stream is an effective tool for stopping one's internal dialogue. Once our mental chatter is at rest, we automatically shift to the spiritual mind, usually without our notice. Our inherent magical consciousness is an aspect of this spiritual mind. I have observed that even wild animals lose their instinctive fear of us when we have shifted into this magical state.

While we were standing in the river's cooling waters, we were captivated by a school of minnows, so perfectly reflected in the sunlight that they appeared as a cluster of sparkling diamonds submerged just beneath the surface of the waters. The image brought us into an awareness of the sacredness of this special place.

Finally, refreshed and in a state of quietude, we stepped out of the water onto a grassy clearing. I had walked to some bushes to relieve myself while Astrid began walking to our car. No sooner had she taken a few steps than a wild dove flew out of the nearby trees landing next to her feet. Although it flew well, she could see that it was a juvenile. She wondered if it simply did not see her, although this seemed unlikely. Excitedly, Astrid called me over to witness this bizarre scenario.

We were as still as mice, fearful of startling it. Unafraid, the dove walked over and began pecking at the ground only inches away from us. Then, to our astonishment, it climbed on top of my tennis shoe and began pulling at my shoelaces with its beak. We were enthralled.

Curious, we backed away to see what it would do—only to find that it followed us. We backed up several times with the same results. The crazy little dove thought he belonged to us.

Wondering how far we could take this, we walked about 20 paces away to see its reaction. At first the little dove seemed not to know where we had gone, but as soon as it heard our voices, it flew over to us. Then, as if to say "You are my territory!" it climbed on Astrid's shoe. We continued to look on in disbelief.

This was just too much! We had become enraptured with the little dove that was following us around like a puppy. Finally, I cautiously reached down and picked it up, placing it on Astrid's head, certain it would fly away. Instead, the dove began pulling on her hair with its beak. Then, as if pleased with its new residence, it settled down to nest in her hair.[8]

Unfortunately, by now it was time for us to leave. This was easier said than done. Even when we opened the car door, the dove did not flinch. Apparently, it was committed to remaining in its new nest. The little dove had quickly endeared itself to us by its strange attachment to us and the hilarious act of nesting in Astrid's hair.

We hesitated before actually entering our car to see what choice the dove would make. For a few moments more it remained motionless watching us. But then its natural instinct must have overridden the strange kinship it felt with us because it flapped its wings once and effortlessly flew away.

We were enthralled by the magic of this experience. But as I pondered what had happened, I felt that there was still something we had missed. I knew that many times in her past Astrid had taken in sick or wounded birds, nursing them back to health. In fact, as recently as six months ago, she had attempted to heal a dying pigeon. It struck me that all these events were somehow related. Could it be that somehow her compassionate acts had bound her to the group soul of doves and pigeons and perhaps I'd become bound as well?

Together we witnessed how our acts of compassion for wild creatures had gone full circle and come back to reward us for such love and caring. From such experiences, I have learned that there are invisible threads that span both time and space to connect us in mysterious ways to life in its infinite diversity.

○○○

This wondrous experience with the little dove demonstrated to both Astrid and me that undreamed-of possibilities exist in our relationship with Creation. This experience was one of ecstatic joy for us. Our attempt to quiet our minds and blend with the natural world around us was rewarded by this extraordinary visitation.

We perceived that by developing these simple disciplines it was possible to heal the ancient rift between the human and animal worlds. How enriched our lives can become when we shift from our existential separation into an ecstatic oneness with life around us!

○○○

ON BENDED KNEE

Cascade Canyon, Grand Teton National Park: Mid-June

Astrid and I had been hiking for nearly six hours in the high country of the northern Rockies. It was late afternoon. We were approaching a series of switchbacks that would take us in a 2,000-foot descent to our campsite at the base of the mountain.

No sooner had we rounded a bend on a narrow path then we spotted a large doe standing on the path, intently watching us. I had the strangest feeling that this was no chance encounter.

By this time I'd become familiar with that peculiar phenomenon I'd often experienced of seeming to draw certain animals to me in the wild. Astrid, too, had begun developing this ability since our remarkable encounter with the wild dove months ago. She is a true daughter of the earth. When we are together, our powers of magnetic attraction invariably were greatly enhanced.

We stopped in our tracks, remaining motionless to see what the doe would do. To our surprise, she remained exactly where she had been. Since there was no way to make a detour around her, we cautiously began walking toward her so as not to alarm her.

When we were 20 feet from the doe, to our astonishment she suddenly dropped to her knees as if to pay homage to us. While we looked on in wonderment, she continued watching us, exhibiting a total absence of fear.

I was transfixed by this remarkable sight. The thought came to me that perhaps she was sick or wounded, but soon I realized that we were looking at a very healthy mule deer, who, judging by the size of her nipples and a slightly swollen belly, would be giving birth in the not-too-distant future. I was struck by the thought that this lovely creature was demonstrating vulnerability and trust much like a dog does when it rolls over on its back showing its belly. I had the definite sense that she would actually allow us to touch her or even scratch her back.

As I often do with animals, I could sense her thoughts. "I was supposed to meet you here!" she seemed to say. "I like you. You two are different from the others. I'm not afraid of you."

The doe was still watching us when we rounded another bend in the trail and disappeared from sight.

I shared my conversation with the doe with Astrid, laughingly acknowledging that perhaps it was my imagination. But she countered that, although she hadn't heard anything, she had felt the essence of what I'd described. She reminded me of how often my supposed communication with animals had been verified in some way. She questioned why I would be imagining it only in this particular case? I had to agree.

By tacit consent, we spoke no more on the way down, not wishing to break the spell of what had just happened.

During the descent, I could not cease pondering over how different our experiences of wilderness were from that of most people. Why does the forest, so vibrant with life, grow silent when humans enters it? Why do both predator and prey flee or go into hiding? Even the wolf is able to walk close to the caribou herd when not on the prowl, like the lioness near the gazelle. The prey knows when its predators' bellies are full.

But with us, it's different. There is always fear! Why is this so? Perhaps we really are exiles from the Garden of Eden and all other creatures of the Garden know it. They sense our state of separation from the rest of life.

We've fallen out of relationship with our Earth Goddess, and we have no idea today how to approach her, to address her, or to even know what she wants from us. Incredible as it would seem, many are even in denial that there's anything wrong at all.

These are the same errors we make in our human relationships, right? Only in this case the potential consequences are much greater.

ooo

Years ago I learned that when I am out of harmony with nature, my own inner harmony eludes me as well. I feel a sense of quiet desperation when my connection with life around me is lost. The greatest hope for our earth is that we humans can stop perceiving ourselves as being separate from the rest of Creation.

We have to rediscover and restore our natural link with life around us. If that connection is restored, then our survival as a species is assured. If it is not, then our survival grows more uncertain with each passing year.

The experiences of the earth and wilderness that are related in *Soul on Fire* are vastly different from the experiences of most people, even many nature lovers. They are part of the new paradigm emerging in our relationship with the world around us. Those who choose to be part of this new paradigm almost appear like a different species of human being compared to who we are now.

I have discovered that there is a language of nature. It is a language that our modern world has lost and desperately needs to rediscover if we are to understand and communicate with our living earth. This language is based on what has been called the "ancient code of Gaia." But a growing number of people around the world are intuitively learning to unlock this code. I find both hope and comfort in this realization.

Still, reflecting over our recent encounter with the doe, I realized that there was now little that could come as a surprise for me. It seemed as if there were no real limits to the possibilities and varieties of experiences on this wondrous earth. The extraordinary had become almost commonplace. The magical had become a way of life. The deep communion with life on this planet had become a natural state of being. Life was ecstatic.

In the days that followed our unusual encounter with the doe, I often had images of that magnificent creature watching us on bended knees with her soft eyes. She seemed to symbolize the innocence, wildness, trust, and oneness with the flow of Creation that our human world has lost.

WARNING THE DEER

East Tennessee: Early November

When Astrid and I moved to a cottage in a country setting outside of Knoxville, we had a family of deer that would graze at the far end of a large meadow next to the our home. They were quite wary of humans, however. I felt that they'd had some dangerous encounters in the past with hunters. Consequently, they quickly disappeared into the woods whenever we took our walks.

One day we saw some suspicious-looking men in camouflage suits checking out the area. I remembered that hunting season was opening in several days. Since we had grown quite attached to the deer, we feared for their safety. It was this concern that prompted us to devise a plan.

The next morning while the deer were grazing in the distance, we stood in front of our house and attempted to send them a mental message. I thought this might work, because in my experience I had found large animals to be very telepathic. The message was that they should avoid their usual grazing area because they would be in danger by hunters. However, they could graze in the area close to our home where they would be safe. When we completed the message, we wondered if it had been too complex to decipher. We waited to see if they would respond.

That evening while Astrid and I were entertaining some friends, we heard a strange yelping sound outside the house. When we opened the front door and stepped out onto our large porch, we saw three deer a few feet from the steps. While two of them were grazing, the third one was facing us with her neck stretched out in our direction as if waiting for us. I was certain that this one was responsible for the yelping sound.

I had the strongest impression that they had come to pay their respects and that she was saying, "You called us!" We both were amazed by this humanlike response. Still, we did not know whether or not they would remain close to our house as we had requested for their safety.

There was no need to be concerned. The three deer remained in the vicinity of our home for most of the hunting season, and during that time three more deer joined their group. In time, several weeks after hunting season was over, they returned to their former grazing habitat.

ooo

As I reflected on this joyous and heartwarming experience with the deer, I could not help but dwell on the religious background out of which I had come. In our Western society, the creation story in biblical scripture has become the definitive statement regarding our relationship to the earth. In the book of Genesis, humans are given "dominion over"[9] all life on Earth. Unfortunately, this verse has been used to justify our right to lord over and use nature as we see fit. Tragically, this belief system has contributed to our exploitation of the environment and has led us to the brink of ecological disaster.

Surely an error must have been made in the translations over the last 3,000 years. If the scriptures are divinely inspired, they must have originally implied something else. When we place this verse in the context of the entire creation story, the meaning is transparent: A human being is meant to be a caregiver in the garden of nature. A caregiver does not lord over, but is in loving relationship with, her charge. She is sensitive to the needs of all in her care. She also understands that her role as caregiver may sometimes include that of protecting those who have no way of defending themselves.

On this fall day, Astrid and I had the opportunity to fulfill our role as protectors for a family of deer that we had grown to love. We discovered that distance is not a factor in this kind of telepathic communication and that our animal friends, even in the wild, are capable of responding to concepts much more complex than we would have imagined.

Since this experience, both Astrid and I have made it a point to release any conditioned attitude of superiority when we encounter wild creatures in the forest, recognizing that this child of the earth has both awareness and purpose. We may say to it, "What can you teach us?" or "How can we assist your species in fulfilling its life purpose?" We have learned that each experience has its own unique energetic signature, and it is best to have no expectations about what we can learn.

○○○

THE PANTHER'S SCREAM

East Tennessee: Fall

After three years of living on the outskirts of Knoxville in a rental cottage in a country setting, my partner and I bought a small log home located on the edge of the Great Smoky Mountains National Park. Although we loved where we had lived, we felt drawn to the mountains almost from the first day we moved to East Tennessee and this new house gave us the opportunity to be minutes away from the national park. Since I returned to my public work four years ago, after a respite for health reasons, I wanted to have easy access to wilderness areas because I need the balance they have always provided for me.

The wilderness preserve just a few miles from our home was teeming with wildlife. Both Astrid and I have strong connections with panthers through our dreamtime encounters with these marvelous creatures, though we had never met them in real life. We felt such an affection for these special creatures that we wished their physical counterparts were close by. Long ago panthers once inhabited the area near our home; however, the last officially documented sighting was around the turn of the 20th century. Like wolves, they had been relentlessly hunted down and trapped to extinction.

From time to time throughout the years, the local people in these mountains have reported panther sightings (locals refer to cougars as panthers), but these were never verified. Skeptics always pointed out that if they were around sooner or later someone would find their tracks or remains of their kills. For decades there were no traces of the panther. Some theorized that the occasional panther sighted may have wandered up from Florida or over from the western states, for these creatures are known to be great travelers able to cover enormous distances.

Independently of each other, Astrid and I had received a directive from the spirit world to assist with bringing the panthers back to our area. When we discussed our impressions with each other, we felt confirmation that we should attempt to bring them back with a ceremony. In spite of the official position of the Forest Service that these felines have been extinct in our area for over a century, we felt that we just might succeed.

After sending out our intent on the spiritual planes, Astrid and I felt a subtle shift in the energies of the wilderness preserve. We especially felt this during our walks there. During this time, our friend Barb approached us with some startling information. She said that Jenny, a research biologist, informed her that for the first time in decades, panther sightings were being reported in three nearby areas. Barb pointed out that these sightings form almost a perfect triangle around our home. Barb continued by saying, "A mutual friend of ours and I discussed this, and we decided that your and Astrid's presences must have something to do with the panther's arrival."[10]

Astrid and I were stunned to receive this information. Naturally, we had not discussed our experiment to call in the panthers with anyone. It was as if our intuitive friends had been innocently eavesdropping on our activity. Barb shared with us that Jenny, the research biologist investigating these reported sightings, wanted us to join her in a backcountry search for panther signs. "She is interested to see if the two of you can intuitively pick up any signals in the areas where she will be making her rounds," Barb said.

Astrid and I knew we could not turn down such an invitation. We set a date to go out into the first area a week later. I could hardly wait.

We met with Jenny as planned and spent half a day with her and a small entourage of her friends checking out half a dozen sights in the Cades Cove area of the national park. All of these sites were no more than a 20-minute walk from park access roads, and they all seemed like good habitats for large felines.

In each of these sites, Jenny had tacked pieces of carpet to the base of trees. She rubbed a salve on the carpet pieces saying confidently, "This scent will attract any self-respecting panther within a half-mile radius." One whiff of the stuff was enough to convince us that it had no drawing power for humans. The salve was a mixture of ingredients sent to her from a friend with the National Park Service in the West who swore by its effectiveness. It included spray (or scent glands) from male panthers native to the western states. Jenny told us that the felines would be drawn by the scent and rub against the carpet to show territorial dominance. She would check the carpets for hairs left by the big cats, which would provide scientific proof that, indeed, these creatures had returned. To our dismay, however, throughout the short backcountry treks, we only sensed the possible presence of a large feline once, although we were unable to pinpoint its presence.

On our trips, Jenny, who was also an excellent teacher, shared her knowledge of the native flora and fauna with the group and spent time answering questions. While Astrid and I appreciated this information and the questions that came from the group, we remained rather quiet, attempting to tune in to our intuitive voices for information about the panthers' whereabouts. We were not able to both listen to this interesting information and simultaneously read the invisible landscape. We realized that in accepting Jenny's invitation to join the group, we failed to share that we would need to be in a meditative silence while we were out in order to sense the possible presence of the panthers in the area. We were sorry that we could not have been of more assistance to her, and we even considered returning to the sites on our own to see what we could discover.

When we returned home, we decided to follow our instincts and made a decision to attempt to draw the elusive phantom of the forest to us using our already proven ability to attract others animals in the wild. In another attempt to connect with the Panther Spirit, we conducted a ceremony in which we explained our ardent wish for their return to this verdant area and to make their presence known to us. We explained that the land needed their presence for the overall balance of the ecosystem (since large predatory animals thin out diseased animals, which make herds stronger). There is also a spiritual element that cannot easily be defined, when a species is lost to an area. The land loses something, and we, as humans, are diminished in some way.

In our ceremony we apologized to the group soul of this species for how it had been savagely hunted and trapped by unthinking humans to the point of extinction. We stated that many people moving into the area now have a different consciousness and that we would try to offer them protection.

A few weeks after this ceremony, Astrid and I began to feel the distinct presence of one of these creatures. From our past experiences, we knew not to discount such feelings as only wishful thinking or our imagination. Still, on our walks in the nearby wilderness area, we saw no traces of their presence, such as paw prints, scat, or the remains of a kill.

During this time, I had made the decision to do a vision quest at a particular site in the same wilderness area because of its strong magnetic energies. We were having an October Indian summer, and it seemed like a perfect time for a vision quest. The night after I had finished packing for my vision quest, a barred owl perched on a tree outside our bedroom window and called a number of times. I felt that this was a distinct sign that I should not do my spiritual quest in the wilderness area near our home. I trusted the sign; however, I could not begin to imagine why I was being warned. We had frequently seen signs of bears, but I knew they would not be a threat because I would not have any food with me to attract them to my tent.

Astrid was adamant that I *not* go, and I didn't. She reminded me that during our eight years together, on several occasions, an owl's warning cry had prevented us from a disastrous mistake. In fact, only six weeks earlier, an owl's warning cry outside our window caused us to cancel a flight we were taking early the next morning. We did not have any factual reasons for making this decision, but later that day we learned that we were saved from making the trip in vain and, subsequently, losing a lot of money.

We had to wait several weeks to learn the reason for the owl's call on this particular night. It happened when we were walking in the same wilderness area and came to the place where I had planned to do my vision quest. It was a heavily wooded area not far from a large beaver pond. As I had expected, everything seemed as it had always been. The place felt benign and safe to us both. We had been there less than three or four minutes when suddenly the silence was interrupted by an ear-piercing scream from no more than 400 feet away.

I have heard such a sound only two other times in my life: once near my former home in Highlands, North Carolina, and once while camping out West. Anybody who has heard this sound agrees that there is no other sound like it in nature. It was the sound of the North American panther. It is literally hair-raising. Then, less than a second after this incomparable sound, an owl hooted several times from only a short distance away as if to warn the forest creatures of the panther's presence. Even more unusual was that both of these highly shy, nocturnal creatures cried out in the middle of the day.

Astrid immediately caught the synchronicity of their calls. "That owl was for you!" she said. "A few weeks ago you questioned the owl's warning outside our window. Just then the owl was letting you know what you were being warned about. Why else would an owl be hooting on the fading notes of a panther's scream?!"

How much danger would I have been in if I had ignored the owl's warning? Perhaps we could never know. We were both aware that there are few instances of panther attacks on humans in this country; however, in the last decade such attacks have greatly increased in several western states as a result of urban sprawl. In spite of my thwarted attempt at vision questing, we were elated by this unexpected confirmation by the great feline herself that our ceremony had been effective.

When Astrid and I finally made the three-quarter-mile-long walk back to our home, we received an unexpected validation of our experience. We saw the 10- and 12-year-old children of a neighboring family playing in their yard.

"Guess what we just heard," I said to them.

Without hesitation, they both enthusiastically chimed in, "A lion," while pointing in the direction from which we had come.

"That's right," Astrid said. "But how did you know that was a sound a lion makes?"

"We learned it in school when we listened to animal sounds on tape," they said proudly.

My partner and I looked at each other in amazement that the piercing scream had carried all that distance and was still recognizable.

ooo

Eighteen months later: A lioness has given birth to three precocious cubs not far from where we heard the lion's roar. Two are tan like their mother, but one is soild black like the true Florida panther, which we suspect is the color of the father. A more fairytale ending to this wilderness drama could not have been possible.

❀ ❀ ❀ ❀ ❀

CHAPTER 3

THE GODDESS

◌◌◌

THE GLOW AND LUMINOUS THREADS OF THE WORLD

Back Roads Between Sun Valley and Boise, Idaho: September

The ascent up the low mountain pass in central Idaho was barely discernible, as it stands only 1,200 feet above the surrounding landscape. Although it was still early September, the green aspen leaves had turned a splendid color. In the morning sun, the brilliant gold of the leaves gave the illusion that the trees were on fire.

While driving down a back road and basking in its beautiful view, I suddenly became aware of the presence of an Elk Spirit. I sensed an urgent message: It was pleading for me to help stop the increasing encroachment by humans on their winter refuges. Such encroachment, it said, had forced the herds to re-treat to higher and higher elevations, where they had no protection from the winter storms.

Just as I was preparing to protest that I had no jurisdiction over such things, I became stricken with anguish so heartwrenching that I involuntarily started wailing in a high falsetto voice. Never before had I wailed, and I could hardly recognize the sounds coming from me as my own.

I was then aware of the unmistakable presence of the Earth Mother herself. I knew that the Elk Spirit, which had just come to me, was a messenger for this exalted being. The grief I was experiencing was not just for the elk herds, but was a universal sadness for Earth, herself, and for the pathos of man who, in setting himself up above the rest of Creation, has taken a wrong evolutionary turn.

My feelings of grief had become unbearable, and I attempted to pull off the road. But as suddenly as the wailing began, it ceased, and everything was transformed. Looking at the landscape around me through the window of my parked car, I wondered at first if I might be dreaming. Every rock, every sagebrush, every lofty pine and blazing aspen, as well as the mountain itself, was bathed in a yellowish-gold light connected to luminous threads. I felt as if I were enveloped in soft down.

"This is not a vision," I said to myself. "I am seeing the world as it really is!"

The mysterious glow surrounding everything seemed to emanate from within all things . . . more accurately, perhaps, from within the Earth, herself. The threads of light were even more extraordinary. Unlike the visible spectrum of light, these felt alive. It seemed that each strand of this "living light" was self-aware and also aware of the whole. I felt that I perceived, on an energetic level, the very essence of the earth—perhaps the nature of Creation itself. I also felt that for a brief, timeless moment, I perceived the "flow" of things, for these luminous threads of light seemed fluid, shimmering, and eternal. These threads of light were connected to all things, thus forming the impression of a vast living web.

There were also strands, which extended upward as if connecting this web to some greater whole. Perhaps they reached into infinity itself.

My heartwrenching anguish had been transformed into utter bliss. It was then that I heard an inner voice telling me that one must know the sufferings of the world before bliss is possible.

When my perception returned to normal, I thought of the Navaho deity, Spider Woman, who wove the web of the Universe. I remembered the opening verse to an ancient East Indian account of Creation, "Father, Mother, spin a web, whose web is the Universe."[11]

I felt that my eyes had been opened. For the first time I understood what these ancient people must have known through direct experience. For the next half hour while standing on that mountain pass, I continued observing the glow of our world with its luminous threads. I knew that the goddess of our world had shared with me both her anguish and her bliss. Through a spontaneous shift in awareness, I had perceived her energetic configurations, while experiencing a joyous and ecstatic union with this great being—the Earth Mother—in her Gaia, or planetary, form.

ooo

Surely it is one of the great ironies of my life that as a priest of one of the most patriarchal institutions on Earth, all of my mystical encounters with Deity have been with the Divine Feminine rather than the Divine Masculine. For over 30 years, I have encountered the Feminine aspect of God in more than a dozen different experiences, which took place in both my dreamtime and when I was fully awake. How paradoxical it is that I was told in these experiences that I was the "servant of the goddess,"[12] when by virtue of my office as a priest I was supposed to be a servant of the Father God.

The deeper, more universal message here is that Western religions have lost their connection with the Divine Feminine. It is time for us to acknowledge our errors of the past. The Divine

Mother certainly has not suffered from our apostasy. It is we who have paid the price.

If Christ were alive today, would he not tell a parable of the prodigal son that strayed from Mother Earth, and, after squandering his inheritance of a healthy environment, was welcomed back home with great rejoicing?

∘∘∘

A TIME OF TESTING

Highlands, North Carolina; Atlanta, Georgia

My seeing the luminous threads of the earth on the mountain pass in Idaho was the culmination of a series of encounters with the Earth Mother that had begun five years earlier. Marilynn and I had just moved from Sante Fe, New Mexico, to Highlands, North Carolina, in the hopes that I might recover from my complex health problems in the nurturing mountains of the Blue Ridge. Marilynn had just graduated from the Sante Fe School of Massage, and she planned to start a practice, while I planned to divide my time between the lecture circuit and allowing myself to be healed by the land.

In the early 16th century when de Soto came through these mountains, he and his men were in awe of the natural beauty of the Highlands plateau. On one spectacular cliff, known today as Whiteside, the Spaniards were so captivated by the beauty of the land that they left writing on the cliff that has been translated as "this holy place." Since then, many thousands have shared those early explorers' feelings.

At one time, the Highlands area was covered by a magnificent, old-growth forest. Few old-growth forests remain. There was also a time, before the chestnut blight, when giant chestnut trees dominated the forests of the North Carolina Blue Ridge. Today their ancient carcasses are scattered throughout the forests like fallen titans. Still one can find enough huge tulip poplar and hemlock trees to appreciate, and perhaps long for what once was.

There are places where the trees and rhododendron are so thick that one finds oneself in a perpetual twilight interrupted only by the occasional shafts of sunlight filtered through the dense canopy in late morning and early afternoon. The Appalachian Mountains, once higher than the Himalayas, are the oldest mountains on Earth. They have a mystical aura that those early explorers must have sensed. Perhaps the enshrouding fog around the cathedral forest, meadows, and sequestered coves influenced the early explorers, too.

Today there is something more that can be sensed by a perceptive visitor. The ghosts of the Cherokee still walk the forest. Traces of a much earlier race that left mysterious glyphs on some of the granite rocks remain as well. Who these early people were, no one, including the Cherokee, seem to know.

In spite of the magic and pristine beauty of my new home, I found myself plunged into a deep depression filled with agonizing self-doubts about the path I had chosen nearly a decade ago. Through my continuing quest for knowledge, I was finding many of the answers that I had sought. With the awakening of my deeper intuitive faculties, I was able to help people in ways that were unavailable to me before. Yet, in spite of the profound changes and powerful revelations in my life, I had begun seriously questioning my decision to leave the institutional church. In the more than ten years since my farewell sermon at St. Jude's Episcopal Church, my life had been filled with so many miracles that it seemed incomprehensible to me that I could be experiencing such doubts.

Yet I was haunted by these questions: "Had I made the right decision?" and "Could I have accomplished more by remaining in the church?" I discovered that one of my calling does not easily become free of the past. The church's hold on me was tenacious. Most incredibly of all, there were times I even experienced a sense of guilt for leaving the church. "How could this possibly be?" I pondered. Perhaps nobody does guilt better than a good church or synagogue attendee, unless it is someone of my station in life.

As a priest, I had been symbolically married to the church.

Leaving it had brought up for me many of the same heartwrenching emotions that one goes through in any divorce—the anguish of separation from someone who has been a part of one's life on the deepest levels. Knowing that it was best that we part company did not in any way absolve me of the pain or guilt of leaving the church. Like many who have gone through a divorce have felt, I wondered if perhaps I could have done things differently.

On the other hand, I realized that I would have been a walking paradox if I had remained in the church. My beliefs had changed so radically that I could not, in good faith, continue teaching the catechism, creeds, and doctrines that I had vowed to uphold at the time of my ordination.

Since making my leap of faith and leaving the church, I had embarked on a truly ecstatic journey. In spite of the wonderful opportunities I had for growth and service to others during my ten years in the church, I had not experienced any of the miracles, epiphanies, and ecstatic moments that have defined my journey since then. Perhaps organized religion had lost its soul. Like so many bureaucracies, it had become self-perpetuating and self-serving, having lost the powerful vision that had brought it into being in the first place.

With the leap into the Unknown, I had left behind everything: a partner and a two-year old daughter who was the apple of my eye. I had left behind the security of an assured income, the benefit of a provided house and automobile, and an excellent retirement program. I had been well taken care of financially.

Now, without possessions of any kind or any assurance of an income, I found these things that I had once taken for granted now took on great importance. I also found myself longing for the close camaraderie I had enjoyed with many of my fellow priests. But it was leaving behind the intangibles of respect and prestige that goes with the territory of a parish priest that affected me the most. I now longed for the security of the known past as opposed to the uncertainty of the future. With all its flaws and obvious contradictions, the church had survived the disintegrating forces of time. Suddenly, the weight of what I had given up or lost had fallen on me with a crushing blow.

One day, while struggling with these issues, I had a sudden flashback to a sermon I delivered at St. Jude's Episcopal Church that marked a definite departure from traditional teaching. It reflected the growing changes in my thinking that I remained silent about up until that time. It was, in effect, a "coming out" sermon for me. The memory of this time was so vivid now it was as if I had been transported back over a decade in time. It began with a reference to the powerful changes in our world.

> For some time I have felt a growing sense of urgency. It is as if something of great magnitude is about to happen, and we are being prepared for it. I have come to believe that our humanity is at the end of a great cycle and is being prepared to embark on a new one.
>
> Our world is like a mother in labor preparing to give birth, a mother who breathes and sighs and heaves and groans as she prepares to give birth to her child. That child is a new humanity, purged of its greed and self-interest, cleansed of its old, outworn understanding of itself and its relationship to the Cosmos.

At this point, I challenged the people I loved and served within the church to take a journey with me. I made reference to a biblical event, which soon would take on new meaning for me:

> We are in a period of great transition. I think of the Hebrew people who long ago wandered with Moses through a desolate wilderness; who, day after day, week after week, month after month, were forced to wander. They began to wish they were back in Egypt. Even being the slaves of the Egyptians was not as bad as all this. Today we have to wander through a wilderness of mind and spirit. Like the Hebrews long ago, many of us long for the security of the known past as opposed to the uncertainty of the future before us. Many would prefer to cling to the old religious dogmas rather than open

ourselves up to the great revelations of the Age into which we are moving. Yet the old dogmas were never really that liberating. They have their own kind of subtle enslavement that prevents us from exploring the New. Today we must make an "exodus" from the dogmas and traditions that bind us and make a "journey inward" to the "promised land" of Spirit.

As I was delivering this sermon at St. Jude's Parish in Atlanta during the spring of 1968, I could see an attractive man with dark hair and penetrating eyes, early 40s, perhaps, writing fast and furiously, occasionally looking up from his notebook toward me. There was an intensity about him that I found compelling.

Had I known at the time that the sermon would appear in the *Atlanta Journal-Constitution* and newspapers throughout the country and later in two national magazines, I might have lost some of my composure. It was through this sermon, however, that I came to know John Pennington, an editor of the *Atlanta Journal* and a Pulitzer Prize winner. As a result of this sermon and successive ones quoted in Mr. Pennington's daily syndicated column, people were drawn from all over the city to hear my increasingly nontraditional approach to Christian teachings.

Throughout my sermon, I had frequently paused, allowing time for the message to sink in. During this time, an electric-like tension had been building. I knew that I was expressing the secret sentiments of some. Others in the congregation were growing visibly uncomfortable, and many were stunned by my next statements:

> The great new revelations of the mind will not be without profound effect on many age-old beliefs. Our religious beliefs will be tested to the very core. Like it or not, we will have to ask ourselves: "Is the Bible a book worth reading? Are the creeds "statements of faith" worth making? Is traditional morality a system of rules worth following? Is the church an institution worth

keeping? Perhaps none of us can honestly say what the final outcome will be, but we cannot deny that the direction of religion will have to change. That institution which in the eyes of so many has perpetuated and upheld a "closed system" of belief will have to open its doors to the wealth of new knowledge that is available. None of us can deny that within Christianity can be found that "pearl of great price," but for many it appears all but concealed by the trappings of ritual observance and correct creed, of dogmas and definitions . . .

Finally, I spoke of the need for the church of today, if it is to survive this century, to "die to itself," even as Christ was willing to die:

> The Christian church has an incredible legacy in the power of resurrection and rebirth. If the church is willing to die to itself, then like the mythical phoenix, it will rise up out of its own ashes. But if the church tries to save itself, if it continues to be self-serving and protective of its belief systems and traditions, then it will cease to be an effective force for good in our world and for the transformation of the human spirit. If the church stays its current course, it will become more and more irrelevant, eventually fading into oblivion. For future generations, the church of today will become only a distant echo from the past. The church's choice to die unto itself remains, at once, its most formidable challenge and its greatest opportunity for transformation and spiritual growth in its 2,100-year history.

It was the beginning of a new cycle for me: a cycle of change, a time of growth. The ideas that I was expressing were born out of a series of personal revelations, which had begun altering my perception of reality.

Jesus once said, "I am the Door"[13]—and he was correct. A door is something to go through. The church, however, has remained at the threshold of the door, worshiping it, afraid to enter.

I felt that the time had come for me to pass through that door and make a journey inward.

Even though such feelings had haunted me in the past, they were now hitting me with such intensity. Deep inside I knew the answer to this question. Shakespeare once wrote: "There is a tide in the affairs of men, which, taken at the flood, leads on to fortune . . ."[14] When I had made the decision to leave the church, I had the feeling that I was riding on the crest of a wave. I had sensed that if I did not remain on that crest, I would not reach my destiny and my life would be a continual struggle.

During the time of my exodus from organized religion, I had felt so caught up in the forces of destiny that there hardly seemed enough time to stop and question the direction in which my life was moving. Now, I was being forced to face issues that I had put on the back burner for more than a decade. It had seemed that everything that was happening in my life at that time was already planned. I had felt that I was acting out a script that had already been written. I had no idea how this drama would be resolved, but I had sensed that I had little choice other than to continue acting out my part.

ooo

THE GODDESS'S PROMISE

Highlands, North Carolina: Late Winter

It was at the height of my personal struggles that a series of events occurred that lifted me out of this period of anguish and guilt over leaving the church, providing me with the validation for my choices that I needed at that time. From this point forward, such feelings never returned.

Nearly a year after renting a hundred-year old house in Highlands, I had the exact same lucid dream three nights in a row—a dream that forever changed my life. In this dream, I was contacted by an utterly awesome goddess who seemed suffused with the primal feminine forces of Creation.

Standing in a large meadow broken occasionally by stands of tall pine trees, I look around and the setting feels familiar, although I know I have never been here. Wyoming? Montana, perhaps? The aroma of sage is in the air, instilling a subtle feeling of nostalgia—definitely somewhere in the West. I sense something very auspicious is about to unfold. And then it happens.

The ground begins to vibrate ever so gently. I hear a low rumbling in the distance, which moves closer and grows louder. I recognize it as the thunder of many hoofs. I see occasional coyotes, wolves, and bobcats emerging from the trees, racing by me silently like the ghosts of the forest that they are. What wondrous creatures! A herd of antelope comes bounding by. A family of mule deer breaks into the clearing. Overhead a pair of eagles soar, then a huge owl and ravens. The ground shakes. The noise is almost deafening, and I'm wondering if I should take cover. No! It's too late!

Out of the clouds of dust emerge the large animals, the bison and elk, in their herd formations. It is as if the entire natural world is passing in review before my eyes. Running with the elk is a tall primal Goddess-like being dressed in skins, who appears to have alpha status with all the animals. She does not seem quite human.

I later discovered that the Greek goddess Artemis Huntress is depicted exactly the way she appeared to me in this dream on some of the ancient temple walls in Athens. I had this lucid dream again the next two nights. On the third night, the woman stopped abruptly and faced me, saying,

"You are the servant of the goddess! You will help bring many back to the Earth Mother! You will have two ashrams, one in the East and one in the West. Fear not! This is your destiny!"

Upon awakening, I continued to feel caught up in the spell of this dreamtime encounter. I wondered about the strange prophecies. What about the ashrams? I am not a guru. A broader, more universal meaning must have been intended. But what? In spite of my confusion, something about her message felt very right.

Lucid dreams are always significant for me. A vivid dream is to the sleeping state what heightened consciousness is to the waking state; and when a dream recurs three times, this usually means that the events of the dream have already been set into motion and the outcome cannot be changed. You can only disregard the dream's significance at your own risk because, no matter what you do, what has been shown will come to pass. In these cases, it's best to prepare yourself and ride the events out as best you can and to learn all there is to learn in the process. It is destiny.

Several weeks passed after the encounter with the goddess in my dreamtime. I continued to wonder how such a prediction could possibly come to pass.

Then, one evening I received a phone call from a woman whom I had met with six years earlier in Atlanta. She had been diagnosed with uterine cancer. Although she was already scheduled for surgery, she decided that she wanted to try spiritual healing first and asked me for help in precipitating her healing. I had agreed to try and help her. When we met, I spent nearly half an hour directing healing into her luminous energy field around her body and to points on her physical body. To the surprise of her family and physician, after the healing session her cancer went into remission and a subsequent biopsy showed no remaining traces of the disease.

"I have always wanted to express my appreciation to you for what's happened to me in the past six years," she explained. "I have wanted to help you in your work, and now I can help you and Marilynn secure a home of your own. I feel it is important that many others have the opportunity to experience what you both have to give."

I realized that her offer was a fulfillment of my recent prophetic dreams. My partner and I were filled with excitement as well as a puzzling sense of urgency. We knew we had to set up this spiritual retreat home soon, because the direction of our work was about to change. We felt this was a direct fulfillment of the prophecy in my recent dreams. The area in which we were living would be the site of our "Eastern ashram," about which the goddess had spoken.[15]

The very next day we began hunting all over the mountain for a retreat home, which would serve not only our personal needs but provide a place where groups could come and visit us and be part of the powerful spirit of this mountain setting. For a month, we checked out every available cove and ridgetop and found nothing appropriate. Either the cost was too high or the place was just not right. I began to wonder if this project would take longer than I had anticipated.

Then I had another lucid dream:

I am standing at a viewing area seven miles south of town. I'm looking out over a huge valley 2,000 feet below and recognize an area known as Blue Valley. As in waking life, I see those familiar mist-enshrouded mountain ranges in the distance.

But there is a striking difference. All about me I can see innumerable points of fiery light suspended above the huge valley far below. I seem to know that those fiery lights represent the presence of angelic beings.

I turn to my partner, who is with me, and I say, "Look! It's the fire of the angels. It's where we'll find our spiritual retreat home."

The next morning I shared the dreamtime vision with Marilynn. We wasted no time getting into our car and driving down the mountain to the Blue Valley overlook. We saw no fiery lights above the valley, but I could feel the same sacredness, the same powerful magnetism I had experienced in my dream. All doubt was removed. This had to be the right area. For several days we drove the area's dirt roads until finally we found our retreat home. We knew it was ours as soon as it came into view. It was a contemporary log house overlooking a 30-acre lake adjacent to the Nantahala National Forest. A hundred yards to the north was another ridge, which looked down on the southern slope of the densely forested valley. The house itself could accommodate 20 people during a long weekend. It would enable us to have the experiential workshops and retreats to teach people how to reconnect with the earth.

I felt that this place would help me work to prevent the dire future scenarios for our world that I received in visions a decade ago. In my visions I was shown that unless we learned to live in a greater harmony with all of life and become better caretakers of nature, we would soon reap a bitter harvest.[16] These visions haunted me, and although I had frequently spoken on this subject, I had wanted to have a more profound effect on preventing these scenarios.

I felt a deep gratitude for my friend's generosity and the divine forces that made this spiritual retreat home possible. I knew in my heart that it was a gift from this goddess who ran with the animals and who seemed to have such authority over matters pertaining to the natural world, as well as my own life.

oOo

VISIONS OF THE FUTURE

Atlanta, Georgia; Highlands, North Carolina

I have said that the disquieting visions of the future I received were one of the principal reasons I left the church, because I realized it was not fully addressing some of the most crucial issues of our time. A full account of these visions will be published in a forthcoming book; however, I want to briefly summarize them for you here.

These visions were like lightning flashes on a dark and stormy night. For a brief moment, they illuminated a hidden landscape but then faded away, leaving only lingering memories and impressions of some greater reality. They also left me with a sense of urgency about the issues they reflected and a need to understand more of what they were teaching.

The visions differed from my intuitive feelings and psychic impressions. I did not consciously seek them, nor could I stop them once they had begun, because I was usually in a cataleptic-like state. I always experience a split consciousness while receiving a vision in which part of me is the detached observer while another part is totally involved in the unfolding drama. An indefinable voice always accompanies my visions. This voice, which conveys such spaciousness that I can only describe it as a "cathedral whisper," always sums up the essence of the vision in a single poignant sentence.

The impact some visions have had on me often lingered for days and sometimes weeks. The impact of a few, like the apocalyptic visions, have never gone away and seem larger than life.

I saw that as residents of this planet, most of us are engaged in inconsequential pursuits, while the deeper more urgent needs of our world are going unrecognized.

The following is a brief summary of some of my early visions dating back to 1970:

I saw a total revolt of the elemental forces that resulted in catastrophic earthquakes, tidal waves, floods, massive storms, volcanic eruptions, and huge fires that could not be extinguished. I saw that many people would want to blame nature, but, in reality, this elemental revolt was the inevitable consequence of humanity placing itself above the laws of nature. Others would believe these events came as punishment from God, but I perceived that God does not punish! Instead, what was happening was the result of our being poor caregivers in the garden of the world. We were reaping a bitter harvest of the seeds we had so carelessly sown. I was told that what was happening would be a cleansing for the whole world and would be the means by which Creation saves us from a much worse fate.

I saw much fear, chaos, and loss of life. I was shown that only those who live in harmony not only with their fellow human beings but also with the elemental forces themselves would come through this safely. These "Earth Children" would have to return to wilderness areas for a time, where they would thrive.

The very next night I had a second vision in which I saw ghostly forms rising up from the earth. I was told that these forms represented all that had ever been: the noblest achievements, the greatest discoveries, and the highest knowledge of our species. Knowing that the earth was dying, I felt unspeakable grief and anguish for her and for humanity. As I gazed in despair at this scene, I heard a voice say, "Do not be saddened, for what you behold will provide the prototypes of a new earth that is being born."

To my amazement, I saw the dying earth and, next to her, a new earth bathed in a golden glow. I understood that this was the glow of her awareness. She seemed to embody all of the purity, hope, innocence, and potential of a newborn child. I felt myself reaching out to embrace her with my love and gratitude.

My next vision of the future occurred on the eve of a winter solstice during the mid 1980s. I was taken out of my body and suspended in space at a distance of about a third of the way to the moon. I was told that I was going to witness the six possible futures of the world and that the fate of the world would not be caused by God's will. Instead, the fate would be the choice made by the Group Mind of humanity and based on the lessons that humankind needed to learn.

Several of these possible futures were unthinkable. They involved great destruction by the elemental forces and environmental collapse. In another possible future of the earth, we narrowly survived a complete environmental collapse. All of humankind needed to spend time and effort on healing the damage that had been done. With this narrow escape, there was good news. The consumer culture that had been responsible for so many of our problems had collapsed. War had ended. People were no longer motivated by greed and materialism.

I was also shown a possible future where we moved into a new level of awareness. People were much more psychic. Although we were living more in harmony, some hardships remained as we worked through the particular challenges of this level. Finally, I was shown a possible future where we made a quantum leap in mind and spirit into an earthly paradise. I was told that it would be unlikely that our world would choose such a future but that, nonetheless, it was still in the offering.

When the visions ended, the first rays of dawn were just appearing in the sky. I could not believe that I had witnessed an epic nightlong vision of future possibilities for the earth. Of course I wondered how many years we had before the time of choosing came to an end. But for the moment it seemed that the human story was open-ended. We could still make choices for the future of our planet, but we were rapidly running out of time.

❂ ❂ ❂ ❂ ❂

CHAPTER 4
THE INVISIBLE WORLD

There's a whole energetic world that surrounds us that is teeming with life and is vaster, more complex, and more ancient than the physical world with which we are so identified. The energies and entities of this unseen world impinge on and influence our world in countless ways. Many of our human problems come from nonrecognition of this elemental realm, but our connection can be restored. A union with the world of the elemental spirits and powers is unsurpassed as a key to restoring balance in our world.

○○○

THE SACRED GARDEN

Highlands, North Carolina: Summer

During our first year in Highlands, Marilynn, my former partner, and I rented a two-story frame house with an ideal backyard for a garden. The rich soil and the eight-hour exposure to sunlight provided the necessary raw materials for our garden. We decided to go for it.

Within weeks, we had created a large garden consisting of raised mounds of soil. Each mound held the seeds of three or four vegetables, flowers, and herbs. This method of companion planting was based on the theory that certain plants thrive growing next to certain other species. An example of this is the relationship between corn and string beans, where the mature bean vines wrap around the cornstalks. Flowers and herbs such as nasturtiums were added because of their proven ability to keep insects away. It was our desire to use only natural means of growing plants in an attempt to be in harmony with the natural world.

We asked my stepson, Rick, who was 13 at this time, to make a scarecrow for the garden. A few mornings later, Marilynn and I found ourselves staring with amazement at what undoubtedly had to be the most sensual-looking scarecrow east of the Pecos. Because of her extraordinary chest measurements, we named her Sophia. I learned to never underestimate the creativity of a 13-year-old boy trying to deal with raging hormones.

Sophia, in fact, became a local legend, and soon local people began frequenting our yard expressing a desire to study our unusual mound garden. We knew better. They had heard about Sophia and wanted to gawk at her. It became a source of pride for Rick.

After planting our garden, we held a ceremonial chanting making tobacco and cornmeal offerings. We beseeched the spirits of the natural world, the nature elementals, to not only bless our garden but to help keep away the animals, birds, and insects who might plunder it when the sprouts began to break through the soil.

In turn, we promised to harm no living being and to leave a large area wild for the creatures adjacent to the garden. We also promised to leave a portion of our bounty close to the garden as our gift to all creatures.

Not completely satisfied with the spiritual contact, Rick and I spontaneously conceived a backup plan. We decided to do a "male thing" of marking the boundaries (specifically the four corners) to let others know that this was our territory. Rick got so involved in this endeavor that I had a hard time convincing him that marking the garden once a week was enough. In fact, more than once I caught him clandestinely marking the garden on his own for added insurance.

Something we did worked, whether soliciting help from plant spirits, adding certain flowers and herbs to serve as repellents, or the "marking ritual." Weeks later we were looking at a beautiful garden, prolific beyond our wildest dreams.

Clinging to the numerous sassafras and elderberry plants surrounding our creation were hordes of Japanese beetles and other predators. In fact, there were so many that at times the branches were bent down with their weight. Yet not a one could be found in our garden. As it later turned out, we were the only ones in this rural county whose tomatoes survived the onslaught of beetles that summer.

Local farmers, long brainwashed and misled by the propaganda of the Department of Agriculture, dropped by to look with awe at this strange garden. They wanted to know our secrets but were skeptical of the veritable simplicity of the combined French

Intensive and biodynamic methods of planting envision by the Austrian philosopher Rudolf Steiner. Some seemed to be convinced we were withholding key information. We were! Of course, we avoided bringing up the "weird stuff" about contractual agreements with elemental spirits and territorial marking. But then, doesn't every good chef leave out some key ingredient when sharing a favorite recipe?

A family of rabbits produced a litter in the dense foliage about 20 feet from the garden boundaries. At first, Marilynn, Rick, and I were apprehensive, but we need not have been. Each evening, about an hour before dusk, we could see the rabbits grazing all around the garden. Yet there was not so much as a single bite into the cabbage leaves or anything else in the garden. In thanksgiving, every few days we began leaving a portion of our bounty for our friends of the natural world.

Any garden of the type we created becomes a natural, man-made power spot. It is impossible to describe the feelings of harmony, healing, and serenity we experienced in our sacred plot of land. Sometimes we visited it simply to experience its power and serenity.

Not all was perfection, however. One afternoon in August while drinking tea in our small kitchen, Marilynn and I saw a raven land on a small feeding station outside the kitchen window. Instead of eating, however, it glared ominously at the two of us. We knew that unusual experiences with black birds can be warnings of sickness, disease, or negativity. Something was wrong. Only once before had a large raven come to the bird feeder. Two months earlier, the exact same phenomenon occurred, and three hours later our kitten suddenly became ill, nearly dying. Once again death was lurking close. But where? Then after a few minutes of contemplation, we both received the same flash of cognition—the garden.

Arriving there moments later, our hearts sank. Overnight a blight had hit, and already 40 percent of the garden was stricken. A day later and it would have been a complete disaster. We rushed to a nearby nursery and picked up a bottle of the least intrusive chemical herbicides at the time.

The dusting of herbicide proved successful, our garden was saved, and another lesson was learned. A truly holistic approach means utilizing not only the insights of the alternative and natural methodology, but embracing some scientific approaches as well. No model has all the answers.

Finally, late August rolled around with a still prolific garden that promised to continue thriving until November. In our enthusiasm, we had planted a garden that yielded far more than we could eat, can for the winter, and give away to friends. At the height of this abundance, a subtle new sensation began haunting us. We began to feel guilty. How selfish it was for us to continue gathering so much more than we needed.

That afternoon while standing at the edge of the garden and offering sage smoke, in a loud voice I thanked the nature spirits for this joint experiment between the human and elemental kingdoms. I added with much feeling, "From now on, we wish to remove the protective boundaries, and share our garden with our winged friends, the hopping ones and creeping crawling ones." Then, we expressed that the animal kingdom could now enter our garden, but to please take only their share.

Our request that animal-world visitors take no more than their share was not heeded. The following day we walked down to find our garden ravaged. Every cabbage, tomato, cucumber, and squash was partially eaten. About a third of our vegetables were chomped on, and even the moles had had a field day, tunneling into the garden for the first time to devour the succulent roots. One thing was clear: It had been our contractual agreement that had protected us for four months, more than the territorial marking or the repellent plants. But how could we complain? We had received so much from our garden, not just in produce but also in great spiritual lessons and blessings.

○○○

This was my first attempt to consciously work with the elemental kingdom. The prolific garden that resulted exceeded my expectations. The concept of unity with all life was given new meaning for me by this experience. I realized through this experiment, and others that followed, that such partnerships between the human and elemental world are unbeatable. I realized that our gardens do not have to be invasive and that they can serve all life, not just humans. I sensed that through such cooperative efforts between the human and elemental worlds, along with a more enlightened attitude, we could quickly solve many of the problems plaguing our environment today.

ooo

PLANT SPIRIT

Canyonlands National Park, Utah: Spring

Marilynn and I intended to have a short leisurely walk into Squaw Creek Canyon to fill several quart bottles at one of our water sources and then return to our campsite for breakfast. The vision-quest group had departed to their solo sites the morning before, and the questers were scattered throughout the trackless expanses of the canyon where they would each be alone for the next two days.

Happy to have some well-earned time alone ourselves, our mood was one of lightheartedness and abandon. While we were walking, we became so enchanted with the spectacular redrock formations and the desert foliage that we temporarily forgot about breakfast. We continued in silence as if being drawn to some unknown destination.

Soon we came upon a partially hidden trail that led to the canyon rim, where we discovered a huge bowl-like depression. The bowl formed a natural "medicine wheel." It appeared almost as if it had been placed there by conscious design. It was a place of power. I knew immediately that this was the location that had been drawing me. We sat down to experience its energies. To the east we looked out over a vast expanse of canyons to the snow-covered San Juans. A golden eagle slowly circled above us while rising on the thermals, eventually disappearing into the sun.

Our meditation was soon interrupted. Within a couple of minutes, my legs suddenly became too weak for me to stand. It had been an easy hike and I was in good condition. My old nemesis, hypoglycemia, was paying me an unwanted visit.

For years, I had found it necessary to eat a full breakfast before exercising to prevent my blood sugar from falling. Past experience had shown me that once my blood sugar dropped, no amount of willpower would get me more than a few hundred yards. Furthermore, I would not recover until I ate something. Our food was several miles away at base camp. Our only option was for Marilynn to make the round trip back to camp to get food, and on the rugged trail this would take too long.

While deliberating what to do, I heard a whisper in my left ear. Assuming it to be Marilynn, I asked what she wanted. Her expression remained blank. The whisper repeated itself, this time from behind me. It said: "Take my berries!"

I turned to see a lone, stunted, cedar tree growing out of a rock with dried purple berries that had fallen from its branches lying beneath it. I was amazed that a tree only five feet tall could bear fruit, but such trees growing from the red sandstone could actually be quite mature.

I sensed that it was the Plant Spirit offering help. I had never eaten cedar berries, but I decided to gather a dozen berries and chewed up a few. They were grainy and slightly bitter, but not unpleasant. Within a minute or two, I felt an unexpected burst of energy followed by a sense of well-being. The transformation was magical. Not only had my strength returned, but my hunger was also completely gone.

We were able to remain in the power spot for several more hours, both of us munching on a few dozen more berries. When we finally decided to move on, I left a tobacco offering for my special friend. My energy was still very high when we arrived again at camp a few hours before dusk. I was so excited! I thought I had found the cure for hypoglycemia! Unfortunately, the cedar berries I later purchased from natural-food stores failed to have such dramatic effects on my blood-sugar levels. Perhaps the secret of the berries I ate in canyon rim was with the connection with the Plant Spirit itself.

It was my first experience of having direct communication with a Plant Spirit in the wild. Like my experiences with the garden in Highlands a few years earlier, I learned much about our relationship with the world of nature elementals. More and more I had begun to see that I was a part of a much greater scheme. I was waking up to find that everything around me was alive and that I was not alone. Another piece of my spiritual life had come together.

○○○

If we are receptive to the whispers and subtle communications of the natural world, then we open ourselves to guidance and assistance in ways we never could have imagined. However, we must learn to listen with an inner hearing and to sense the pulses, rhythms, and heartbeat of the world around us.

The earth has a deep awareness that we seldom touch because it has a much slower rhythm than that of most humans. In contrast, our modern consumer culture has caused us to move through life with greater and greater speed. Amazingly, this rapid pace of living and thinking is often considered to be a virtue.

If we are to be connected to and be in harmony with life, then we need to learn to slow down our consciousness to match the much slower rhythm of the world around us. Had I not been out in the desert for several days, I most likely would have missed this rich opportunity to find help within nature. It was this experience and others like it that taught me the importance of slowing down my speed so that I would be in harmony and communication with the Creation around me.

○○○

PARTNERSHIPS BETWEEN THE WORLDS

Boulder, Colorado

It has been a great joy for me to guide others into working closely with the nature elementals in the care and protection of home and property. On one occasion, a friend spoke with me about a problem he and his father were having on some mountain property they had acquired. They had just dug a deep well on their land in a proper and likely spot . . . without finding water. This was unusual in our area, which has a high annual rainfall.

At his insistence, I visited what he had described as beautiful country property. I was horrified by what I saw. The land had been ravaged by his father, who was a contractor and who was accustomed to using heavy machinery to alter the land to meet building specifications. Trees, plants, and topsoil had been removed when it was not at all necessary to do so, leaving an eyesore and a threat to the local watershed runoff.

I spoke with the sensitive young man about the need to be better caregivers of the land and work in harmony with the invisible world. I explained that some of the nature elementals were upset about what had happened. I could feel the anger and frustration in the land itself.

I outlined a specific plan for restoration that could help heal the land, adding back the foliage that had been stripped away and restoring the topsoil. I also suggested that he speak with the earth and water elementals at the site, acknowledging the mistake that he and his father had made, and promising to work cooperatively with them. Knowing certain fragrances to be powerful in attracting and pleasing these beings of a subtler realm, I gave him some sage and sweetgrass to burn as an offering, too.

Soon after I left, he asked the land for help in filling his well with water. He apologized for his and his father's insensitivity and promised to do certain things to restore the balance of the land. As he spoke, he felt a distinct shift in the energies around him, and he was certain he had connected with the elementals.

The next day, to his delight, and to the surprise of his skeptical father, their well had filled with water. It remained full in the months ahead. At my insistence, he returned to the well to offer his thanks and placed some crystals in the area as an offering to the land. My friend was elated over the success of his deal with the nature elementals, and his father became a believer himself. He also learned how to be more sensitive to the natural world.

I was happy for both of them, but such a quick response from the nature spirits didn't surprise me. I'd found these beings to be very willing to assist and trust humans who acknowledge them or express willingness to offset past errors.

During the same time period, a former student spoke with Marilynn and me about a problem she was having with the house into which she had recently moved. The place, she said, had a history of former occupants who were involved in abusive and violent relationships. As a highly sensitive person, she had been finding it increasingly difficult to feel good or balanced where she was living because of the lingering field of negativity she had failed to notice before moving in.

Upon becoming aware of the problem, she began performing ceremonies for clearing her home, but they had been ineffective.

When we asked whom she'd called upon for help, she replied, "The ascended masters."

"That's your problem," we replied simultaneously.

"You're calling on the 'higher-ups,'" I told her. "This really is not the responsibility of such beings. They have loftier responsibilities." I realized how bizarre these statements must have sounded.

We urged her instead to call upon the nature elementals for assistance with this sort of issue. I explained that many jobs are best performed by middle management, and that there's a place for the blue-collar workers of the invisible world. They are quite efficient at their tasks and welcome the opportunity to assist when they are acknowledged.

That night our friend offered a ceremony invoking the nature elementals, although she found it difficult to believe it would work. After all, if the higher-ups didn't help, why would these "elementals"?

The next morning, she awoke to a house that was completely cleansed of its former depressing and disturbing energies. In fact, her home felt wonderful. For the first time in this place, she felt happy and relaxed. In addition, that night she dreamed that the "little people" gave her a flute melody she could use to call them when she needed them. At our insistence, she played it for us on her piano. It was as lovely as it was haunting. I had heard that some divisions of the elemental kingdom have their own music, which would explain why we had not heard anything like it before.

Not all of our attempts to encourage people to cooperate with the invisible world were as successful. A few months after assisting my former student with her house cleansing, Marilynn and I were contacted by the owners of a huge development of resort homes in the northern Rockies. They were having financial problems as well as other peculiar problems they would not identify, and they wanted to fly us in to determine if there was any kind of psychic interference with their project.

When we arrived, we immediately walked over the land to see if we could discover anything wrong. But we found nothing obvious.

The development was in a long valley with mountains on either side and several streams running through it. When we communicated with the spirits of the land, questioning why there were so many problems surrounding this development, we got an unexpected answer: The resort was situated in the middle of the winter habitat for elk herds of the area, and the extensive development was forcing the herds to winter in higher elevations where they had no protection from the storms.

The area's spirit guardians told us that if the owners were willing to leave some particular areas wild and untouched for the animals, they, in turn, would stop protesting the development and would offer their assistance. They explained that there was enough space for both humans and the nature kingdoms, and they welcomed the opportunity to work cooperatively.

To our surprise, the owners not only believed the message we had received, but agreed to the proposal. Marilynn and I left with the feeling that our efforts had paid off and our time had been well spent.

We were soon disappointed, however. A few weeks later, the owners decided that they could not leave sections of their property undeveloped and set out to continue with their original plans. They actually called to apologize to us, explaining that they simply couldn't afford to carry out the proposal we had passed on to them. We were unable to dissuade them from going against our warnings.

Our hearts sank. We knew they would pay a much higher price for their decision. It was not long before one unexpected thing after another began to go wrong. Contracts were broken, employees quit, and there was growing strife and dissension among those who stayed. Soon the development was bankrupt. The stress led to a falling out with the partners erupting, at least once, into a fistfight.

We were sorry for their problems, which could so easily have been avoided. But we were more sorry for the elk herds because their plight was all too common in our modern world, which is obsessed with more and more development based on greed instead of true need.

OOO

Many potential problems unrecognized by our modern society arise when we perform acts that are invasive to the land, our homes, and even our office spaces. We humans often act as if we are laws unto ourselves. This is usually the result not of malice but of ignorance. We have become deaf to the voices of Creation, blind to the signs from the mirror world around us that would have been obvious to people of other ages, and insensitive to the subtle emanations from the invisible landscape.

The village and tribal shamans of other ages understood the importance of maintaining harmony with the world around us and restoring harmonic balance when it had been lost. I have seen the enormous need for people to be educated about the reality of the invisible threads that connect us to the physical and etheric life around us.

The spiritual leaders of the future will be the priest-shamans who are able to read the invisible and visible signs and know what is needed or required of us for harmony and balance. These women and men will differ widely in their spiritual expression but will all serve the same Universal Spirit. Their churches will be magnificent cathedrals of Creation; their sacred scriptures will be etched in the stony hieroglyphics of nature. These talented and compassionate individuals will be the true leaders of the Church Invisible that is to come.

OOO

THE ELF PRINCE

Nantahala Forest, North Carolina: Midsummer

A few weeks later while on a four-day retreat with a group of students in the Nantahala Forest, I received information about the interdependence between the human and elemental worlds.

I had chosen to sleep under the stars in a cloistered area of ferns and mosses, surrounded by large hemlock and white pine trees, to whose energies I'm very connected. Shortly after first light on the first day after our arrival, I awoke with an awareness that I was in the presence of other beings. With my eyes still closed, I could see a number of little people standing all around me. I could clearly hear the flutelike melody one was playing and sensed they were sharing with me some of their music.

I opened my eyes, expecting to see them, but saw only the vegetation around me. They had disappeared. Disappointed, I closed my eyes and again they were there. One particular elemental seemed to stand out. I knew that he was their leader and spokesperson and was held in great esteem by the others. He was much larger than the others, perhaps the size of an eight-year-old human and very boyish looking. I wasn't deceived by his appearances, however. Even before he spoke, I knew he had the wisdom of the ages.

This Prince of the Elves, as he introduced himself, began speaking to me about the need for cooperation between the human and elemental kingdoms. He also described the purpose for his particular order of elves.

"Humans," he repeatedly emphasized, "must regain an understanding of their place in creation. Humans are to be caregivers in this garden that is our world. Of course, this does not mean that everyone should become a farmer. Some farmers," he noted wryly, "are in fact very poor caretakers of the earth."

At our best, we must have the consciousness of a good gardener, who loves and is in a relationship with all that is living. The gardener does not create the elements of the garden, such as water, soil, and sunlight. Nor does he or she cause the plants to grow. The gardener assists in the care, nourishment, and protection of all that is a part of the garden.

The wise prince went on speaking specifically about our relationship with animals. By loving and caring for animals, we help them to realize their own uniqueness. In this way, we can assist them in becoming self-aware and ultimately achieve individualization. This transition is necessary for them to make the leap into the human kingdom. For just as we need higher guides and angels to enable us to transcend our humanness, animals require our assistance to transcend.

"This assistance," the Elf Prince emphasized, "is a very sacred responsibility. Humans must assist the plant and animal kingdoms in fulfilling their evolution by helping them make the leap into the human kingdom."

I knew that this lovely being of the elemental kingdom was right. All that he said resonated with me; his words rung true. I felt such love and an utter lack of judgment from him, and at the same time, a pressing sense of urgency.

Again, I opened my eyes, half expecting to see this one who spoke of himself as the Prince of Elves, but I found only ferns and mosses, and the first rays of sunlight filtering through the canopy of evergreen above me. I was filled with elation, intermingled with sadness. It was the first time the little people had ever appeared to me in that form. I was also saddened to realize how far we humans had strayed from our appointed role as caregivers in the garden of the world.

❂ ❂ ❈ ❂ ❂

CHAPTER 5
COMMANDING THE ELEMENTS

*O*ne *goal of the ancient shamans was mastery of the four elements of earth, air, fire, and water within oneself. Each element provides certain powers. The element earth gives one the power to ground and manifest things in the physical world. It is the element of the practical. The element air is the element of freedom of movement and expansion, and rules the mental realm. Fire is the element of activity, transmutation and change. It rules our passions and inspiration. Water is the element of dreaming, memory and the past. It rules feelings and intuition.*

It was recognized that there is a direct relationship between one's ability to control the outer world and personal inner world. The degree of inner mastery was often measured by the ability to influence or control the physical counterparts of earth, air, fire, and water. Tests were often set up to demonstrate control of the wind, the water spirits, fire spirits, or earth elementals. Although few achieved complete mastery over all four elements, there were many who were able to demonstrate prodigious feats of consciousness and power in some form of mastery of one or more elements.

A more pragmatic reason for controlling an elemental force also exists. Shamans were often called upon to restore balance, not only for the community or tribe, but also for the natural world and all of its non-human representatives. A shaman was given the task of making sure there was rain or sunshine when it was needed, that crops would grow, medicinal herbs could be found; and that deer, elk, or buffalo would be in the right place at the right time. Shamans would also need a mastery of the elements to know if a person experiencing an illness had a particular element that was out of balance, so they could use their knowledge to help the person return to health.

Shamans never perceived the power of command over the elements as belonging to themselves. They recognized that they were simply mediators between the visible and invisible worlds. When invoking such powerful forces, one had to use great discretion and careful discernment. It is a cardinal rule that one does not arbitrarily invoke these elemental powers, lest one inadvertently unleash energies beyond one's control. The practitioner must have a valid need. One's motives must be pure and never rooted in self-gain or self-aggrandizement. Shamans themselves must be in a state of balance. Otherwise such forces, like floodwaters, could run rampant, creating chaos not only for the practitioners, but for those around them as well.

For me, the awakening of such abilities to master my inner world occurred with a spontaneity that may have been a result of my spiritual practices, and I quickly perceived the need to refine and explore the parameters of these abilities.

PROTECTION OF THE FIRE SPIRITS

Highlands, North Carolina: Early Spring

A growing sense of uneasiness had pervaded me the week before a workshop I was to conduct at a retreat center northeast of Montreal, Canada. I was rarely anxious about my teaching, but in this case, I had grounds to be. From reliable sources I had heard of a faction that had managed to keep several internationally known metaphysical teachers away from eastern Canada through both direct threats and directing negative or psychic energy.

I had a personal connection with the area, however, since two of our apprentices lived in Montreal. They both worked for the Canadian Broadcasting Corporation as the anchor newswoman and anchor weatherwoman. I had been looking forward to the opportunity of spending personal time with them and also to seeing eastern Canada for the first time. I had agreed to lead a retreat with the condition that we would not do any advertising and that all promotion would be done by word of mouth. By miscommunication, my trip had been advertised, and the publicity surely contributed to my uneasiness.

I grew increasingly agitated for a week. Each night I had disturbing dreams of the sort that usually indicated psychic attack. Although I used my usual means of protection, the problems persisted. Such situations were not new to me. For years I'd been on the lecture circuit making guest appearances on TV talk shows. Being in the public eye so much can make someone like me somewhat of a sitting duck for certain types of people who might be jealous of the attention I was receiving, who would want to test my power, or even try to stop me or anyone else engaged in helping others spiritually.

Finally, late one evening, I asked my friend and colleague Larry White Oak to join me for a fire ceremony of protection against the growing bombardment of negative energy I was receiving. Larry, a young healer of Native American/Scots ancestry, had been living with me for several months during a transitional time in his life. On more than a few occasions we had worked together and had always had excellent spiritual magnetism between us.

A ceremony or shamanic ritual is a means of bypassing the conscious mind and directly influencing the "second attention," which is our magical consciousness. This is achieved by the use of movement, gestures, chants, songs, and prayers as well as ceremonial objects. When the second attention is reached, it is possible to get information not accessible to normal awareness or to influence, even at a distance, the outcome of a situation. It is also traditionally used for healing and personal empowerment.

My decision to use a fire ceremony was not just for the symbolic value of a fire but to ritualistically draw in the power of the elemental force itself, or what could be called the fire behind the fire. Fire has a great power to draw out negative energies as well as protect one from those invasive forces that can travel through the subtle ethers.

The use of the elements of earth, air, fire, and water are a central part of the spiritual tradition I follow. These are believed to be the fundamental powers of Creation. Because man is a part of the Creation, something of the essence of each of these is within him. Mastery or command over the physical elements is the equivalent of mastery over the spiritual elements within oneself, which is the practitioner's ultimate goal. It is only when we find balance in our life with these forces that we can experience growth and evolution.

At 11:00 P.M., with Larry sitting across from me near the wood stove in my living room, I lit four candles, one in each of the four directions. I called upon the fire spirits to show me the direction from which the psychic attack was coming. Even as I spoke, the candle to the north began flickering wildly, while the others re-mained calm. This persisted even though the doors and windows to the house were closed and there was no draft that I could de-tect. We had little doubt now that the source of psychic attack was in eastern Canada, far to the north of our Highlands. Larry was just as concerned as I was, because he had been invited to accom-pany me on this trip to assist with the program.

I initiated a ceremony for protection by lighting a bundle of sage to cleanse our energy fields. As was my custom, I invoked the aid of the fire elementals. As I drew the sage toward me, my abdominal area suddenly burst into flames. Instinctively I began slapping my body in hopes of putting out the fire. Each time I slapped the flame, it spread further over my body—first down one leg, then the other, then to both arms and around my back.

Meanwhile, Larry had come to my side to assist me. Ordinarily a fearless warrior, Larry's face was pale and frozen with fear. When he tried to beat out the flame on my back, it spread onto my neck and into my hair. I must have looked like a human torch.

Then sensing this was no ordinary fire, we both stopped and looked at each other in shocked silence before bursting into ca-thartic laughter. Unbelievably *I had combusted!* And, yet, in defi-ance of every known law of physics, I was unharmed.

Even in the midst of all this intensity, we had not failed to notice how ludicrous the situation was: two shaman frantically trying to beat out the very flames that one of them had just called forth—flames that only spread with each slap of their hands. Such a scene certainly struck a blow at any self-importance we might have felt. Here in high resolution is one of the great mysteries of the spiritual journey. With every transcendent experience there is usually some crazy, absurd aspect of it that serves to keep us humble.

Seconds later the fire went out on its own. "Do you know what just happened?" I asked.

"You called on the fire spirits for protection and they gave you what you asked for," Larry said. For my part–Native American friend, there was no mystery. For me, however, the mystery only deepened.

"*More* than what I asked for!" I corrected.

"It does seem like overkill," Larry deadpanned.

As we discussed what had just happened, I became aware of how different I felt. Completely cut off from the negative intrusion I had received during the past week, I had become my old self again. I took a few deep breaths as my body relaxed. I walked around a little, remembering how much I enjoyed the feeling of the ground beneath my feet. Not only was my wool sweater unburned, but it also had no smoke odor. Nor did I remember any trace of smoke during the actual fire.

"Maybe this is what some traditions have called 'the fire that burns but does not consume,'" I mused aloud, remembering Moses' encounter with the burning bush.

Smiling, Larry pointed out three burn holes in the carpet. It took a few moments for it to sink in.

"How could fire that can burn a carpet have no effect on me at all?" I asked. But it was a rhetorical question, for I knew that I had been placed under the protection of the wondrous and mysterious elemental spirits of fire.

OOO

Later I remembered a wonderful episode in the movie *The Right Stuff,* an authentic account of astronaut John Glenn's experience as the first American to orbit the earth. There was a dramatic scene in which he prepares to reenter the earth's atmosphere for splashdown. Upon discovering that he had lost a portion of his heat shield, he and NASA ground control realized that he had little chance of survival. His space capsule would burn up long before he reached Earth.

Meanwhile, at a tracking station on the remote Australian outback, a group of aborigines showed up and questioned the worried Americans about what they were doing. They replied simply that they had a man in the sky and that he would probably burn up.

An old shaman offered to help, and immediately he and the others built a bonfire and began a ceremony to invoke the fire spirits to protect the "man in the sky." Simultaneously, John Glenn saw little flicks of light like moths surrounding his space capsule as he began reentry. He was intrigued by the flicks of light and even felt that they were friendly and protective in some mysterious way. He kept questioning what in the world they could be.

Of course, the rest is history. Glenn miraculously returned without burning up, as it seemed he must.

While watching this movie, I was intrigued by the idea of anyone being able to invoke Fire Spirits for protection, or for any other purpose for that matter. The scene had such an impact on me that it lingered in my mind for weeks.

In retrospect, I now believe that on some level I recognized that I also would soon be working with the elemental force of fire. Of course, not in my wildest imagination would I have been able to anticipate my experience with the fire that burns but does not consume . . . except for three patches of carpet.

OOO

A FIERY LESSON
Boulder, Colorado: Mid-Spring

During his senior year at Boulder High, Jack began dating a girl who was addicted to cocaine. The temptation was too much, and soon Jack was also experimenting with the powder. It was not long before his mother noticed its adverse effect on his school-work and then his personality and finally decided to bring him to me.

Jack had maturity well beyond his years. My conversations with him were always very open, deep, and understanding. Each time we talked, he readily agreed with what I was saying and vowed to stop.

Yet it soon became apparent that my conversations and his good intentions were not enough. In spite of our efforts, cocaine was too available to Jack, and he was too socially accepted by his peer group as a user. Each of his attempts to come clean was short-lived.

After speaking with Jack one afternoon, I'd finally had it. I told his mother that I was going to ask the Fire Spirits to light a fire under his ass. She told me she wanted me to do whatever I felt inclined to do.

This idea was prompted by an incident that had occurred the summer before when a student of mine was spending a week at Metatante, an outdoor school that teaches the Native American philosophy of the earth. My friend and mentor, Rolling Thun-der, was the founder and resident shaman. Rolling Thunder had a strict taboo against drugs, particularly among his students, and possession resulted in an automatic dismissal from Metatante.

One evening when everyone was seated around a council fire, Rolling Thunder threw some herbs into the flames, while asking if anyone in the group had brought in drugs to Metatante. A tense silence ensued. He then threw some more herbs into the fire and said a few inaudible words, apparently to the Fire Spirits, while everyone watched in apprehension.

Suddenly a stream of sparks began shooting in the air like a Roman candle, all shooting in the direction of a certain couple. The shaman then burst into a tirade about their possession of drugs, ordering them to leave the community. They were so dumbfounded and so taken by surprise that they made no attempt to deny the accusation. Everyone was astounded and wide-eyed. The Fire Spirits had correctly identified those who, unbeknownst to the other students, had brought in drugs.

Remembering this story, I conducted a simple ritual in our ceremonial room, specifically requesting that a fire be lit beneath Jack to give him the will to refuse cocaine when it was offered. I then returned to the living room just in time to see him and his buddy coming down the stairs to the first floor. From the far side of the room, through the side railing, I could see only the lower half of the two young men's bodies as they descended the stairs together. I would never have anticipated what followed.

First, one of them shrieked. Then I heard "Son of a bitch!" quickly followed by "Oh, shit!" At the same time I heard the loud, frantic slapping of hands against a body.

Something must be terribly wrong. Jack was just not that volatile. As Jack came into view, I saw that his pants were charred and smoking around his front zipper and crotch. Both young men wildly explained that Jack's pants had simply burst into flames as they began descending the steps. Neither of them smoked nor had any matches with them that could have ignited.

At first I grew anxious, until a deeper realization began to sink in that this bizarre occurrence was somehow related to the fire ritual I had performed moments earlier. Once Jack's mother and

I finally figured out what had happened and saw that Jack wasn't hurt, we both doubled up in convulsive laughter. The situation was unimaginably funny. While his friend was totally confused, Jack had grown suspicious. Turning to me, he said accusingly, "You did something, didn't you?" He had come to know me too well. He again asked if I had done something to cause this. Making no effort to contain my laughter, I said, truthfully, "Yes, but I didn't expect you to burst into flames!"

The Fire Elementals are very powerful allies. But I saw then that they also could be quite literal. When I said that I wanted to light a fire under Jack, I meant it metaphorically. Yet they did just that. I made a mental note on to how to ask for help next time, and when I did, to be prepared for their response.

Still, the fire worked. Jack was so impressed and impacted that he stopped using cocaine and never went back to it. I've since wondered if the Fire Spirits actually understood perfectly well that my request was metaphorical, but decided that a literal response would be most effective. If so, I have to bow, not only to the power, but also to the intelligence inherent in the invisible world. Who knows? Perhaps Jack and I were paving new roads for drug rehabilitation.

I knew that Jack was longing for me to explain what I'd done. I told him that I had only been the mediator. Describing the ceremony I performed to him would have no more illuminated the resulting incident for him than for me. The ways of the invisible world remained as inscrutable as ever for us.

I couldn't resist a parting shot, though. I suggested to Jack that he should go change right away and get rid of those pants. If the girls at Boulder High ever found out about his hot pants, he would never have a moment's peace!

○○○

This and other accounts of spontaneous combustion in this book are also found in *Ablaze!*, Larry Arnold's definitive work on spontaneous combustion. Of the hundreds of stories in Larry's book, my experiences were atypical because they are the only incidents in which spiritual practices were involved. Remarkably, too, no one was burned as a result of these fires. Larry and I share the same explanation of this phenomenon: that the spiritual practices provided protection from burning. Years ago Larry asked me to appear on the national television show *Unsolved Mysteries* with Jack and Larry White Oak, who witnessed spontaneous combustion with me, to talk about our experiences. Although they were both willing, I was not. At that time, I felt that I needed to deepen my personal understanding of this phenomenon before relating it to others.

In my reflection on the continuing series of spontaneous combustion I have experienced over the years, I began to realize that the idea of a mastery alluded to in traditional shamanism goes far beyond anything that I could ever have imagined. In every instance of my experience with spontaneous combustion, either a sacred ceremony was involved or the need for elemental fire was so great that it seemed to have precipitated this remarkable response from the fire element. I am well aware that I could not have preformed such feats based on a whim. The proper conditions needed to be in place for this to happen.

I sensed that these experiences were related to the deepening of my connection with the elemental forces themselves—achieved through spiritual practices. For me, as well as for the innumerable women and men who have gone before me, the elemental forces have provided a direct path to God that no organized religious system of our time could have possibly duplicated.

○○○

POWER$ OF THE WIND AND $TORM
East Tennessee Home: Late Summer

When Genevieve and John got out of the car with their eight-year-old daughter, Carrie, I knew by the expressions on their faces and sense of exhilaration that something extraordinary had happened to them. I'd been standing on the front porch of our home awaiting them when they arrived shortly before dusk.

I didn't have to inquire. Breathless, Genevieve began describing the strange weather anomaly they had encountered on the country road leading to our home. Rounding a curve about a mile from our home they saw what at first appeared to be some kind of mirage. Four hundred yards in front of them, spanning the entire road and beyond, was what appeared to be a miniature tornado turned on its side. The center of the vortex was aglow from the fading sunlight in the west, while the swirling periphery was dark and filled with all kinds of flying debris.

Genevieve, John, and Carrie said they all felt awe instead of fear at the sight. Never before had they encountered anything like this, nor did they know that such things could occur in nature. John had started to apply the brakes, but Genevieve instinctively knew that it would be safe to drive through this vortex. In fact, Genevieve saw it as a sign from the Creator that the help she was urgently seeking for her family would be available.

It was as if this amazing natural phenomenon represented a rite of passage for them. They were about to pass through the eye of another more dangerous kind of psychic storm, unscathed by the chaotic winds that three times on the previous day had threatened the health and lives of John and Carrie.

While playing golf at the local country club the day before, John was suddenly thrown from his golf cart when it unexpectedly hit a bump. As he was being ejected from the vehicle, his foot had become caught in the seatbelt. By some miracle, he barely managed to wrestle free of this entanglement just as he was beginning to be dragged across the ground by the runaway cart.

When he arrived home, still shaken, he learned that during this same time period his daughter had experienced two strikingly similar accidents. In the first, she'd been riding her horse when it stumbled, throwing her off. When she hit the ground, however, one foot was still caught in the stirrup. Fortunately, like her dad, she managed at the last moment to break loose just as her startled horse had panicked and began to run.

As if that wasn't enough trauma for one day, later, while riding her bike, Carrie collided head-on into a tree that she had mysteriously failed to see. In this case she barely missed hitting her head, in spite of the fact that her bike was almost totally demolished.

Alarm signals started going off in Genevieve when the second accident occurred in the space of a few hours, and she began to suspect that something was very wrong. Her daughter was winning blue ribbons at the local horse show and was an excellent gymnast. Such bizarre accidents were simply out of character for the talented and agile Carrie.

When Genevieve learned of her husband's accident, she realized that it was time to call me for help. A few weeks earlier, when Astrid and I had visited her home, we both had become aware of what seemed to be a sinister presence lurking in certain parts of the house and had warned her of the potential danger to her and her family. Genevieve had already known that there were spirits in the house, which had been in her family for many years, but had believed them to be benign.

I had felt otherwise, and was more than concerned about their safety. Most ghosts are harmless, but there are notable exceptions to this rule.

It had been only a couple of months earlier that I'd been asked by a friend to check out a home she'd been renting to a woman with two children. After hearing about some near tragedies that had befallen her tenant since having moved in, she wondered if something could be wrong with the house itself or the surrounding land.

Shortly after they'd moved into this house, the woman's son, who had always been emotionally and mentally stable, was found one afternoon hanging on a rope tied to a rafter. Fortunately, his mother had found him in time, and he lived. The rescue unit managed to bring him back to consciousness. To her amazement, her son had no memory of what he'd done.

Then weeks later the son was discovered on the bathroom floor with his wrists slit, having already lost a considerable amount of blood. The mother had quickly enrolled him in therapy after the first episode, but obviously it wasn't helping. As if all this wasn't enough, the mother, since moving, had been experiencing what seemed like unbelievable bad luck.

My friend, who was renting out the house to the mother and her two children, had offered to pick me up and drive me to the home. Even before we arrived at the house, I saw with inner vision exactly what the problem was.

I told her that a very negative man who had once committed suicide in the house was still hanging around. She did not know about the history of the house, but later, upon inquiring, had learned that such was the case.

I said that he was experiencing something akin to what in physical reality we refer to as a psychotic state. Whether from malicious intent or simply out of confusion, he had become energetically attached to the 11-year-old boy who now began reenacting his earlier successful attempt at suicide.

It was relatively easy to rid the house of this highly dangerous spirit, and the change in the son's personality was immediate and dramatic. Amazingly, the very next day his mother experienced an entire reversal of the misfortune she had been experiencing, and she began having one stroke of good fortune after another.

With this experience so fresh in my mind, I told Genevieve that we had no time to lose. They needed to come over to our house that evening. My usual preference is to visit the site of the problem in person, but my schedule and the considerable distance to their house made me decide otherwise.

I knew that it was possible, though certainly more difficult, to perform this kind of extraction from a distance. But I knew I would need help. It was these circumstances that made me decide to seek the aid of my old friends the Storm Devas. In situations like this, one needs all the help one can get, and the Storm Devas, if they agreed, would be powerful allies—as powerful as the Fire Spirits who had bailed me out on other occasions when I was trying to ward off dark energy.

Ten minutes before Genevieve and her family arrived, I lit some copal, notifying Astrid that I was going out on the porch to solicit the help of the powers of wind and storm. The afternoon had been overcast and I'd heard some distant rumblings of thunder. I said that a storm would greatly empower the ceremony we were about to perform. By the time Genevieve drove up to our house, the wind had become wild and there was continual rolling thunder.

The ceremony itself was the essence of simplicity. Astrid and I asked that this sinister presence be removed from the home of this family and not be allowed to return. We asked that the house and surrounding grounds be cleansed of all disharmonious and unbalanced energies and that all who live therein be protected. We also requested that the house and its occupants be blessed and protected. At a certain point during the ceremony, an almost palpable force came in and was noticed by everyone. It was at that moment that I knew things would be okay.

When they returned to their home later that evening, Genevieve, John, and Carrie were startled by the enormous change in the way it felt. There was a sense of harmony and peace that pervaded the whole house. It had never felt so good since moving in two years before.

But would it last? We all felt that whatever it was that had come so close to harming them three times in one day would never return. Even if it should try, Genevieve, John, and Carrie would be able to identify the sinister presence and would know how to handle it.

ooo

Once more I was reminded of the enormous assistance that can come from Creation Herself when we are faced with difficult or dangerous situations. In the two previous stories ("Protection of the Fire Spirits" and "A Fiery Lesson"), I reported how my invocation of the elemental forces of fire brought immediate and miraculous assistance. This time, the personal danger to a family was extreme and needed immediate attention, and my calling on the powerful Storm Devas (who are also known as Thunder Beings in Native American traditions) brought assistance that was just as immediate, powerful, and miraculous. As always, I was most grateful for this assistance from the Infinite Creation in which I trust.

All of these episodes played themselves out with such awe that it left no doubt in my mind that there is a deep consciousness in the elemental forces of Fire, Wind, and Water. Perhaps there are few limitations to what is possible through them. I also recognized that I had developed what is known in shamanic cultures of India and the Americas as a "command over the elements." Command, however, does not mean "power over" as it does in our modern understanding of the term. It means that one has achieved such a connectedness with the universal forces that there is a merging of one's essence with that element.

I realized that I had moved into a new level of spiritual power as a modern Western shaman. In some ways the personal triumph was bittersweet, for I could not help but grieve over what has been lost in our organized religions. What I have come to know since I left the church are things I would have learned about and developed in my training as a priest had this knowledge not been purged from the institutional church.

Our religious leaders of today have been left spiritually

impotent because of the imposition of certain false belief systems. It is time to challenge the consensus reality of our time and to reclaim our power. This is the real truth behind the legend of the grail. The quest of the grail is, in reality, the quest of every person for that which is holy within one's self and has been lost. It is our magical nature, our true spiritual power, which has been denied us. Our connection with the elements is our connection with the Divine Feminine that was purged from the church.

ooo

PALL OVER HIGHLANDS

Highlands Plateau, North Carolina: Summer

When I saw my friend Larry White Oak walking down the gravel road to my home, I knew that he hadn't come to pay a casual visit. Larry, who did not own a car, lived three miles away. At first he was surprised to see me standing in the driveway of my home waiting for him. I had sensed that he was coming. Judging by the look on his face alone I knew something was wrong. Larry wasted no time getting to the point of his visit.

"What's wrong with this place?" he asked. "The entire area has felt so negative for weeks. The merchants in town are all angry and uptight. Even some of my friends are acting a little crazy. I'm beginning to feel this way, too."

I could hear the frustration in his voice.

"The land itself feels out of balance. I've even gone to some of the natural sanctuaries around here . . . places that always feel good, but they aren't right either. It's as if a pall is hanging over the entire area."

I listened with great interest. His words could have been my own. He was accurately describing my own assessment of the Highlands Plateau.

This was the confirmation that I'd needed. Sometimes it's difficult to determine whether or not feelings like these are more than the result of personal issues surfacing. I knew now that what I'd been suspecting was accurate: The problem was impersonal and pervasive.

"It's the weather!" I stated, relieved to have some validation of my instinctive feelings. "This drought has had a negative effect not only on the land but on the people."

For the past several months, the Highlands Plateau, at 4,000 feet above sea level, had been under siege by the worst drought in recent history. The abundant streams and cascading waterfalls for which the area was well known were down to a trickle. Wells and springs were drying up for the first time anyone could remember.

I took the opportunity to share certain esoteric concepts about the function of storms. I pointed out that a primary role of storms is not only to replenish the land but also to cleanse and recharge the electromagnetic field of the earth. The energy of such storms helps to neutralize the negativity built up in the subtle ethers. Humans contribute to this buildup through negative thoughts, feelings, and actions. Our negativity pollutes the subtle levels, which give rise to feelings of being limp, lethargic, depressed, and without purpose. Who among us has not experienced these conditions many times and wondered what was wrong?

"I thought that was it!" Larry said, reeling somewhat from this confirmation.

"I hate it!" he said emphatically. "We really need rain."

"Perhaps that's why you're here," I said. But my friend missed the cue.

"What do you mean?"

"You and I should do a rain ceremony and see if we can tip the weather scales." Aware of some of my endeavors in the past, he was intrigued by the idea. I knew that with his natural love for and connection to the land, my neighbor of Native American/Scots ancestry would be a good ally for this sacred ceremony. We had worked together in many ways for almost ten years and always felt a strong and positive spiritual and psychic magnetism with each other. We decided to go at once to a secluded place that was special to Larry. For the first time in weeks, I felt a sense of elation. I took it as a good sign that we'd made the right decision.

After gathering certain power objects we'd be using for our rain ceremony, Larry guided me along back roads to the secluded place he had in mind for our ritual. My off-road vehicle kicked up huge clouds of dust as we headed out, an unusual sight in this region, which received 70 inches of rainfall each year. It was a reminder of just how serious the drought at hand was.

Parking our car where the road narrowed, we began following an animal trail. Soon we came to an unusual formation of large rocks where a rushing stream began its rapid descent down the mountain. Just beyond our vision, we could hear the sound of a waterfall that was somewhat muted by the dense foliage on either side of the stream. To my surprise, Larry pointed to the entrance of a cave only ten feet away. Its dark mouth blended so completely with the shadows cast by the rocks that I had completely missed it.

When we entered the cave, I felt as if I were stepping into another dimension . . . timeless, dark, and still. From the entrance, I could catch glimpses of the beautiful Nachoochee Valley 2,000 feet below. Just beyond the cave opening, the diffused sunlight was reflected off the water flowing over smooth, solid granite carved out of the mountain.

"When I was living at the barn with Chief Ken (Two Trees) and helping him with his horses, I would come here to be alone," Larry explained. "It was my special place of power. You're the first person I've ever brought here."

"I'm honored, Larry. I won't tell anyone."

As we prepared for our ceremony, I experienced my usual self-doubts. Who was I to think that I could influence the powerful elemental forces of wind and water? What if my unbroken string of successes were just coincidences or simply due to incredibly good timing?

At the same time, I also felt that growing sense of elation over what we were about to attempt. Perhaps it was the challenge of the unknown. Perhaps it was the very audacity of attempting such an inconceivable feat that was drawing me closer to the Great Mystery. I wasn't bothered by the apparent contradictions in my feelings, because on the path that I traveled paradox seemed to be the way of so many things. From a detached stance, I watched my mind for a moment until the chatter ceased.

We began our ceremony by calling in the powers of the Sacred Directions and stating our intent. We had opened up a sacred space, a window to the invisible world, in which we could draw on the powers of that other realm. Once such a window is opened, there is no limit to what is possible. A different set of laws become operative when linear time and three-dimensional space have been transcended.

Our next step was to set our human egos aside so that they were not in the way. We needed to become completely detached from the outcome of our ritual. Any need for certain results could block our access to the very spiritual forces we had invoked.

Our ceremony was the essence of simplicity. No one raised their arms to the heavens, commanding the powers in stentorian voices. That makes good material for movies, but the reality of these ceremonies is very different. We spoke in a natural, unassuming way to the Storm Spirits. Finally, we closed our ritual with the release of the sacred powers we had brought in so that they could fulfill the purpose for which we had intended.

The following day the rains came in from the west, riding on the winds of a major weather front that no one had foreseen. Once the dry earth was saturated, the lakes and streams began to rise, rapidly overflowing their banks by the second week. Soon the local newspaper was printing articles about the flooding problem that had replaced the prolonged drought. I even wondered whether or not our spiritual intervention in the stagnated weather condition had resulted in overkill. Perhaps some of those legendary shamans and medicine people of ages past would have known how to avoid having the pendulum swing to the opposite extreme. Yet something inside me told me I was only obsessing. Larry and I had accomplished what we set out to do. Besides, we were only mediators and midwives. It was the Earth Mother herself who gave birth to the storms, ending the drought.

○○○

The repeated success of my Earth ceremonies demonstrated to me the power of intervention in extreme weather conditions to achieve a more balanced environment. I saw that it is possible to enter into a direct relationship with and influence the forces of nature. I was haunted by the ramifications of the numerous miracles in my life since making my leap of faith from the womb of organized religion into the uncharted waters of spirit.

OOO

SUN CEREMONIES

Smoky Mountain Foothills; Canyonlands National Park

I had been doing rain ceremonies for years. This time, however, I needed to do the opposite: to "stop" the rain. I had scheduled an outdoor Earth Magic Seminar for a weekend in April. The seminar had quickly filled up, but when the weekend rolled around there were predictions of several days of rain. Such weather would be disruptive for the group's learning, since most of the exercises we would be doing required us to be outdoors.

As the weather reports predicted, rain began to fall around 8:00 A.M. on the day of the seminar. I asked the spirit world for permission to perform a ceremony to stop the rain. After receiving permission, I felt it would be acceptable to do so. Within a half hour after the ceremony, the rain stopped. However, it started to rain again the next morning. I performed a second sun ceremony, and the rains stopped almost immediately and held off just until the close of our seminar.

On both days the weather was spectacular. The wind blew in from every direction in powerful gusts. When the sky grew cloudy, the wind always seemed to push the clouds away. There were times during the seminar that we stopped what we were doing to experience the power of these wild winds. It is said by the native peoples of our land that a "four directions wind" is the most powerful of all directional winds and brings with it special blessings of plenitude and success in all current endeavors.

A month later, I was faced with a similar rain situation when Astrid and I were outside of Canyonlands National Park with a group of people on their first vision quest. Our first night together we experienced a violent storm that uprooted several of our tents. Then, on the morning we were prepaing to go out for a three-day solo quest, an even more violent storm with strong winds and continual lightning began rapidly approaching. As it became apparent that the storm was moving in our direction, I could sense concern growing in some of our group. We gathered together in a circle and joined hands. I thanked the Storm Devas for their gift of rain and asked if they would provide gentler weather for our vision questers.

According to one member of the group: "It was an amazing thing to see. It seemed as if the storm just parted and passed on either side of us enabling us to remain dry on our way to our individual quest sites."

The next day Astrid learned that the National Park Service had been forced to close down a section of the park near us that was flooded by a ten-foot wall of water that poured down through one of the major washes.

ooo

The winter that followed our return to East Tennessee from the vision quest in Canyonlands was the wettest on record. It rained nearly all of January and February. In February alone, the weather bureau announced that it rained 26 out of 28 days.

By the end of February, the ground was saturated, and most people were feeling a little waterlogged and frustrated by the weather. This imbalance was putting stress not only on humans but also on the earth herself. Intuitively, I had received strong impressions from the elemental spirits that I should do a ceremony for sunshine and clear weather, because the weather was largely out of balance.

Since I had received such clear guidance, I began making preparations. No break in the weather had been predicted, so I knew that I was up against a real challenge. My allies of the invisible world had never failed me, so I was cautiously optimistic. Besides, the true power and know-how for this effort comes from these marvelous beings from the ethereal realms; humans involved in this ancient endeavor are only mediators and conduits.

When I informed Astrid and several of my friends of my decision to do a sun ceremony, they were very supportive. Astrid remarked, "It's about time! I wondered why you waited so long to make that decision." It really had not even occurred to me to intervene in the prevailing weather before I had received guidance to do so.

In the late afternoon in the field beside our home, I performed a ritual for sun and clear skies asking the Wind Devas to blow the rain clouds away and release us from this oppressive weather system that had steadfastly refused to move on after dumping record amounts of rain. I was told that the rain clouds would be dispelled in 24 hours.

When I shared this promise with Astrid, she was delighted and passed on the good news to several of her associates. Apparently, I had gained somewhat of a local reputation for this sort of thing.

Twenty-six hours later, blue skies appeared in the west, and since the wind was blowing in from that direction, I knew that we were finally in for some sunny weather. An hour later, the clouds dispersed and, before the sun went down, we had our first hour of sunlight in quite a long time.

I was grateful that my ceremony worked and began thinking about how the traditional shamans in other ages had been responsible for helping to maintain the balance of the natural forces in their respective areas. Rolling Thunder used to say that there are always many problems that arise in areas where there are no "medicine people" living. He would point out that there are many such places in our own country. Rolling Thunder also said, "Those of you of European ancenstry killed off all of your shamans, and you have been paying a terrible price ever since." He was refering to our own dark history of infamous witch trials and inquisitions during which the main victims were often the village healers, herbalists, and midwives.

Rolling Thunder also would say that the very presence of these shamans was often enough to hold the balance of elemental forces. I could not imagine how my "presence" alone could make that kind of difference, but I was grateful for the honor of being in the company of a long lineage of women and men of every tradition . . . a lineage that may go back to before we even began recording time.

ooo

ROLLING THUNDER

Smoky Mountains, Tennessee: Spring

Astrid and I had driven to the nearby Tuckaleechee wilderness area that borders the Great Smoky Mountains National Park the day before our group was to arrive for a vision quest. Having finished working out the rather complex logistics that go with planning vision quests, my thoughts turned to the weather.

Weather in the Smoky Mountains of Tennessee and the North Carolina Blue Ridge Mountains can be very unpredictable. During the last two vision quests that I had led in these areas 20 years ago, it had rained the entire time of the seven-day wilderness experience. It was these disappointing experiences that motivated me years ago to only lead wilderness quests in the drier western mountains, canyons, and deserts.

However, I was no longer the person that I had once been. During my spiritual development over the past two decades, I had repeatedly been able to demonstrate a command over the elemental forces. It is this very command over the primal forces of Creation that, more than anything else, defines the way of the shaman. It has a higher priority even than the ability to heal or have prophetic visions and dreams. This is because of the fact that commanding the elements without is based on commanding the elements within. Attainment of such abilities constitutes the complete mastery of self. The path of the four elements is a complete path to enlightenment and God.

Besides my repeated efforts to restore the natural balance in specific areas, my purpose behind the public weather ceremonies has been to demonstrate the divine powers that are latent within all of us. I believe that such demonstrations will help to liberate the individual spirit from the prison of the belief systems of our times—the very dogmas that the leaders of both scientific and religious communities so zealously seek to protect. It was the result of my repeated success with the weather that caused me to decide to lead a vision quest in the Smoky Mountains once again.

When I addressed the weather elementals on the day before our group arrived, I stated my intention for fair weather, especially during the three-day period when everyone was out on their actual quest. However, in what would appear to be a contradiction, I gave the strong directive that we have a powerful storm at the very beginning of our week together. The purpose for this directive was that of both cleansing the land and of purging ourselves of any possible negative energy. Usually, I simply ask for fair weather or for rain when there is a major drought. This time, since my directives were much more specific than they had been in the past, I attempted to speak with as much clarity in stating my intent as possible.

When our group arrived at the base camp the next afternoon, I spoke to them about my ceremony the day before offering the suggestion that they set up their tents as soon as possible. Soon after I spoke the sky began to cloud up. An hour later I knew that I had my storm. However, none of us were prepared for the type of storm that hit.

Without any warning of an approaching storm, the sky suddenly lit up with a brilliant flash of lightning and a simultaneous explosion of thunder over our heads. This prelude was followed by more simultaneous lightning flashes and ear-piercing cracks of thunder directly over our base camp. We quickly scurried for cover. From the vantage point of our shelters, we were able to witness the unfolding of this natural drama. Astonishingly, the storm had begun right over our heads, as if out of nowhere. This impressive display was followed by a 40-minute deluge of rain.

I had grown suspicious. It dawned on me that my late mentor,

Rolling Thunder, had a hand in this. In the dozens of storms that I had invoked over the years, there has never been one with such intensity. I became certain of his involvement when finally, with a long roll of thunder, the storm announced its departure. This phenomenon was repeated again and again. This was my former mentor's unmistakable signature. Suddenly, with my recognition, I sensed his presence. "I thought you'd never say, hello, he said." I thanked him for assisting me with my demonstration.

"My pleasure," he said.

In my mind's eye, I could see Rolling Thunder drawing on his small medicine pipe that I had come to associate with him while he was on Earth. During his 70-plus years in a physical body, the Shoshone-Cherokee shaman had truly earned his name. He had achieved a mastery over the phenomenon of weather and had frequently demonstrated his ability to call in cooling storms on hot summer days when there wasn't a cloud in the skies. On at least one occasion, he was seen to manifest a tornado, demonstrate control over it, then dissipate it.[17] I had heard it said among native people that Rolling Thunder was their most powerful medicine person but, of course, he would never have made such claims himself.

The next two days brought fair weather, and then the three-day quest was idyllic. What a gift we all had been given with the cleansing storm and the perfect days that followed. I asked, and I received. I wished that everyone could realize how simple such things are when we seek the greater good with our requests.

Most people seek God everywhere except within themselves. Yet Christ himself taught that the Kingdom was an inner one. If this is so, then we do not need mediators to connect us with God. The ecstatic journey that I have traveled for more than three decades is the path of direct experience with God. One great truth has defined this journey: that the divine powers are present within all of us. Theologians, priests, and pastors must rediscover their role as the servants of God. We have outlived our usefulness when we position ourselves up as intercessors and authorities.

On our final full day together, after everyone had returned

from her or his solo quest, it was the group consensus that we have a sweat-lodge ceremony to close our vision quest (just as we had opened it). With this decision, I sensed that I was not finished with my rendezvous with the weather spirits.

An hour before our ceremony was to begin, while the rocks were heating in the fire pit, I announced to our group that I would ask permission for the Thunder Beings to join us in our lodge. Such visitations during an actual sweat-lodge ceremony are considered very sacred by the native peoples of our land. On such occasions the Storm Devas always bring special blessing to all those participating in the ceremony. Everyone in our group seemed up for such an experience.

I walked back to my campsite, which was in a secluded spot not far from base camp, where I performed a brief ceremony inviting the Storm Devas to be present. An hour later we entered the sweat lodge. The first group of hot stones were brought in, and the powers of the East were invoked.

Approximately 40 minutes after we entered the lodge, we had finished honoring the directions of the East and the South, and I asked that the door be opened in honor of the West. Our fire tender brought in seven glowing, grapefruit-sized shale, and we began the portion of the ceremony that involved the spiritual forces of the West. In the traditions of the indigenous people of the land, this particular direction is associated with the Thunder Beings, whom I sometimes call "Storm Devas."

Within seconds after I had made the specific reference to the Thunder Beings, we were startled by a long roll of thunder. We had forgotten about my earlier request and all began to laugh at our short memory. Amazingly, the thunder continued to roll throughout the entire time we were celebrating the westerly direction, yet there was no rain, just the deep voices of these awesome beings. This extraordinary synchronicity had the effect of greatly empowering all of us.

There was no doubt in anyone's mind: We had been paid a very special visit by the magnificent Storm Spirits as well as by a powerful native shaman. I felt a mixture of exhilaration, gratitude, and awe welling up within me. With the help of such powerful allies, I had been able to give a demonstration that none of us would ever forget, one that would greatly enrich the total experience of the vision quest for everyone who had attended.

I had made what seemed to be impossible requests, and yet they were answered with precise timing and in exact detail. The cleansing storm had come in with great fanfare. This display was followed by idyllic weather. Finally, the rolling thunder signaling the presence of the Thunder Beings, as well as that of my former mentor, came when I invoked the powers of the West in the sweat lodge. My connections with the Weather Spirits and my command over these primal forces had become more profound.

As so often had happened on such occasions, I felt the need to pause and reflect on the place from which I had come. I remembered how often my prayers as a priest in the church seemed to be answered with deafening silence. It was not my fault and certainly not God's. I simply had not understood what true prayer really was. I did not understand how to make connections with the spiritual powers that are available to all who truly seek. I had not realized that our ability to invoke the assistance of the transcendental reality is related to our oneness and unity with the Creator.

CHAPTER 6
SPIRITUAL INTERVENTION

In some of my more recent visions, I was shown that the time in which we can use physical methods alone to avoid ecological disaster has passed. Had we listened in the 1970s and 1980s to the voices warning us about the dangers of our disregard of environmental protection that was so urgently needed, it would be a different story. But we did not listen.

I am told that because of this, nothing short of spiritual intervention will save us from some form of environmental disaster. Fortunately, I was shown how spiritual intervention could be carried out and had numerous opportunities to experiment with this kind of technology to realize its enormous power. Therefore, I have chosen to include the following group of stories as examples of how the technology of spiritual intervention can be a protocol in the years ahead for healing our earth.

GREENBELT VIOLATION
Highlands, North Carolina: Late Spring

An underground source brought word to my former partner, Marilynn, and I that a certain builder was getting ready to develop an area that had been set aside as part of a greenbelt. When selling off lots, he had promised home owners that this section would be left undeveloped for all to enjoy. Now he was about to disregard his agreement. He planned to come in with equipment very early the following morning and clear-cut the area. By the time word got out to the surrounding home owners, it would be too late for any organized opposition.

When we heard about the pending secretive operations, we realized that we had no time to go through normal channels to try to block him. We were going to have to use another way.

Once faced with a similar situation, my friend and mentor, Rolling Thunder, put it this way, "If they can use deceit, then I have the right to counter it with my medicine." And he did so quite effectively.

On the evening before the bulldozing was to begin, we drove over to the site and began preparations for a simple ritual. We entered a state of inner silence and offered tobacco and cornmeal to the Earth Elementals and to the Infinite Spirit. Using a medicine pipe given to us by our friend Ken, we called upon the assistance of these beings to protect this greenbelt that was under siege.

Through our attempt to work closely with unseen forces, we hoped to preserve a small piece of land. A delicate ecological balance still existed in our area in spite of the fact that it had been under siege by the forces of greed and exploitation. As our final words were spoken, we heard the sound of distant thunder in the west. We felt a definite shift within and knew that our petition would be answered. The world around us has a way of reflecting back to us whatever we send out.

The next morning, as we returned to the site, we felt a deep sense of being protectors for Mother Earth. Someone had to be, because the land, the animals, and trees had no voice in their fate.

From several hundred feet, we watched as the large dozer started up and began moving to topple the first tree. When it was six feet from the tree, the huge blade mysteriously snapped off. We were astonished!

The developer was so determined to get the job done before word got out about his deceit that he sent his flatbed truck out for another dozer. The truck broke down on the way back, and the dozer had to be transferred to another truck. Then, when the dozer finally arrived on another truck, it wouldn't start.

Meanwhile, his contractors had made many attempts to drill for well water and had come up dry. His planned resort would have no source of water. In an area that receives 70 inches of rainfall a year, this was nearly unheard of. Finally, it was all over. The frustrated developer gave up, deciding instead to build on a lot he'd recently acquired near the local country club. We thought that was a good idea. Too bad he hadn't asked our opinion in the first place. We could have saved him some time and money.

Later, as I reflected on the series of events that blocked the development of the greenbelt, I realized that the odds against this happening by chance would have had to be infinitesimally small. The power of our intent and of our love for the earth, ritualistically focused on that small tract of threatened land, and empowered with help from the invisible world, was enough to change the outcome.

We were under no illusion that there were good and bad guys in this bizarre scenario. To believe that our side alone was the "right" side would have been the height of "spiritual pride." The welfare of the developer was important, too. No doubt he could have persisted and eventually executed his plan. I saw that by being blocked, he was given the opportunity to elect a more honest and appropriate means of pursuing his livelihood. Our intent had helped him, as well as the land itself.

ooo

I learned from this experience that intervention for the earth is possible using ceremony and intent. Significantly, our ceremony did not override freedom of will. Instead, new options were revealed that made higher choices possible.

This was our first attempt to intervene in complex situations involving human affairs and the earth. We chose to keep quiet about what we had done. However, one of our teenage children related what he had seen to one of his friends, who happened to be the child of some of our friends. As a result, no more than a few weeks elapsed before we were called to perform this kind of service again.

ooo

SAVING THE MOUNTAIN

Highlands, North Carolina: Summer

It was a scenario reminiscent of another era, somehow in the wrong context for an age of Dow Jones, fast food, and computer technology. Like Druids of old, we were gathered on the mountain one summer night, drumming, chanting, and calling upon the powers that be to help us protect the land beneath us. Although our props were those of our times, the scene might well have been from some movie about Merlin of Arthurian days.

In our center, we had built and lit the sacred fire in the traditional direction of the east. It was now dusk, that mysterious pause between the inbreathing and the out breathing of the earth. It was a time of power and heightened sensitivity to the inner planes.

To our east, a full moon was rising over the treetops. To the west, where the sun had just slipped beneath the horizon, a storm was gathering. Although still a few mountain ranges away, the storm was moving rapidly toward us, creating a pyrotechnic display against the background of rolling thunder. I realized that we had little time to complete the ceremony.

Marilynn and I were with a couple who worked as biologists and professors at a local college. Both were dedicated environmentalists with whom we had worked to influence the passage of local laws to protect the fragile environment of the area. Yet the time for political activism had run out. Spiritual means would have to achieve what political pressure and environmental education had been unable to accomplish.

Our close friends had called us to show them what could be

done spiritually to save the mountaintop. Many people in the area believed that it was a sacred spot with special, magnetic healing energies.

We held our friends in high esteem. They were warriors for the earth who had fought many environmental battles and had tried to educate others to work within the laws of nature. But even in Highlands, which they loved with such passion, they had seen one beautiful tract of land after another go the way of development. There seemed to be no stopping it. So many people were living only for the present moment. No one cared to look down the road to the future. There were those who knew better and didn't want to take responsibility. "We know the land should stay in its beautiful natural state, but if we don't develop it, then somebody else will!" they would rationalize. These were the people that made me the most angry.

Highlands, so endowed by the Creator with misty old-growth forests, chalk cliffs, and innumerable streams and waterfalls, is a microcosm of the whole planet. The environmental battles raging here are fought throughout the world. Sometimes I say to students, "If you can pass by a forest that's been clear-cut and not feel the anguish of the land, then you're not yet connected to the Earth Spirit."

The feeling of sacredness is not some arbitrary choice or romantic ideal. Power spots do exist throughout the world, serving as charging and distribution centers for cosmic energies to the surrounding area. Everything would be thrown out of balance, and chaos would reign if these were not left in their natural state.

Each year, we held a summer solstice ceremony on this mountaintop that was attended by a sizable group both from the area as well as many other places. Unfortunately, this site, which many had assumed was in the public domain, had recently been acquired by a builder who decided to develop it. If this came to pass, not only would there be the loss of a sacred site, but the large surrounding area that was already in a state of fragile ecological balance would be disturbed. In spite of the uproar of letters, phone calls, and newspaper articles, the developer adamantly refused to change his mind.

After drumming for a while, we prayed for the protection of the land from exploitation. As we conducted our ceremony, we shifted naturally into a deep attunement with the elemental forces. Every sacred ritual is by nature "alchemical." It is no different from a chemist combining different chemicals to produce a certain product. In ritual, however, what is combined are different energies in order to bring about specific results.

More favorable conditions could hardly have been possible. In addition to the storm, the full moon and the powerful energies of dusk, there was a sacred fire, the heartbeat rhythm of the drums, and four people with unbending intent to protect a sacred portion of the earth. All of these were the ceremonial objects of nature to be placed upon the altar of our love for the earth. This was one of those auspicious yet rare times when many different streams converge into a mysterious sea of magical consciousness.

Through an extraordinary synchronicity, each time any one of us spoke our intent, the thunder echoed in antiphonal response. We had become so intertwined with the elements that we felt that our intent to heal the land was healing us as well.

Further reflecting this synchronicity, at the exact moment the last words were spoken, the rains began. We all ran for cover, but still we were thoroughly soaked. We could not have cared less. We all knew the needed energetic shift had occurred. It was time for the healing, cleansing rains to take over.

The next day word quickly spread that, after months of stonewalling to community opposition, the owner of the land had abruptly changed his mind. He announced that he was closing the land permanently to development. The mountaintop was just too beautiful in its natural state, he added. He was leaving the mountain open for all to enjoy. Everyone was astonished by this sudden about-face, except the four of us involved in the sacred ceremony the night before.

It was almost a letdown for me. It was far too easy. Who would believe that a simple ceremony would accomplish what months of organized opposition did not? In the case of the mountaintop ceremony, there was enough spiritual power to open not just someone's mind but also his heart. In this sense, our intervention was even more powerful than with the greenbelt several weeks prior. The developer's eyes and heart were opened, and he saw for the first time the ramifications of his building on such a place. I could easily envision his driving up to the washed-out dirt road leading to the top on the morning after our ceremony.

Perhaps he was captivated by the panorama of mist-enshrouded mountains, or maybe he just sensed the peace of the land. Perhaps it was the pristine beauty of the wildflowers and a few old-growth hardwood trees nearby. Whatever it was, something happened that caused him to make a quick reversal of his plans and let the mountain "forever remain in its natural state for all to enjoy."

ooo

The episodes described in "Greenbelt Violation" and "Saving the Mountain" were my first attempts at spiritual intervention in human affairs for the purpose of environmental protection. I saw that there are times in which a spiritual methodology can bring about changes in a way more swiftly and efficiently that any political action or environmental measures could ever duplicate. While political activism and environmental education are vital for saving our earth, people's hearts must be opened for large scale and lasting change. I sensed the enormous untapped potential of sacred ceremonies, positive affirmations, and the power of intent to block the abuse and misuse of sacred sites and areas where the ecological balance is delicate and essential for the well-being of all. The startling success of our efforts provided the inspiration and foundation for me to forge the technology for spiritual intervention described in this collection of stories.

ooo

SACRED SPRING

Oak Creek Canyon, Arizona: Mid-February

One of my student teachers, Kathy, had graciously offered to help drive my Pathfinder to Oak Creek Canyon in Arizona, where I would be on sabbatical for the next several months. Kathy's husband, Denny, would be flying out to join us, and they would help me get settled in my rental home. They are both kindred spirits, and I looked forward to our time together.

After four days of driving, Kathy and I came upon the exquisite beauty of the Oak Creek area. Six miles to our south, the canyon opened up into the sculptured sandstone red rocks of Sedona, which has become something of a mecca for people on nontraditional spiritual paths. We turned off to the east on a narrow gravel road, crossed Oak Creek on a wooden bridge, and began a winding ascent of several hundred feet up to the top of a mesa that hosted a more desertlike vegetation. The guest home was small but adequate. It was light and airy and was out of sight of other homes. Perfect!

Kathy and I planned to leave early to hike around and explore the immediate area, while Denny checked out Sedona. It was late, and we were all ready to retire after a hastily prepared meal. Tomorrow awaited us.

Following a light breakfast of bagels, cream cheese, and herbal tea, Kathy and I left at first light. We strode out across the mesa that overlooks Oak Creek on one side and meets a steep rise on the other. There were not any paths, only deer trails that crisscrossed, often fading out, leaving us with no choice but to be savaged by the prickly desert growth.

The vegetation in this area is mostly chaparral and mesquite, interspersed with prickly pear and barrel cacti as well as desert thorn bushes. We were too preoccupied with the excitement of exploration and discovery to worry about being scratched, but I noticed that my knees and calves were bleeding and that Kathy's were faring only slightly better than mine.

As we continued walking, we soon came upon a steep incline of sandstone and shale that dropped into a narrow ravine, opening into a wash. We decided to follow the wash in hopes of avoiding further carnage to our legs.

Soon the foliage grew much thicker until we were forced to walk carefully through a dense stand of nettle that lived up to its reputation. My legs soon felt like they were covered with fire ants. This countryside had no mercy.

Following the wash, we detected the first hint of moisture, which told me that there would be water and cottonwood stands ahead. By this time we were thirsty and wanted to soak our legs. Soon the wash opened up into a beautiful glade of fern, deadfall, and large cottonwoods. Through this ran a stream with large pools so clear that it was difficult to determine the depth.

The water was just too inviting to resist in this mid-February Indian summer. We removed our shoes and outer garments, easing into the water, which was cool enough to take our breath away. It brought relief to our chewed-up legs and overheated bodies. We felt that it was our reward for enduring the recent punishment to our bodies.

Following a refreshing swim, we dried within a few minutes in the arid air. We decided to explore a little further upstream. I had assumed that the stream, because of the large volume of water flowing through it, continued for miles up the canyon. But to my surprise, the source of this stream was only a hundred yards farther. I could see a torrent of water flowing out from under a huge boulder, and growing out from the rock was an ancient cottonwood. Because of the large volume of water, it occurred to me that this was actually snowmelt from the San Francisco Peaks many miles away. The water must have traveled miles underground while descending thousands of feet in elevation.

We both felt the sacredness of this place. Like many springs in desert areas, this had powerful spiritual energies that quickly reduced us to silence. There are certain places where the human voice feels alien and disruptive to the energies that abound.

We each found comfortable places to meditate. I felt my consciousness merging with the aura of the spring. It was as if I had become water itself. I knew its essence, as though I was connected to all water everywhere.

Following our meditation, I suggested to Kathy that we take advantage of the magnetism of this place by doing a ritual for healing the land. In February 1990, parts of Northern Arizona were still under siege from a prolonged drought. Streams and water tables were dangerously low. Springs were drying up. We needed winter storms so there could again be snow pack in the high country.

Our ceremony was simple and direct. We called upon the Storm Spirits to bring rain and snow to this parched land so that the balance could be restored. Not having a ceremonial object, such as cornmeal or a pipe, was no problem. I had become independent of these, realizing that they are only useful insofar as they help focus our intent. Although we had traveled light, we had with us the sword of pure intent, the chalice of hope, and the wand of magical consciousness. Late that afternoon Kathy and I shared our experience with Denny. He was intrigued by the idea of a ceremony to end the drought, but he was a little skeptical.

I awoke the next morning at daybreak to the sharp sound of a tree limb breaking, followed by another. I opened the curtains of the bedroom window and gazed out on a desert winter wonderland. The countryside had been virtually transformed! The storm must have developed quickly. No doubt there already was heavy snowfall up on the San Francisco mountains to the north.

Whatever doubts there may have been about the ceremony of the previous day had been dispelled. It turned out that this was not just an isolated snowfall. It was to be the precursor of a major change in weather conditions.

Several days later a second storm moved in—this time with heavy rains in the desert, but more snow in the high country. It turned out that the first storm was the largest of the decade.

We had an extremely wet spring, unusual for this arid region. Water tables returned to normal, springs were flowing, and wells were full. I was thankful for the honor of having a small part in all this.

◯◯◯

My intuition proved to be correct: This special desert spring could be used as a means of connecting powerfully with the Storm Devas and end a prolonged drought. When I felt myself become water, I realized that the watery element within me was enabling me to merge with the spring and all water beyond. I understood that the watery element everywhere is the physical manifestation of a great universal being who, like each of us, serves the wondrous Creation of which it is a part.

◯◯◯

A LITERAL BOLT FROM THE BLUE

Grand Canyon National Park: Summer

After the major storm hit northern Arizona following our successful rain ceremony, my friend Kathy told me a remarkable story about one of her friends, Jean. Jean had been camping in the Colorado River Gorge of the Grand Canyon for a week. During this time the weather had been idyllic. She found the natural rhythms of the canyon in sharp contrast to the frantic pace of Southern California where she lived. Jean had moved into a meditative silence almost as soon as she had set up camp.

On the last day, having experienced a profound sense of renewal, she felt an overwhelming need to perform a healing ceremony for the earth. It would be a way of giving something back to the land for the blessings she had received.

Throughout the week, Jean had been drawn to an unusual rock close to her campsite. The huge rock seemed to be the center of a natural vortex of energy, and she decided that it was the obvious site for her ceremony.

The ceremony itself lasted no more than 15 minutes. When it was over, Jean walked away just in time to avoid a bolt of lightning that struck the rock. Above her was blue sky. For a moment she stood in shocked silence. Sensing a relationship between her ceremony and the lightning, she felt that something of incomprehensible significance had just occurred. But what could this mysterious phenomenon possibly mean? She did not need to wait long to find out.

When Jean returned home, her phone began ringing the moment she opened her front door. Still caught up in the power of her experience in the Grand Canyon, she had no desire to break the spell by talking with anyone. Yet when the phone continued to ring, something compelled her to pick it up. An unfamiliar male voice said, "We wish to thank you for the ceremony you did. Southern California was about to have a major earthquake, and what you did restored the balance enough to avert it. This kind of spiritual work that you and others are doing is greatly needed at this time."

Then before Jean could respond, there was a dial tone. For a time she continued to hold the phone to her ear, in the hopes that somehow the voice would come on again.

By this time, Jean's mind was reeling with a barrage of questions that would probably never be answered. She knew that she had neither seen nor spoken to anyone while returning. And she had made certain that other campers in the canyon had not seen her perform her private ritual.

Who, then, was this mystery person that seemed to know her deeply, and who were the others he alluded to so matter-of-factly? How was it possible that something she did several hundred miles away could have an effect on the geological stability of the area in which she resided? Considering that bolt of lightning and the mysterious phone call, she now felt that anything could be possible.

OOO

Hearing this remarkable story, I was filled with wonder that two simple ceremonies performed by ordinary people less than a hundred miles apart could possibly have had such an enormous effect on the environment. I realized how we can never know what effect we might have on the world around us. A tiny pebble thrown into a pond creates ripples that move outward into ever-widening concentric circles. Perfectly balanced scales are shifted by the weight of a small feather. A single act with pure intent has incomprehensible powers. A simple prayer, an act of kindness, a courageous stand for a principle, or a ritual for healing the earth can have effects far beyond the scope of our awareness. None of us can rightfully say, "What difference can I make? Who am I among so many? There are others better suited to do this."

Whenever I reflect on the transforming power of these two simple ceremonies, I realize what wondrously endowed creatures we humans are and the limitless possibilities within us to make a difference in our world. I knew in my heart of hearts that I had to find a way to communicate these ideas to others. We do not have to be helpless pawns. We do not have to have economic or political power to act powerfully in the world. We no longer have time to solve the possible environmental tragedies that are looming through physical means alone. Change will have to come as more and more people realize the healing power of their intent and the power that comes to us when we are reunited with the Earth Spirit.

ooo

COMING FULL CIRCLE

Tennessee, Utah, and Wyoming

Two weeks before Astrid and I left Tennessee for the vision quest in Canyonlands National Park described in "Sun Ceremonies," I learned from two of my apprentices who live near the park that the area had been in a drought for the past two and a half years. The places in the backcountry on which we had always relied for our water sources had nearly gone dry.

This was not a situation that I wanted to deal with during our vision quest, because it would mean we would have to make several trips to and from the nearest town to bring in enough water for a dozen people for the week. As unpleasant and distracting as this would be for the vision quest, I also knew how very important these water sources were to the desert fauna and how much they must be suffering because of the drought. The high deserts of the American Southwest are far from being "empty" deserts. Even though at first glace they may appear to be barren, in reality they are teeming with all kinds of life forms, many of which are secretive and nocturnal.

I realized that it would be a blessing, not only for the people on their spiritual quests, but also for the flora and fauna, if the precious gift of water could be brought back into this thirsty desert area. I discussed the proposition with Astrid, who was enthusiastic about the idea. We both knew that when one works with any of the elemental forces distance is inconsequential. As I often do, I asked Astrid to work with me, since our combined energies always seemed to make any ceremony we performed more powerful.

Early the next morning, after we gave offerings to the power-ful Storm Devas, we made our specific request for the blessing of rain in Canyonlands. We thought no more about it. Two weeks later, in mid-September, we arrived in Canyonlands and looked upon an unusual sight for the high desert and canyon country of the Southwest: All across the landscape many of the natural depressions were filled with standing water.

We learned from our friends at the "outback store" near the park entrance that the area had just received a full week of torren-tial rains, and that the drought was officially over. Upon hearing this news, my wife and I felt a rush of exhilaration. Although we had not requested a torrential downpour, I had experienced this phenomenon on a number of other occasions. When a prolonged drought is corrected through a ceremony, the weather pendulum tends to swing to the opposite extreme as if to make up for the lack of rain. We were told that the storm system had passed, and the weather predictions were for clear skies. (As I described in "Sun Ceremonies," it turned out that we did not have totally clear skies. We were hit by two storms shortly after we arrived with our group before the fair weather came.)

The rain was wonderful news, however. It meant that we would have water in the backcountry for drinking and personal hygiene, and, more important, it meant relief for the desert flora and fauna. It also instilled in me a new confidence in being able to work with any of the elemental forces no matter at what distance.

When the following summer rolled around, I had the oppor-tunity to test this theory once more. One morning Astrid asked me to do a ceremony to give some of her friends in the Northeast-ern states a reprieve from wet weather. According to her, they had been experiencing so much continual rain that people's gardens were beginning to rot away. The morning after I performed a cer-emony, the weather system in that area moved out and gave every-one a much-needed break from the rain for the next two weeks.

Apparently this was an El Niño year, and on three more oc-casions we were on the verge of receiving an overabundance of rain. In spite of the fact that the official weather reports called for continual rain for several days, I conducted ceremonies and always brought in a reprieve from the rain. It was during this time that my relationship with the nature elementals took on a new level of responsibility.

One morning during my meditations, I was told that as the resident shaman in my area, it was my responsibility to make regular offerings to the powers of the earth, air, fire, and water, not just when there was a need for an intervention. I was told that it had always been the responsibility of the local shamans or medicine people to keep the channels open for the purpose of maintaining the proper balance of elemental forces. In other words, as a mediator between the world of humans, the natural world, and the world of elemental spirits, I was to be a bridge between the worlds as well as an anchor to help ground their powers in the material world. I was told that there is such interdependency between these kingdoms that the elemental spirits must be respected and honored to maintain the delicate balance of the universal forces. I was also told that there is a dire need for individuals and groups everywhere to assume this responsibility to offset the increasing imbalance in the weather that our country and other parts of the world are experiencing.

OOO

I began my unusual journey into the mysterious world of the Nature Devas and the Elemental Spirits in July in the mid 1980s with a ceremony to end a drought in western Wyoming. In July of 2003, while my book was being edited, Astrid, her 11-year-old son Aidan, and I went on a nine-day camping trip in the Grand Tetons. Upon our arrival, we discovered that a drought and unseasonably high temperatures once again had struck the area. In addition, a large forest fire was burning 30 miles to the south of the park near Hoback Junction. I experienced immediate déjà vu.

Knowing that fires are part of the natural cycle of the earth, I was reluctant to intervene during the first week of our trip. Finally, two days before we left, I did a ceremony in the late afternoon and requested cooler temperatures and showers. For the first time, remembering how the response to these ceremonies is often so extreme, I asked that this weather change be moderate.

The next morning we watched the thunderclouds moving out from the peaks of the Tetons, and soon we were basking under a cloud covering with a temperature shift from the 90s to the 70s. As the showers and cooler temperatures arrived, I felt that I had done the right thing to intervene in the natural cycle at this time because the drought had been causing much suffering for the plant and animal life.

Once more things had come full circle for me. It is perhaps fitting to end my stories about spiritual intervention with the above episode since it all began two decades ago almost to the day in the same magnificent, panoramic location. I realized that the changes in my relationship to the elemental spirits were happening at an exponential rate, and that the insights I am sharing now, which took place while this manuscript was being edited, might need to be expanded upon as a result of further revelations. Nevertheless, I trust that the current information I am sharing is true and will be helpful.

While writing these paragraphs, I also remembered for the first time in years a story that was told to me by a Tibetan lama with whom I studied 25 years ago. He spoke of a time when a large group of Tibetan monks decided to make a dangerous escape from Tibet to Nepal when the Chinese Communist Army was invading. The Chinese army had already set up checkpoints along the few roads leading out of Tibet to prevent anyone from escaping. This lama said that to protect the monks on their way out of the mountains, some of their powerful shamans created a fog bank to cloak their descent. It was an amazing sight, he said, to see this cloud of fog slowly descending down the mountain slopes. It was the invisibility the fog provided that enabled them to get out of Tibet safely.

When he shared this story with me, I was awed that anyone could have this kind of command over the elements. Today I am still impressed by this story, and I know that it is not unbelievable because I am aware that such command over the elemental forces is quite possible.

I know that my relationship with these magnificent beings will continue to take on new dimensions. I hope that these stories will inspire individuals and groups to take the initiative to carry out this sacred work in the subtle realms. I will tell you a secret. Those of you who experience a visceral resonance with these stories do so because you also have some ability to do similar things. What you are experiencing is a "recognition," an ancestral "bodily" memory of a time in which you were involved in such practices. If you meet this description, my advice to you is to stop vacillating and get started!

Our own Earth Spirit, Gaia, is a mother in labor who is about to give birth. The child she will birth is that of a new humanity. But at this time she is having a most difficult labor. Without enough human midwives to assist her in this transition, she could abort.

OOO

Christ once said to his followers, "A new commandment I give to you. That you love one another as I have loved you . . ."[18] In spite of monumental problems in our world, there is more love today than ever before. This love has the power to transform our humanity.

What if Christ were alive today? What would his concern be? I think he would be concerned about our disconnection with the earth and the problems that have resulted. In my opinion, the greatest single failure of organized religion today is its failure to recognize and address the massive environmental problems that threaten the quality of life on this planet for our children, grandchildren, and all living beings. In response to this disquieting situation, Christ might say something like this: "A new commandment I give to you for this new millennium. Love the earth with all your heart, soul, and mind. Love, honor and cherish her. Obey her laws! For she is your true Mother and is responsible for your being here. She has given you life, blessings, and abundance."

Begin fulfilling your appointed task as "caregiver" in the Garden of the World. Never defile or exploit the earth any more than you would your own biological mother. If you take from her, then, in accordance with the "universal law of exchange," give something back of equal or greater value. Offer healing to your own true Mother with your prayers, sacred songs, and dances! Offer ceremonies in natural power places! Bring healing not only to her physical form, but to her etheric levels as well by dispelling the "bad medicine" that is so pervasive in places throughout our world today.

Those of you who have been given the power, assist with bringing rain to the parched areas and bright sunshine to the places in deluge! Restore the environmental balance in the sacred sites and protect them, for in doing so you also provide protection for yourselves and for all living things.

Finally, do not just pay lip service to environmental stewardship. Truly be good stewards of the earth by walking your talk. I end this series of stories, therefore, with a call for help. A summons for those who resonate with these stories to commit in this way to the great work of healing our planet which is suspended like a precious gem of exquisite beauty in the Infinite Creation.

❍❍❍

SPIRITUAL INTERVENTION

No one was more astonished than I when I realized that the dozens of ceremonies for healing or protecting the land that we performed during the last two decades had *all* been successful. Furthermore, the results were often dramatic. When I finally became aware of this phenomenal record, I wished that I had emphasized this type of spiritual intervention more than I did. From a purely pragmatic point of view, very little effort often yielded extraordinary results. The size of the land or even the degree of opposition did not seem to be a factor.

When I first arrived at Canyonlands, there were government signs posted around the park notifying the public that the area was a site being considered by the U.S. Department of Energy for radioactive waste burial. I was appalled. Was no place sacred?

Over the next two years, we performed powerful ceremonies with my groups of apprentices in an attempt to stop this desecration. When I returned to Canyonlands the third year, the signs had disappeared. I learned that an activist group had moved into the area and managed not only to get the proposal withdrawn but had also succeeded in getting strip mining, which had been practiced for years, banned in the county.

Years later, I learned that a vast track of beautiful land bordering the park was in danger of being sold to developers. This land, which was owned by Dugout Ranch, provided a buffer to the park itself. Since our base camp had been there, our connection to the area was strong. We performed ceremonies asking for protection of this awesomely beautiful landscape. A few years later, to my great relief but not surprise, the land was sold to the Nature Conservancy, where it will remain forever preserved in its natural state.

I am not suggesting that we should take sole responsibility for any of the above. Perhaps there were other groups and individuals who were working to protect the land. What I *am* saying, however, is that a sacred ceremony or ritual for the earth performed by a few people with pure intent has enormous power to tip the scales. I have also seen how a number of my former students have been able to carry this philosophy of spiritual intervention into the local environmental movement and effectively bring about changes.

We can no longer continue working on the physical level alone to heal and to protect our earth. Spiritual intervention must become a protocol in the years ahead.

This methodology works because we are using higher energy fields and thought forms to override physical plane situations. This approach to conservation of our environment is a radical departure from the methods with which most people are familiar. In the past, environmentalists have met the enemy on their own grounds where the enemy is the strongest. This approach alone is limiting because those involved in the environmental movement cannot hope to match the economic and political resources or access to media that is available to the corporate world. Important battles have been won, often through near heroic efforts, but the war is being lost and time may be running out.

However, there is an alternative: Take the conflict to a higher level. In other words, the energies of rituals and ceremonies expressing focused intent and prayers, love for Gaia, and a passion for the nature kingdoms can override and transform existing situations that have become stuck or are in the process of deterioration. This should bring unprecedented success because, to reiterate, the subtle planes control the physical plane.

This is no idealized statement. It is a natural law. Higher magnetic fields will invariably override the denser ones. My advice, however, is not just to accept my personal testimony, but for groups to try this out for themselves. The approach of spiritual intervention will revolutionize and empower the struggling environmental movement and help our world avert some worst-case scenarios. It should also help bring the many different groups together that have been divided over whose project takes precedence and which funds should be allocated where.

Spiritual intervention can be just as powerful a tool for healing the land as it can be for its protection. I realized that *every* rain ceremony I've performed has been effective. The same has been true with the sun ceremonies. As astounding as these stories might seem, when we begin to accept that there is an awareness that pervades the natural world and that there are ways to connect with that awareness, then these feats seem less extraordinary. One of my purposes in writing this book is to demystify some of the ancient shamanic principles that were written off long ago by our culture as merely superstitions.

I have discovered that many people who use ceremonial practices seem to experience "recognition" of having done this sort of thing before. No doubt there is an atavistic memory of ritual and ceremonial practices that were at the heart of village and tribal life in other ages. When sacred space is opened up, there is, for many practitioners, the experience of an almost palpable presence of a non-ordinary reality that is at once magical, nonlinear, and beyond syntax. This palpable sacred space has the power to influence events in ordinary reality.

When I'm involved in these ancient practices, I am more truly myself than at most other times. Such practices attract nothing less than the energies of the world of radiant energy which is the primary reality for all beings. This is in sharp contrast to the illusion that we call physical reality, and to which we become so attached. Ceremonial practices, therefore, can be powerful forces in our lives, not only because of their ability to effect physical reality but also because they help us reconnect with the transcendent reality to which we all belong.

With the mounting environmental crisis, I'm certain that if we are to survive the years ahead we must stop viewing these problems in a linear left-brain manner. The spiritual procedures that I'm recommending for healing the earth are not based on some kind of "airy-fairy" idealism but upon certain, yet little known, natural laws. They worked for me again and again. They can work for others as well.

Sometimes people ask me, "How can I get these powers that you have?" I tell them that there is nothing to "get"! Everyone has the potential to awaken these same powers. They are already present in each person. Our inherent nature is that we are all magical beings.

When we surrender to the Earth Goddess, She in turn surrenders to us. The key is to surrender our lives to a higher purpose. When we offer our lives to Her services as I have done, She gives back to us unimaginable blessings and gifts beyond measure.

People have difficulty believing me when I tell them that there are forces that do not want you to access this power and knowledge. These forces are very organized and have a great deal of control over what is presented in the media and taught in academia. They seek to discredit any information about spiritual and natural laws that comes out or use disinformation as a weapon to create confusion and keep us powerless and in ignorance. They may try to do this with me, unless of course they decide that I am so "far out" that I am a harmless eccentric or a raving lunatic.

❁ ❁ ❂ ❁ ❁

CHAPTER 7
THE PATH OF RETURN

○○○

A RETURN TO EDEN

In the preceding pages, I shared a few of many excursions I made into the eastern and western mountains, as well as the remote canyons and deserts of the American Southwest. Sometimes these were for personal quests. Other times they were to help prepare groups for vision quests and other sacred wilderness journeys. These were defining moments for me.

Through days of solitude, through ceremonies and vision questing, and through bonding with the natural world, I became connected to life around me in the deepest, most intimate way imaginable. I became one with rugged canyons, the misty mountains, the empty desert, and one with the flowing waters, cooling breezes, and the blazing council fires. I became brother to the plant spirits, the silent forest, the deer, and the prairie wolf.

I discovered a world that is vastly more personal, complex, and more ancient than I would have imagined—a world that is nonlinear, magical, and beyond the syntax of our culture. To my great joy, whenever I took groups with me into wilderness areas, I perceived that they too could reconnect with the natural world. When we were together, whether in workshops or in wilderness retreats, in classrooms or in canyons and forests, we were, as a group, able to experience something of the magic of creation that had touched my own life so very deeply and personally.

Our world is more than the consensus reality world of our culture. It is vast and incomprehensible, beyond definition; a magical world that is alive and filled with so much beauty and love that if average people had any idea of that which encircles them, they would want nothing else but to open up to that greater reality.

Living together as an extended family in these wilderness areas had become so natural and basic for me and our group members that with each experience it became more difficult for us to return to the madness we knew as our world—one set apart from and in opposition to the earth and her creatures. I understood that this is the condition of the humanity of our times.

I had come to realize that most people are haunted by an acute loneliness that is not assuaged by relationships, devotion to the arts, or to humanitarian causes. This loneliness is the result of our separation from the earth.

I saw that, contrary to conventional beliefs, the human problem is not found solely in hunger, disease, or man's inhumanity to man. Indeed, when we do address these problems, seeking to eradicate them, they seem to keep coming back in new and more terrible forms. I saw that these were only symptoms of a condition that was endemic to us as a species, and was to be found at the very roots of consciousness. It became clear to me that we had lost an ancient original and primal connection with the earth. If my inner vision was correct, an energetic umbilical cord connecting each of us to the earth had been severed or damaged. When this happened, we lost our inherent magical nature.

This discovery left me in a state of shock. I knew that the biblical story of the "fall" was an ancestral memory of such a catastrophe. It had developed into such mythic proportion as to leave us clueless as to what the real problem was much less what to do about it. Whatever happened, humans ceased to be the magical beings they were meant to be and instead were reduced to the petty, self-serving, self-absorbed creatures we know ourselves today.

I saw that the separation from the Earth Mother causes us to behave like homeless children: frightened, unruly, and lost. Yet here the analogy ends because adult children, unlike young children, can be quite dangerous because they have more dangerous toys and far bigger playgrounds.

Another disturbing perception was that I realized that much of what we accept as normal and even proper behavior would actually be considered aberrant behavior in a society that has not lost its direct connection with the earth. An example of this is our Western ethic of "ownership of land." When we are bonded with the earth, we instinctively understand, as a Native American understands, that the earth does not belong to us; we belong to the earth. She is not something that we have a right to buy and sell, divide up, and parcel out. It is no wonder that the original people living in the Americas found European values almost incomprehensible.

Indeed, we are like trees whose taproots have been severed but continue to live through lateral roots. We remain stunted because we can no longer draw on the nourishment from deep within the earth. Until our deep connection with the Earth Spirit has been restored, we can never be the complete beings we are meant to be. It is this very sense of incompleteness that drives us to become attached to material things and values that have no spiritual power or substance and are neither life giving nor life sustaining. This is our single greatest problem today.

The greatest challenge for us is to recognize the earth as a living, sentient being and to enter into a relationship with her on the most intimate levels as if she were our mother, sister, and child.

The earth herself offers an impeccable pathway to wholeness and transcendence because she has given us life and is the source of everything that we have and are.

I believe that our ancient connection with the earth and her creatures still exists within the deeper consciousness of every individual. This connection can be restored in every one of us. Such a restoration will lead us back to the Edenic state of harmony and oneness with her creation.

The parable of the Garden of Eden and other Creation myths are memories of the loss of an original condition in which we existed in blissful harmony with the Creator and Her Creation. Whether or not we accept the testimony of the biblical scriptures, we all resonate on a visceral level with the story of the fall and of being "cast out of the garden." We feel it in the marrow of our bones; we experience it on the cellular level. Each of us, at one time or another, has felt that indefinable longing for a "lost good."

The angel with the fiery sword who barred man's return to Eden is symbolic of our rational mind. We can never return to nature's garden through this faculty. We cannot access higher wisdom. Nor can we know God with our minds. Because our analytical mind has no direct connection with the things of Spirit, we have to find another means of reconnecting to our Source. It is through our hearts and deepest intuitions that we are led back to the earth—to the Divine.

Without a shift in people's awareness, all the environmental laws in the world will not be enough to protect the earth and save humanity. All the protests and demonstrations will be for naught. We cannot hope to change the physical world apart from spiritual transformation. This is an extraordinary claim, but we are living in extraordinary times faced with extraordinary problems. It will take extraordinary solutions by remarkable people to avert the unthinkable scenarios that loom as very real possibilities in an uncertain and fluid, not-too-distant future.

In certain visions that began when I was still a parish priest, I saw future scenarios that could usher in a requiem for humanity and perhaps for the earth herself. However, I also saw that if we rediscovered our lost Eden, there would be no need for a requiem. Eden is found in the roots of consciousness. It is a state of being in which we are in harmony with our Mother, the earth, and with all life.

It is not too late to turn back to our primal source, the earth. If it were, I would not be writing these things. The real meaning of the parable of the Prodigal Son, like that of man's exile from the Garden of Eden, is an allegory of the human situation. We *are* the prodigal children who have strayed, and in some ways, strayed enormously.

The earth is continually calling us back to herself as part of herself. It's time to come home again! Like the Prodigal Son, we are a people who are spiritually bankrupt, and when that occurs it is only a matter of time before economic, social, and political bankruptcy follow.

When the Prodigal Son returned home, there was celebration and rejoicing. It will be the same for us when we return to our Source. The angels themselves will celebrate our return and the whole of Creation will rejoice.

And when this happens, we will remember for the first time what the song of the humpback whale is really all about, or the cry of the timber wolf, or the song of the meadowlark. We will understand the laughter of the dolphin, the playfulness of the otter, and the ecstasy of the storm. We'll know that all these are but expressions of the ecstatic joy of being at one with the Creation. When we finally have discovered this, then we too will know our own place in the great Medicine Wheel of Life.

OOO

MANDATE FOR HUMANITY

Many of the stories in this book feature episodes that are so re-moved from consensus reality that they seem miraculous, yet they are as much a part of the rhythm of all things as the rising and setting of the sun, the ebb and flow of the tides, and the changing of the seasons. When viewed as a whole, these experiences point to the existence of a single, all-pervading consciousness that is behind the physical world in which we dwell.

Wherever I have traveled, from the Arctic Circle to southern Mexico, from the San Juan Islands to the rocky coast of Maine, I have witnessed the same conscious life that flows from pole to pole and throughout all the earth. I have sensed the connection of all life to this One Being whom I've come to realize is aware of me and nurtures and cares for me as a mother would care for her own child.

Wherever I go in the insulated world of people, I am reminded of how separated we have become from all that is of nature. I know that this separation is what has brought about the sense of disconnectedness and isolation that so many today experience. You can take a human being out of the wilderness, but you cannot take the wilderness out of a human being.

We have isolated ourselves from the natural world. Asphalt carpets more and more of the earth, high-rises block out the hori-zon, and pollution in our cities blocks out the stars at night. Our televisions, radios, and stereos blare continually, drowning out the elemental sounds of wind, thunder, and rain, the serenading of birds and the coyote's nocturnal song. The pervasive energies of electronic pollution from high-tension wires, computers, and microwaves, like silent assassins (unnoticed by our human eyes) do deadly work on our health.

And then there is the ravaging of our woodlands. Anyone who has visited our cultivated "for profit" forests, which are no more than tree farms, has experienced firsthand the diminishing power and lack of diversity of such places. They are poor substitutes for the healing possibilities of an old-growth forest, pristine mountain streams and waterfalls, and alpine meadows and marshlands.

Today we have forgotten the Spirit that lives and moves in us and in all things. Our rational mind, which we rely on so heavily today, does not have direct connection with intuitive wisdom or our magical consciousness, that, as these stories suggest, are part of our natural and original state.

Our cultural conditioning has rendered us blind, deaf, and dumb. We are blind to the true nature of the world around us. We are deaf to the Voices of Creation that have so much to teach us. Our dumbness lies in the fact that we are unable to speak with the certitude that comes from direct spiritual experience of the Creation. We know only that which comes through the mediation of the rational mind, which has no direct connection whatsoever to spiritual realities. Data perceived by the ordinary mind is always secondhand knowledge subject to doubts, ambiguities, and confusion.

We look but do not see, and listen but seldom hear. We touch but fail to feel, and gather more and more knowledge but little wisdom. We are clever but not wise.

It is not through thinking that we can perceive the spiritual realties, but through our dreams and visions, through sign and symbol, feeling and intuition, and synchronicity. Spiritual unfolding comes through inner vision, and the phenomenon known as direct knowledge or revelation. Through our spiritual minds we learn to see without eyes, hear without ears, and know without thought.

The spiritual mind is the faculty that connects us to the broader universal consciousness that is embedded in our modern understanding of quantum physics. The spiritual mind exists in quantum superposition to the world around us. Because of that superposition, and the phenomenon known as "entangled photons," it transcends space-time reality. When tapped, it has the potential to be connected to any part of the Creation or to all of it simultaneously. It can extend across the whole span of time. When this happens, we experience what is known as direct knowledge of the Creation. It is what constitutes true knowing, which is very much a lost art.

The imbalance in our world can no longer be offset by ecological measures alone. We've failed to heed earlier warnings and have let the path of destruction go too far. Spiritual methods are needed to complement and empower physical methods of environmental protection if we are to heal our ailing planet.

This means a radical change in the consciousness we have toward the earth and our relationship to her. She is the source of all that we have and are. When we are in a harmonious relationship with the earth, the relationship is never static. It is open and flowing, dynamic and transforming. Nor is our love for her a passive one. It is wild and passionate and bold.

There's a pervasive thinking in our consumer culture that the land is something for us to use and to do with as we wish. Such assumptions only show just how much we are out of touch with our primal source.

As caregivers, we never seek to lord over the earth, but are in relationship with her. We approach her with the consciousness of the good gardener that loves and is in relationship with her garden. On another level, we come to our earth as a child comes to its mother, empty and open to receive. Because of this, a child will always be filled, nurtured, and content.

Our land-use programs for our national forests, as the very name implies, are doomed for failure because they are based on greed and personal gain. The land is not another commodity. When we take from it, we must give something in return that is of equal or greater value. This is in accordance with the universal law of exchange. That is one way we can become good stewards of the earth.

A proactive love for the earth can express itself not only through our caregiving, but also through healing ceremonies, sacred dances and music, prayer and meditation, and even spiritual intervention as described in these stories. This can be accomplished most effectively in the sacred spots and magnetic vortices that are found in every part of the globe because of the enormous amplification of power that occurs in these places. Group participation is more effective than individual efforts because the power of a group increases exponentially rather than sequentially with each new member.

With this principle in mind, one can realize that the power of mass prayer would be almost incalculable. If a rain ceremony performed by one or two people can end a drought, or a healing ceremony for the earth can prevent a possible earthquake (as I have described in this book), what could a large number of people with pure intent engaged in prayer or a ceremony do?

In my visions, I have foreseen that there will come a time in which mass prayer for our world will be absolutely necessary. This will come at a point when the long-documented patterns of weather no longer can be relied on, as is already beginning to happen. Life-support systems such as the ozone layer begin to fail, and the earth loses her ability to heal herself. The inherent checks and balances of the elemental forces are lost.

Still, I have a stubborn hope for us because I believe that our species, with all its idiotic mistakes and blindness, has the capacity to rise above itself and unite, ultimately prevailing against what seems to be overwhelming odds. In ages past, human beings have often shone most brightly in their darkest hours.

In this book, I have described how simple ceremonies for the earth performed by a few people were able to accomplish what activist politics and environmental measures alone could not do, at times bringing healing or protection for the land so swiftly and efficiently that we were amazed. The true stories in *Soul on Fire*, and the lessons implicit in them, can point to a radically new way for us to rediscover and heal that ancient union we once had with the earth, the nature kingdom, and with all life. As the native peoples of our land have rightfully said, the sacred hoop of life has been broken and must be restored if we are to have any meaningful future. When this begins to happen, there is hope. We will then be assured of a worthy future for our grandchildren and their grandchildren.

CHAPTER 8
TRANSFORMATIONS

*T*here are sacred unions that span any distance and
extend both forward and backward in time. These
are unions that exist on the level of essence. There are
times, however, when the power of one of the unions
manifests on the physical world, and we experience
what seems like divine intervention. The truth is that
there are contracts that we have made on other levels to
intervene when necessary in one another's lives. Such
interventions always leave us with a sense of awe and
mystery, and they invariably become powerful tools for
our transformations.

○○○

A PRAYER FOR A FUTURE LOVE

Tennessee

Dan and Helen had been married for six months in what could only be described as a blissful union. From the moment they met, they had known they were destined for each other, and they were engaged within a few months and married soon after.

One afternoon when they were together in the car, Helen told Dan a story of a peculiar incident that occurred two years before they met. She awoke one night around 2 A.M. with a feeling of great anxiety. She then heard a voice telling her that the man she would someday marry was in grave trouble and desperately needed her prayers. At the time, Helen was not dating anyone and was not even really looking for a life partner, but the urgency of the message convinced her she'd better follow this mysterious advice. For the next hour she lay in her bed, praying ardently for someone that she was not sure even existed.

At a certain point her anxiety lifted and she felt that her prayers got through somewhere, and the crisis was over. Still, she wondered what all this meant and wondered even if the voice could have been her imagination. So she recorded the experience in her diary in case it later turned out to mean something to her.

While listening to Helen, Dan turned pale and began to tremble. With a sense of urgency in his voice, he asked when the episode had taken place. Helen, who always carried her diary with her, had no difficulty locating the entry. When she told Dan the date and time, he felt such strong emotions welling up in him that he had to pull off the road, no longer able to drive.

"That's the night I made the decision to take my life," he said. "I'd bought a gun and was prepared to shoot myself. At the very last minute I felt a profound sense of love and peace come over me. I'd never felt anything like that in my whole life. That's the only reason I'm still here."

OOO

I was profoundly moved when these students of mine shared their story with me. To me, the great truth is that love knows no boundaries. We have soul connections that exist beyond this lifetime with people we are not even aware exist. In this case, a love reached across the barriers of space and time to assist someone in his hour of greatest need. Perhaps we can never fully know the power of our love or prayers to make a difference, even in the lives of those we have never met.

OOO

PROTESTING TOO MUCH

Ketchum, Idaho: Early Spring

The site for my workshop was a spacious log cabin sequestered six miles north of Ketchum, Idaho, next to the picturesque Wood River. Two hundred feet east of the cabin, a mountain rose sharply a couple of thousand feet before leveling off into an alpine meadow where a large elk herd and mule deer resided a good portion of the year. Probably since the receding of the last glacial period, this bountiful land had hosted these herds as well as antelope and, of course, the various predators that help keep these herds healthy.

Except for a lovely garden area of mostly indigenous flowers, the lot was filled with medium-sized aspen, which by mid-September had turned gold and appeared to be on fire when illuminated by the autumn sun. In one corner of the lot was a recently built sweat lodge. I hoped that we could fit the nearly 30 people who signed up for the class into the living room.

The lingering haze and diffused light of the early morning gave the surrounding countryside a shimmering effect that reminded me of a Monet landscape. Through a large picture window, I saw our group milling around. This was a land of plenty, and it was supposed to be work? I knew I wouldn't trade my life with anyone.

But all was not as it appeared. The tranquility of the setting was deceptive. Soon after I entered the house, a very angry man whom I had never seen before accosted me. By his skin tone and features, I could see that he was of East Indian descent and probably close to my age. In a loud voice, he told me that his name was Moksha and he would like to have his money back because he came against his better judgment. He complained that mutual friends of ours had pressured him to come. I could understand his feeling, as several of my local apprentices could be quite evangelical. I made a mental note to suggest they tone down their zeal a little.

I told Moksha that his preregistration was not binding and that he was welcome to have a refund. For some reason this did not satisfy him. He continued as if he never heard me, stating that he did not believe any of what I would be teaching and that he did not belong here.

I agreed with Moksha, explaining that I had no interest in converting him to my philosophy and that the seminar was not an indoctrination but an exploration. Again, I told him his money would be returned.

For some reason I was not getting through. Moksha began insisting that he had no desire to change his personal life and that he was happy with himself the way he was. On the surface, Moksha appeared arrogant and judgmental, but something was wrong with that picture. The more I insisted that he could have his money back, the more agitated he became. I was offering what he claimed he wanted, but he was not hearing me. I began to suspect that there was some hidden message. Then I saw it. Moksha, like Lady Macbeth, was "protesting too much."

On some level, he wanted to be forced into attending this workshop. It has been said that the greater the resistance to an experience, the greater the potential power it has for the individual. If this was so, he had the potential for a major breakthrough in his life that day.

It looked as if Moksha was begging for an excuse to stay. Having heard that he was an entrepreneur, I decided to make him an offer he could not turn down. Moksha could have his money back and would be my guest at the seminar. If at any point he decided that he had heard enough, he could simply leave without paying. If he ended up staying for the entire program, he could pay me if he felt he had benefited from it. Moksha readily accepted these conditions.

After a brief introduction, I opened the seminar with group drumming before starting my presentation. Twenty minutes into the program, Moksha's body began trembling. I was the first to notice it and stopped my presentation momentarily. When I questioned him about what was going on, his trembling became more and more pronounced. Then, as I was anticipating, he burst into tears.

Several well-meaning people instinctively rushed to his aid. I told them to stay where they were. He did not need consoling. It would only make him angrier. He needed to release a cellular pain, which I figured had to be a carryover of an early period in his life or possibly from a past-life embodiment.

He was embarrassed about his tears, insisting that he had never cried in his life and had no earthly idea what it was all about. As he sobbed profusely, he repeated over and over that he could not believe all this was happening. Moksha was still protesting, but I knew he was running out of things to protest. Soon he was shaking so badly that I asked several of the men in the group to hold him so he could not hurt himself with his flailing arms and legs. He was clueless as to what was going on.

I knew this violence in his body was the result of his own resistance. His conscious mind and will was pitted against an even more powerful unconscious. If only I could look deeply enough into his unconscious, I might be able to help. Almost immediately I saw with my inner vision a scene of unspeakable horror.

In my mind's eye, I saw a young East Indian boy being buried alive in a pile of mutilated bodies. The vivid details were almost too horrible to believe. I wanted to deny what I saw, to make it go away . . . to believe it was my imagination. I could not, because now I could also feel his pain, terror, and revulsion.

It seemed impossible that what I saw had any basis in reality, yet I had no choice but to share my vision with Moksha. I had to do so not only for his sake but for mine as well. This vision did not belong to me, it belonged to Moksha, and for me to be free of it I had to release it to him since it reflected his life.

I asked Moksha if he had ever been buried alive as a child. He responded as if he had been struck by a thunderbolt. For the first time since the program began, he began to speak.

"It was the time of our independence," he said. "The British had withdrawn and almost immediately our village was raided by a group of Pakistani men who proceeded to kill the men and boys of our village using huge knives. My mother, desperate to save me and my brother, hid us in a pile of bodies. To this day I remember it vividly! The bodies were bloody and horribly mangled. The stench was terrible. We had to stay under the bodies for many hours until it was safe to come out."

In light of this massacre in the name of religion, I could easily understand his lifelong animosity toward anything spiritual. I also saw why he had not been able to cry for all these years. In order to survive and live through that nightmare when he was a boy, he had to suppress his tears and terror. Stoicism meant survival. The young boy carried into adulthood this unconscious philosophy, restricting his experience as an emotional and spiritual being.

My perception of the source of Moksha's problems shocked him so deeply that he stopped blocking his own healing. Until I told him what I had envisioned, he had no idea what was wrong with him. Finally, he was able to release the pain and terror of that experience.

Within minutes, Moksha had become fully calm and was somewhat in awe of what had just transpired. His entire process had taken half an hour, yet it had not been lost time for the rest of us. I have learned that whenever any one of us experiences a breakthrough, it is a triumph for all. Whenever one person is healed, every one of us, each in our own way, is also healed. This miracle of collective healing is related to the wondrous intrinsic unity we all share beyond the manifest duality of the phenomenal worlds.

Six months later I returned to Sun Valley for another workshop. On the day I arrived, the first person I met in town was Moksha. As we spoke, he seemed much softer and much more at peace. However, I knew that something was bothering him. Finally, it came out.

"Peter," he said, "I want you to know that you have really changed my life. I am a better person for having met you. But I want to apologize in advance because I will not be coming to your seminar this weekend. I do not want to have to go into convulsions again."

I was taken aback. Did he really believe that one always goes through convulsions in such seminars? I assured him that this was not the case. The terrible core pain he had released from his boyhood trauma was gone now, and he would not have to go through that experience ever again, but I saw that Moksha would not be convinced. Perhaps he would always be protesting something. This was just his nature. Besides, he was accustomed to getting his way. He had made a fortune over the years in the business world by being in charge.

For a moment we just gazed at each other, in mutual respect. So different we were, and yet so much alike. We were both warriors— he in the competitive, often cutthroat world of high finance, and I in the world of spirit. Like warriors whose paths crossed briefly for the fulfillment of a single purpose, we wished each other well, gave our bear hugs, and continued on our separate journeys.

OOO

Sometimes we may be carrying deep wounds from traumas that occurred earlier in our lives, even wounds that have been forgotten. These burdens greatly restrict our ability to act freely and consciously in our quest for happiness. While conventional Western wisdom holds that healing such wounds can sometimes occur through a lengthy therapeutic process with a skilled clinician, I perceive that healing can happen in an instant through a very different process.

In being a catalyst for Moksha's dramatic healing, I recognized the power drumming and chanting have for enabling someone to bypass his intellectual belief systems and unconscious defense mechanisms to tap into the source of repressed emotional pain.

Our drumming and chanting had struck a chord in Moksha. The opportunity to bypass his defenses, and the presence of a loving support coming from the group in attendance at the seminar, gave Moksha permission to connect with his childhood trauma. My "seeing" the source of Moksha's protesting and pain acted as a powerful trigger for release of his unresolved tears and terror that he had suppressed since he was a young boy.

This dramatic episode demonstrated to me a quicker and much more powerful approach to connecting with and releasing core pain that is buried so deeply under our natural defenses that it is almost impossible to access using conventional methodology.

∘∘∘

THE HUNTER'S LEGACY
Idaho

Early one morning I received a call from Ron, a resident in the resort town of Idaho Springs where I was working at the time, claiming he urgently needed an appointment. Since I had to be in Boise by early afternoon, which was four hours away, I told him there was no way we could meet. The man was insistent, saying a situation had come up in his life and he was desperate. With some misgivings, I agreed to meet him in an hour at my hotel room.

I was puzzled as to why he was seeking my help. He had been telling others in the community that he thought I was a phony and that what I did had no basis in reality. Naturally, I wondered why he suddenly needed to see me.

When he arrived, I noticed a haunted look I'd not seen in him before. He quickly got to the point and explained that for the last three days he had been in emotional turmoil, often bursting into tears. He insisted that he hadn't cried like this since childhood and had no idea what could be wrong. He wanted to know if there was any way I could tune in to him and discover what his problem was. He reminded me about his skepticism about my work, but he said he had exhausted other possibilities.

It did not take long to focus on him with my inner vision. I saw the image of a large deer in his aura and suggested that it might be the source of his problem. Surprised, he acknowledged that he had shot an elk three days ago while hunting but could not see how it related to his emotional turmoil.

By that time, I was in communication with the spirit of the

elk and could see that there was a definite relationship. The information I received was that he had not killed the elk in a sacred manner, and, consequently, the elk spirit in its distress and fear had inadvertently become trapped in his energy field. I explained to him that the elk was even more unhappy about the situation than he was.

The whole concept was new to Ron. But remembering that he had some Native American ancestry, I took the opportunity to explain to him how the Native Americans would apologize to the animal they had killed, telling it that they needed food for their families. They would then help release the spirit of the dead animal by thanking it and praying for its safe journey to its source.

I pointed out that he had been feeling the emotions and confusion of the elk that had become attached to him. Ron's present predicament made it obvious that this Native American tradition was more than a romantic ideal. The practice served to protect both the hunter and the hunted from a harmful symbiotic relationship that could manifest very much like a possession.

While I spoke to Ron, I detected a shift in him. For the first time, some aspect of himself acknowledged the validity of my views. Our next step was to actually release the elk spirit. Ron was more than ready. With my guidance, Ron spoke aloud to the elk spirit about his regrets about the killing and his desire that the elk spirit be free to continue on its path, empowered with his love and blessings. Then together we prayed that the elk be reunited with its own group soul.[19]

When I then placed my hands on Ron's head to assist with the release, he felt something almost physical lift from his energy field. Immediately, Ron felt like himself again for the first time in three days, the overpowering sadness and confusion completely gone.

I knew that this experience would have a profound effect on Ron. At the least he'd think twice before ridiculing spiritual concepts he had never investigated, as he had been doing in such a cavalier manner.

It was past time for me to get back on the road, but Ron wished to linger and speak more about what had just happened. Unable to comprehend the dramatic and sudden disappearance of his grief and despair, he said he felt open for the first time to the spiritual philosophy I taught.

How often I've found honest skeptics easier to work with than "true believers" who sometimes frighten me with their zealousness. Once convinced, these skeptics usually become the most committed students. The "true believers," on the other hand, are often so set in their mental concepts of spirituality that they have trouble letting their beliefs go long enough to have real spiritual experiences.

Ron went on to study with me for several years and eventually became a healer and teacher in his own right. What a gift that elk spirit gave Ron because it helped set him on his path.

ooo

When we kill an animal, whether deliberately or unintentionally, we can become connected to its spirit by etheric threads or filaments of light. This phenomenon can create problems for both humans and animals. The human, without understanding why, begins experiencing the confusion and emotional turmoil of the animal because the animal's spirit has become trapped in the human's energy field. In fact, with the killing of large predator animals, there can even be danger for humans who are vulnerable to the psychic force of the animal's frustration.

Like the native people of our continent always did, when an animal is killed, we perform a service for both the animal and for ourselves by honoring its spirit, praying for its journey to its source, and stating our intent that it be released from its body. This is something I often do when I encounter an animal that has been recently killed on roads or highways because I can sense that the animal's spirit is often still attached to its physical vehicle and unable to comprehend what happened to it.

Each of us has an "inner shaman" that already knows and understands all of this. When necessary, we can call on our inner shaman to assist and guide us in such endeavors.

OOO

A BAD WAY TO START THE DAY

San Diego, California: Spring

During a visit to the San Diego area, I was the houseguest of Robyn, my local promoter and student. Upon arriving at her condominium that evening, I was surprised to find her ill. I offered to stay elsewhere since I had many students in the area, but Robyn insisted that I not change my plans. She felt a need to discuss her situation with me in the hopes that I might have some insight. I agreed to try and help.

Later, after resting from my drive, I met with Robyn. For several days she'd felt nauseated and had flu-like symptoms. In addition, she'd become increasingly agitated. While listening to Robyn describe her symptoms, I began hearing alarm signals going off in my head. I'd run into this sort of situation before. Still, I needed more information.

Then, while my student was speaking, I began to perceive with my inner vision a dark, reddish-orange vortex of energy spiraling into her solar plexus. I myself began to feel sick and had to quickly detach. I knew what this sick feeling meant, and that Robyn was in more trouble than she realized. My worst fears had been confirmed. She was under some kind of attack.

I shared my perceptions with my friend, but neither of us had any feeling about the source of what was being directed to her or why. However, I knew that she was in need of immediate protection. I began taking these measures at once. First, I lit some copal (one of the most powerful sacred incenses) I'd brought with me and performed a simple ritual for protection. Following this procedure, I held my hands a few inches above what seemed to be the disturbed area, which I'd identified as the solar plexus area, the seat of the emotional power center.

While holding my hands, I was aware of a dark negative energy being directed at Robyn. But by whom and for what purpose? While holding my hands over Robyn's solar plexus, I began to feel an uncomfortable sensation of heat being drawn out of her. It felt like a sphere the size of a volleyball that began to increase in temperature and intensity. This energy felt highly negative.

While the healing progressed, Robyn complained of considerable pain and nausea. My hands by now had grown quite hot, as if they were on fire, and the invisible fireball seemed huge. I explained to Robyn that the negative energy was coming from someone's jealous rage and that this energy would need to be returned to this person while holding the pure intent that no harm would come to the sender. In that moment, we both instantly knew who the sender was.

As I began the process of returning this fireball, nothing happened at first, but then the fireball was gone, and I knew it was being returned to the sender. Robyn was now free of the pain and nausea that she had felt all last week. Instead, she had become extremely drowsy, and I knew that this was her own natural healing energy taking over. I left her so she could get a much-needed restful sleep.

The next morning the pandemonium began! The woman who had been psychically attacking Robyn, as well as two of my other students, was driving to work where she held an important position with a software company. On the way, taking some back roads, she was startled by the sound and bright flash of a transformer exploding ahead of her. This was followed by a power line falling across the road in front of the car but continuing to dance around shooting off sparks and flame. Frightened, she began backing up, only to hear another transformer behind her blow up and a dancing fallen cable block her retreat. Uncertain of the danger of driving over a live power line in her car, she decided to remain

in her automobile until a power-company truck arrived a few minutes later.

When Robyn and I heard what had happened, we realized that
my strategy had been effective beyond all expectations. At that
point, no longer able to contain ourselves, we erupted into convulsive laughter. The visuals were so hilarious. The point that was
made was so perfect. Later we heard that her friend had correctly
interpreted the bizarre lesson she had been given. I was deeply
grateful because I had met this person and knew her to be a very
special individual. I gave my thanks to my friends and allies, the
Fire Elementals, for their assistance and marvelous creativity in
staging this incredible scenario, which worked beyond all my expectations.

○○○

BE CAREFUL WHAT YOU ASK FOR

Tucson, Arizona: Late Fall

There's a saying that we should be careful what we ask for because we just might get it. A friend of mine discovered the wisdom of these words late one evening.

Monica was a 50-year-old professional artist who now lived alone after raising two lovely daughters. A striking woman with silver hair, she had a keen sense of humor and was an excellent raconteur. She shared with me an extraordinary and rather traumatic experience she'd had shortly after having a ten-day retreat at the holistic health center in New Mexico that I helped direct.

For five years, Monica had practiced celibacy to enhance her spiritual growth. She had committed to the Eastern path of Kriya Yoga, brought to this country by the late Paramahansa Yogananda. After her retreat with us, she had hesitantly decided to release herself from her experiment in celibacy. She thought it was no longer necessary, as she had achieved the goals she set for herself when she first made this vow. Monica felt it was time to be less of a hermit and begin enjoying a more social life.

I remained silent when she informed me of this decision, sensing the potential problems if the fires of her passions were awakened too quickly. After hearing her decision, I did, however, ask my allies, the Fire Spirits, to protect her from the potential chaos that could result from her decision.

It was not long before Monica was asked out on a date. Nervously, she accepted the dinner invitation. The evening went wonderfully, and, not wanting the evening to end, she invited her date into her home for a nightcap. One thing led to another, and before long the two of them were in bed together. As their passions increased, Monica grew more and more anxious. Had she made the right decision? Was this the right person to be her paramour?

She prayed for a sign—for some revelation that would guide her into the right course of action. Finally, in spite of a sense of foreboding, she let go of her fears and decided to give herself over to her desires.

At that moment, deafening sirens and red and blue lights flashing outside her window startled her and her expectant lover, and she heard a persistent banging at her door. A ladder appeared beside the window of her second-story bedroom, and a man in fireproof garb entered the window, hose in hand. A moment later, an ax splintered through her front door, and another man rushed inside.

For Monica, this was more of a sign than she'd bargained for. The fire bells and flashing lights, the man with the large fire hose and protective suit, and the ax breaking through her door all symbolized invasive male energy threatening the sanctity of her spiritual home.

Monica listened in disbelief as the fire chief told her about the call they had received from a neighbor, who had reported seeing smoke pouring out of her condominium windows. After failing to get a response from ringing the doorbell and vigorously knocking, the firefighters concluded that Monica must have been overcome by smoke, so they broke in. They were relieved to see that the source of the smoke was only a pot burning on the stove because Monica forgotten to turn off the range.

The firemen's embarrassment didn't compare to Monica's. She recommitted to transmuting her sexual energies into her spiritual disciplines, at least until she was absolutely certain that it was time to release her vows of celibacy.

When Monica related her experience to me in her inimitable style, I broke into convulsive laughter. For days afterward, when the visuals of this impossibly funny scenario returned, I burst into laughter all over again.

It was not until months later that I remembered that I had asked the Fire Elementals to intervene, if necessary, in Monica's decision. Now, upon reflection, as with Jack's "blazing crotch,"[20] the Fire Spirits had made their point in a most unforgettable way.

OOO

The mirror world around us reflects our inner life. Without realizing it, we may symbolically act out our deeper issues. Occasionally, those very symbolic acts are so obviously stated that it is downright ludicrous, the mirror world crashing down on our consciousness in such a way that it's impossible to miss the point.

CHAPTER 9
A SHAMAN'S WAY OF DEATH

○○○

WHISPER ON THE WIND

One afternoon in 1973 while Marilynn and I were at the metaphysical center in Atlanta we founded shortly after I left the parish ministry, a Tibetan lama appeared unannounced at our doorstep. He explained that a mutual friend who was a psychic surgeon had suggested that he get in touch with us.

We learned that he was of the "red hat" lineage and bore the title of "dugpa," which is something comparable to the abbot of a monastery. The red-hat lamas, we were soon to discover, were not the kind of meditators who have become so beloved in our country and Europe. They are powerful shamans and magicians whose path is one of power in contrast to the more contemplative path of the yellow-hat lamas to which the current Dalai Lama belongs.

In the course of our conversation, he must have sensed that I was experiencing some skepticism that he was who he claimed to be. The lama, whose name was Dorje, suddenly shifted his posture and for the next five minutes proceeded to tell me things about my childhood and life that no one else could have possibly known.

Dorje explained that he had been trained as a healer in the three main branches of Tibetan medicine: acupuncture, herbal medicine, and psychic surgery. In time, I came to realize that he was accomplished in all of these areas and a master in the art of the latter.

For the next three hours, Dorje kept us spellbound with stories about Tibet and his training as a monk. When he finally got up from his chair to leave, he made the cryptic remark that he would be getting in touch with us and that it would be sooner than we would think.

We thought no more about the remark until that evening when we suddenly began to detect a distinct fragrance in our living room. It smelled like a sweet-smelling, aromatic tobacco. To our astonishment, the fragrance seemed to be emanating from the empty space in the center of our living room. We had no explanation for this phenomenon until the living-room lamp and overhead light began to blink off and on. Almost simultaneously, we detected the presence of Dorje in his subtle body.

We were amazed! Prior to this we had never met anyone who had the ability to project at will in his or her astral body and effect physical phenomena while in that state.

Once we had detected Dorje's presence, we became aware of his telepathic communication with us. We had a general agreement on the content of his messages, including one that we were to call him the next morning.

The next morning we called Dorje on a phone number he had scratched out on a piece of paper the day before.

"Congratulations," he said, before we even had a chance to open our mouths. "You've just passed your first test. You not only detected my presence, but you accurately interpreted my telepathic communication, including my request that you call me first thing this morning. This is what we, in Tibet, call 'whisper on the wind.' It is part of the training a chela (apprentice) experiences with his teacher."

We were stunned by this revelation, not only by the phenomena that we had experienced, but also by our realization that this was Dorje's way of saying that he would be willing to teach us. During the weeks that followed, we spent time with Dorje both in his physical and his astral form. I learned that part of the power of whisper on the wind, other than overcoming the inconvenience of separation by distance, was that abstract concepts that are difficult to verbalize with accuracy could be easily understood in this modality. We learned through Dorje that didactic-style teaching was a waste of time. In true "red hat" shamanic tradition, he chose to teach by manipulating seemingly ordinary events into powerful learning experiences.

One day the lama informed us that he would be leaving town for a few weeks. He asked when I would be holding my next class of students. When I told Dorje a class was scheduled for the next evening, he said, enigmatically, that he might visit us. Momentarily forgetting who it was that made such a promise, I was puzzled as to how he could visit my class when he was hundreds of miles away.

During the night of the class, I began sharing, for the first time, our experiences with Dorje. At the moment I spoke of his whisper-on-the-wind communication with us and the accompanying physical phenomena, the lights began to blink off and on, and we all smelled a tobacco fragrance. At first some class members were a bit frightened, but then their fear turned to elation when they realized that they had the privilege of sharing an experience of which few persons would ever be privy.

When Dorje returned to town, I thanked him for his remarkable demonstration for my class. I assured him that it was an experience that none of them would ever forget. As it had with Marilynn and I months earlier, the experience with Dorje had instilled in my students a sense of awe, and a realization of the untapped potential within each one of us.

○○○

During the next five years, we maintained contact with our friend and mentor, occasionally visiting him in another part of the country where he was residing. During our visits we would assist him with the organizational aspects of his healing practice, which involved his seeing 15 people a day several days a week. Having gained a reputation as a healer, most of Dorje's patients flew in from different parts of the country, Canada, and Europe. These were often desperate people who had exhausted the possibilities of modern Western medicine.

It was during one of our special times with Dorje that he shared with us the story of how he had embarked on his own spiritual path. He said that after several years of searching, he had met his own teacher in Sikkim, a small country bordering Tibet. Dorje explained that he was drawn to this particular teacher because he was a maverick among the lamas, who rejected a lot of the formalism and rigid discipline of most of the Buddhist monks in Tibet. When Dorje first met his teacher, there was immediate recognition on both their parts. His teacher said, "I've been waiting for you a long time." Surprised, Dorje had questioned him about his statement, and the lama explained that some years ago he had seen Dorje's face in mediation and recognized him the moment he saw him.

When Dorje asked him why he had agreed to be his teacher, he was surprised by the answer. The lama said that Dorje possessed somewhat of the same essence as that of a particular lama who had died many years ago. Dorje was well aware of the significance that the monks place on what they speak of as "reincarnations" (of those who had been lamas in previous lives).

Dorje's first teaching involved being taken to a tiny alpine lake in the Himalayas. The lake was so clear that it perfectly mirrored the sky and clouds overhead and yet was transparent to the rays of the sun penetrating its depths.

To his surprise, his teacher took a stick and began stirring the bottom of the lake until it had become clouded with silt and debris.

"What do you see?" the lama asked.

"I see water that has become cloudy," Dorje replied.

"That is the mind of most people on this world. They are so clouded and polluted with the thoughts and cares of the mundane world that no light can get through."

The two men sat quietly for perhaps 15 minutes gazing at the waters until once more it was clear and transparent to the sun's rays.

"Now what do you see?" the lama asked.

"The water has become clear and transparent to the sun's rays," he said.

"That is the mind of the lama, a holy person!" he said. "You will learn to control your thoughts until your mind is like this body of water, clear and transparent to the rays of the Infinite."

Dorje never forgot that first lesson. It was following this that his teacher took him to a cave and told him that he would remain there until he had learned to control his mind. The lama then proceeded to pile stones at the entrance to the cave until it was completely sealed off. He left, however, a small opening, which emitted no light into the cave but through which water and a bowl of rice could be passed to Dorje every three days.

"At first I believed that this would be easy," Dorje told us. "I'd just sleep most of the time until I was let out of the cave. But after what must have been several days, I discovered that I could hardly sleep at all. At that point I began to panic and had to fight the feeling that I was going mad! I felt claustrophobic, and my mind seemed totally out of control," he said. "I knew that at any point I could have removed the stones and walked away, but if I had done so the teachings would have immediately ended, and my relationship with my lama would be severed."

While Dorje was speaking, I was mesmerized by the story of his experiences. I even tried to place myself in his shoes, wondering if I could have passed such a test. I felt that it would have been unlikely.

"The only thing that enabled me to stick with this test," he said reflectively, "was the knowledge that there were others in the past who had done so, even though these were in the minority." Dorje continued, "One of my first crises was that of enduring the cool temperatures with no blanket and wearing only a loincloth. I was shivering all the time," he said. "Then almost miraculously, I discovered how to raise the 'tumo,' which is the internal heat that the lamas learn to master. From that time on, I was not bothered by the cool temperatures, and even today, I am comfortable in most extreme cold temperatures."

Dorje explained that some of their lamas have contests during the winter months to see who can melt the most ice around them. At other times they see who can dry off the most number of wet sheets that are draped around them while they are sitting out in the snow without clothing. He said that this was an amazing sight to watch.

It was during this time that Dorje learned to awaken and raise his internal fire, known as "kundalini," which later he used extensively in his healing practice. He also became adept at leaving his physical body. He explained that once he had been able to achieve this, being sealed off in the small cave no longer posed a problem for him. In his subtle body, he could go wherever he chose.

Dorje remained in the cave an incredible 11 and a half months before his teacher appeared one day and began dismantling the stone barrier.

"Now you are ready," he stated, "to begin instructions in the deeper aspects of our teachings."

Dorje explained that the Tibetan "short path" is much too rigorous and austere for most Westerners. "Westerners," he explained, "simply don't have the psychological makeup for this kind of austerity." This, of course, was something I had already figured out.

"However, Westerners can achieve the same ends," he explained, "by more gradual methods. These I am able to teach you." My partner and I marveled upon hearing of Dorje's remarkable training, and we were grateful to have embarked on a more moderate "middle" path.

I had always felt a deep love for Dorje and thrived on a lot of the information he shared with us. On the other hand, his particular path seemed too austere for my predilection, and so I never felt that I could commit to the totality of his teachings. Nevertheless, the genuine affection I felt for him remained, and this feeling was mutual.

Then two years passed without our having had any contact with Dorje. We were not even certain where he was until one evening I answered the phone, and it was our old friend and mentor. There was sadness in his voice that I had never experienced before, but his reason for calling seemed more of an expression of sentimentality.

"I had always wanted to tell you and Marilynn how much you both have meant to me all these years. You were the first people in America who welcomed me and took me in. I have never forgotten this."

I expressed how much his sharing such feeling meant to me, and then Marilynn got on the phone and said pretty much the same thing. Finally, we said our good-byes. Neither of us realized that this was Dorje's way of expressing his final "farewell" and that neither of us would ever speak with him nor see him again in his physical form.

The next night we received a phone call from an associate of his saying that Dorje had died sometime during the night, and that the examining physician could find no apparent cause of death. In fact, his death was a mystery to the doctor since it appeared that he had been in perfect health.

Of course we knew immediately what had happened: Dorje, having felt that his work in the West was complete, chose to voluntarily and permanently leave his physical body. The associate informed us that Dorje had also called up several other friends, and that no one had gleaned the real reason for his calling.

We learned that upon hearing of his death some of his fellow lamas had performed the ceremony out of the Tibetan Book of the Dead to assist this special soul on his journey through the "bardo" (lower worlds) into the higher world. Privately, we remembered our former teacher in our own way. I realized then, perhaps more than ever, how much he had meant to me.

Two weeks later I was delivering a lecture in Charlotte, North Carolina, in a public auditorium when my thoughts filled with fond, poignant, and sometimes humorous memories of our times with Dorje.

I began speaking about the time he visited my class years ago in his astral body. At the moment I began talking about his calling card with the lights, the auditorium lights suddenly went out. Then, after a pause, they began going on and off repeatedly. I could hear gasps and then a murmur going through the audience. Everyone was stunned into a kind of incredulity. Later some in the audience confessed to me that at first they thought I had staged this. But then there was nervous laughter, and soon the entire audience was caught up in enjoying this marvelous cosmic joke. It was the inimitable red-hat lama, of course, up to his old tricks again.

OOO

SEQUOYAH'S FINAL COUP

Highlands, North Carolina

While living on the Highlands Plateau, we developed a close association with Ken Two Trees, a Cherokee medicine man. Ken's work as a native medicine person had been featured in a national psychology magazine as well as a full-length story in *National Geographic*.

Although he had been raised on the Cherokee reservation in Oklahoma, as a young man Ken rebelled against the old ways of his ancestors and sought a career in the military. It was around the time of his retirement that his searching led him back to his own tradition.

Ken had a burning desire to help others through alternative healing, combining Western holistic medicine with Native American philosophy and teachings. We had been especially impressed by his medical clairvoyance, and we had witnessed demonstrations of this talent with total strangers who had come to him for help.

We first saw his connection with the natural world when Marilynn and a mutual friend, Elizabeth, a freelance writer, first visited him. After a brief introduction, he took them to a clearing near his stables. Blindfolding each of them, he asked them to begin walking forward slowly, stopping only if they experienced any change in their surroundings. After about ten paces, both women stopped in almost the same place; they had sensed that at that point they had passed through some kind of veil. Marilynn experienced a sudden quieting of the world around her. Before she had been aware of the sounds of horses, birds, a barking dog in the distance, and of a gentle breeze blowing. But as soon as she passed into the spot, it was as if all those sounds were absorbed into the deep silence of the place she'd entered. She felt a sense of peace and detachment.

When Marilynn described her experience, Ken was exuberant. "Congratulations," he said, "you've just passed the test I gave you. This is a place where the four directions come together. It's a sacred spot. I'm glad you recognized it."

Ken also had a close spiritual connection with the elemental forces. One summer the Highlands Plateau had suffered from a prolonged drought, a rare phenomenon in these verdant foothills of the Blue Ridge Mountains, which average 70 inches of rainfall a year. Consequently, his ground spring had dried up.

Ken relied on his spring to provide water for his horses, his garden of medicinal plants, and himself. Yet, instead of worrying about it, he did the most natural thing in the nonrational world of shamanism. He simply went to the dried-up spring, made a tobacco and cornmeal offering to the spirit guardians of the water source, and requested that his spring begin to flow again. In keeping with shamanic protocol, he explained the reasons he needed the water, in turn making a commitment to do certain things for the local environment.

The next morning when he returned to the spring, Ken was not surprised to see that his well had water again. Yet something was wrong. His well had more water than he'd had even in times of excessive rainfall. Suspicious of his new overflowing spring, Ken began walking above his spring toward a distant ridge. When he came to a pond on a neighbor's property, he found his answer. The earthen dam had sprung a leak. The water escaping from the dam ran for a few hundred feet downhill toward Ken's property, then disappeared into the ground.

When Ken returned to his property, he made another offering to the water elementals, saying, "Thank you for filling my spring, but please don't let it be at the expense of my neighbor." The next morning Ken discovered that the situation was fixed. For although he had much less water in his spring, his neighbor's dam was no longer leaking.

One Sunday morning, Marilynn and I received a strong impression that our neighbor Ken needed to see us. There was a certain urgency that seemed to be riding on the wings of this feeling.

Ken did not have a phone. We would always just know whenever he wanted to see us. Likewise, he usually sensed when we were coming to visit him at his riding stables, eight miles down the mountain from our home.

Although in those early years I lacked the confidence I have today in my telepathic abilities, there was nothing that extraordinary about this level of the relationship with Ken. I had experienced the same method of communication with Dorje as well as with Rolling Thunder, the late Shoshone-Cherokee shaman, who informed me that this was the way their medicine people communicated with one another when separated by distance. My limited experiences with this method of communication with these talented persons had taught me that there existed a deeper level of communication that bypasses the ordinary barriers of distance.

To develop an ability in this mode of communication is not so difficult as might be imagined. To experience it is more like a "remembering" of something one once knew but has simply forgotten. The faculty for this kind of communication seems to be found in the roots of the mind involving an arcane and very primal level of one's being.

Upon completing the eight-mile drive on a winding, steep mountain road to the horse stables, Marilynn and I were not at all surprised to find Ken standing beside the road, looking toward us in anticipation. "Good," he said, "I thought you'd hear me calling you. We need to go to Cherokee right away. Amaweeti (Sequoyah) came to me in a dream last night. He's in some kind of trouble and asked for our help."

There was no question in anyone's mind that the dream message was valid, and soon we were making the 90-minute drive to Cherokee, North Carolina. Marilynn and I had heard much of Sequoyah, the ancient resident medicine person of the Eastern band

207

of Cherokee. We were aware of Sequoyah's miraculous healings of many physical afflictions using his vast knowledge of herbal medicine. He was reported to be more than one hundred years of age.

Sequoyah, as a traditional Cherokee, had a vast knowledge of plant medicine. In fact, he had had a steady stream of patients, including white people, coming to him for help. Furthermore, he was able to cure certain cancers and other diseases still beyond the scope of Western medicine. I spoke with a white man from a large city, who after months of suffering and failure to find relief from his traditional American medical doctors, had recently been cured of shingles by Sequoyah's plant medicine.

No one knew exactly how old he was, but we had heard from Ken and others that he had been Buffalo Bill's "Eagle Dancer" in his traveling "Wild West Show." Later Marilynn and I saw proof of this when we visited him at his tiny trailer on the reservation. Hung on one wall were actual photographs of him standing next to Bill Cody, as a young Native American, in full dance attire. No doubt about it, it was the young Sequoyah. "What sort of help does the ancient medicine man need?" I wondered. "What can any of us present do for someone like this?"

When we arrived in Cherokee, we learned that Sequoyah was seriously ill and had been taken to the native hospital the night before. As we arrived at the hospital, we were told that the old shaman had been in a coma and was not expected to live. Apparently, a few hours earlier he had stopped breathing and was pronounced dead. Then to everyone's amazement, he seemingly came back to life, experiencing the return of all his vital signs.

Upon hearing this, I knew that he had known we were coming, and I wondered if this knowledge was enough to bring him back. We were treated with great deference at the hospital. Apparently, it is considered an honor to be visited by a medicine person, but a rare tribute for anyone to have three medicine people visit. Having been in many hospitals in the past, as a visiting priest, it was a new experience to have such a reception. In fact, we later heard that Sequoyah himself boasted to the hospital staff about his visit by three medicine people.

When we walked into Sequoyah's room, the first thing I noticed was that even though his muscles were atrophied, his skin was as smooth and youthful-looking as a child's; and his long, black hair had only a few streaks of gray. I wondered if his herbal knowledge had anything to do with his incredible youthfulness.

We began administering healing on the old medicine man at once. Our combined energy fields and intent were sufficient to bring Sequoyah out of his comatose state, and within minutes, he was sitting in bed laughing and telling stories. Although Marilynn and I were shocked by the transformation, Ken appeared to have expected it and took it in stride.

Sequoyah lived in good health for another six months. As with all traditional native people, he felt that to die in a hospital or from a lingering sickness was not a warrior's death. In fact, by his philosophy, it was about the worst thing that could have happened to him.

During the months following his leave from the hospital, Marilynn and I visited him several times. I also met the very nice young couple who were staying with Sequoyah and who were caring for him in exchange for learning the native tradition. The wife was pregnant, and it was their intention to raise the child with a spiritual knowledge they had learned from Sequoyah.

One evening Sequoyah asked the couple caring for him to gather all his power objects and bring them to him. Then, as he lay on his bed, he had them carefully place his eagle wing, medicine pipe, pouch, and other objects in different configurations on or around his body. Turning to the woman, who was now eight months pregnant, Sequoyah said, "I am going to be leaving now. But I will be coming back soon, and it'll be through you."

The next morning they discovered that Sequoyah had died during the night. It was only then that they realized he'd been telling them good-bye. However, they forgot about his promise to return until their child was born. They were soon aware of a familiar birthmark on their baby. It was the same birthmark they had seen many times on Sequoyah and, in fact, it was in the same location on their child's body. They had known that the Cherokee saw birthmarks as a sign that a child is special and destined to become a shaman and healer. There was no doubt in their minds that their child was their former mentor for whom they had cared in his final days.

We had no further contact with the couple, but a few years later we heard that they had brought their child to the Hopi elders to assure that he received training in the "old ways" as he matured. The elders, their deep intuition having confirmed what the young white couple already knew—acknowledged that a venerated Cherokee shaman was back.

Before the young couple had left the hospital, however, they shared with us a number of their experiences with Sequoyah. One of the stories that actually took place after their teacher's death was riotously funny. It seemed that for years Sequoyah had been verbally attacked by fundamentalist Christian clergy who had churches on the reservation. The clergy had strongly disapproved of his "pagan" ways and his refusal to be converted. Sequoyah has steadfastly resisted the strong social and political pressure that these men of the cloth exerted.

This made it all the more shocking when it was discovered that in his will Sequoyah requested that these same ministers, who had been his worst enemies, serve as his pallbearers. The clergy themselves speculated with a sense of triumph that the old medicine man must have converted on his deathbed. They prided themselves on having saved this "sinner" from a miserable afterlife.

They began to wonder about the meaning of this final request, however, when they learned that Sequoyah had requested that he be buried at the top of the highest, unpaved mountain on the Cherokee Reservation in the heart of the Smoky Mountains. We heard later that these men had enormous difficulty in their struggle to carry the body of their former nemesis to the top of the mountain. One of the men even had to be hospitalized from overexertion.

When I heard this story, I doubled over with laughter. Having witnessed Sequoyah's bizarre and sometimes slightly dark humor, I had no difficulty imagining that stubborn old shaman riding in his casket, laughing at his former enemies who were struggling to get his body to the top of the mountain. It had been against Sequoyah's spiritual principles to attack his persecutors in response to their tirades from their pulpits. However, it was permissible for him to engineer and craft this incredible scenario. It was the old shaman's final coup!

ooo

The deaths of Dorje Chen and Sequoyah both evoked memories for me of some difficult moments in my priesthood. As a priest, I had seen members of my congregation fall apart over the loss of a loved one. It was not simply their personal loss that brought about their disintegration, but also their urgent need for answers. They had sought reassurance that was based not just on blind faith, but also upon concrete evidence that there is life beyond the grave. I had always felt inadequate at such times because I could not give them what they needed and most certainly deserved. Unlike a few of my peers, I could not bring myself to offer trite reassurances by reiterating church doctrines or reciting appropriate passages from the scriptures.

Although each Sunday we had recited together the words of the creed, ". . . I believe in the resurrection of the dead and the life everlasting . . . ,"[21] to my dismay, I discovered that such words had no power to give hope at these times of personal loss. Over and over again, I had seen that belief systems were not able to sustain a person through a personal crisis such as the loss of a loved one. Real faith for me was not about the ascent to certain doctrinal statements, but it was a childlike state of openness and trust.

Two remarkable men in my life, a Buddhist monk and a Native American medicine person, demonstrated to me tangible proof that one survives physical death, and that life continues beyond the grave. What comfort I could have offered bereaved members of my congregation if I had been able to tell the amazing stories of these two people who were not Christian. They both had not only died a warrior's death, but also provided the most powerful testimonial to the survival of a bodily death that I had ever encountered.

From my association with Dorje and Sequoyah, I learned that dying can be a powerful and conscious experience. Incredibly, both of these people not only died consciously, but chose the time, place, and manner in which they died. Both in their own way demonstrated, almost irrefutably, that there is no finality in death, and that our personality continues its journey beyond the grave.

As a result of my connection with these two deeply spiritual and powerful warriors, the words of St. Paul that I had so often read in our burial services took on new meaning for me: ". . . Death is swallowed up in victory. Oh death where is thy sting, oh grave where is thy victory."[22] It was an understanding based not on more "belief," but on knowledge born out of powerful personal experience.

❖ ❖ ✸ ❖ ❖

CHAPTER 10
DARK SIDE OF SPIRIT

In the more than three decades in my life as a shaman-healer, a number of people who were unknowingly victims of invasive psychic forces would have ended up committing suicide or institutionalized for life had they not been referred to me. A few of these people would have died from multiple syndromes and afflictions that were not their own to experience.

Although these stories are not directly related to the theme of this book, I decided to include them because the New Age and Human Potential movements, as well as the clinical psychology profession, have consistently been in denial of the reality of the dark side of spirit. With the New Age half-truth that we are creators of our own reality and the tendency of contemporary psychology to focus on classifications such as psychosis, people who are under psychic attack often have nowhere to turn for help. There are symptoms described in this sec-tion that, in any shamanic culture, would have been immediately recognized by the village or tribal healer for what they were—effects of the dark side of spirit—and treated appropriately.

○○○

COYOTE WOMAN
Boulder, Colorado: Fall

I received a call from an old friend, Connie, who had introduced me to the spiritual community in San Antonio and had made arrangements for me to teach workshops there. When Connie called, she only stated that she had a problem she needed to discuss, and she requested an appointment with Marilynn and me as soon as possible. Detecting a note of urgency in her voice, I arranged for her to visit us late that afternoon.

When Connie arrived, I was shocked by her appearance. She had aged considerably since I'd last seen her four years earlier. She admitted she had been in a prolonged state of depression and had been unable to break out of it. She had no idea what the source of the depression was. Connie had lost interest in the things that once fascinated her and had been unable to work. She was beginning to lose interest in life itself.

I was reeling at the enormous changes in my old friend. She normally had an effervescent personality that could literally transform the energy of a group. She was a caregiver who had spent much of her life in humanitarian service.

A feeling of heaviness came over me. I was so saddened by the changes in my friend and co-worker that I sensed that there was something very wrong about all this, but I had no idea what it could be.

Connie continued describing her state for several minutes. Occasionally we interjected questions, which she answered briefly. I began to grow more and more uneasy, feeling that we were on the wrong track. I understood the sadness inside me, but the anxiety welling up didn't seem to fit the situation.

Suddenly I felt an abrupt change in the atmosphere of the small room where we were gathered. With my inner vision, I saw standing behind Connie a tall woman dressed in skins, a coyote head tied on top of her head. I recognized at once that this being was Artemis Huntress, the essence of primal feminine power. She was the elemental goddess that had spoken to me in my dreams only a few years earlier. Her coyote headdress told me there was some kind of trickery, perhaps even treachery, involved. Her lips were moving, and I distinctly heard the message, "Tell Connie that she must go south to the desert to reclaim her power. An evil sorcerer took her power away while she was in the desert." Once more, Artemis, who had appeared four times in my dreams, had given highly accurate information.

When I related the message to Connie, she reacted to my words as if she had been struck by a thunderbolt. Visibly shaken, she began to describe a tragic and terrifying experience she'd had two years earlier in New Mexico. She and a close friend, who was one of the spiritual leaders in Austin, had acquired some land 30 miles outside Santa Fe to start a spiritual-retreat center. They had been warned against moving there by local Hispanic people, who explained that a very evil "curandero" lived there who hated white people and would attempt to harm them.

Caught up in their idealistic vision, the two women ignored the warnings and acquired the land anyway. Three months later, Connie's partner decided to visit the curandero in hopes of establishing some kind of rapport. Her decision was a fatal mistake.

The very next day after the visit, tragedy struck. The woman and her one-year-old son were killed in a head-on collision with a drunk driver in downtown Santa Fe. Connie was so stricken by the loss of her close friend and associate that she immediately put the land up for sale and moved to Boulder. Since that experience, Connie had not felt like herself and had even wondered many times if the sorcerer had put some kind of spell on both of them.

Certain I was on the right track, I asked Connie if she remembered the name of the curandero. Ordinarily this would be a normal request because a person's name easily becomes a honing-in method for my inner vision. But in this case it was the worst possible thing I could have done. I should have known better. In tribal traditions throughout the world, it is no secret that speaking the name of a dark sorcerer can bring in that unwanted energy.

No sooner did Connie pronounce the curandero's name then a sudden gust of wind blew open the back door of our ceremonial room, made a right turn through the foyer, then with great force blew open the door to our ceremonial room. Now it was too late. We were stunned. High winds coming off the mountains nearby were common in Boulder, but it had been a calm day.

Never had our back door blown open, much less the interior door to our ceremonial room. It was no ordinary wind. We had to work fast. Clearly we had inadvertently caught the sorcerer's attention, and his awareness now made our work more urgent and more dangerous. There was little time. Connie was terrified. Neither of us needed to say anything; she sensed what had just happened. Then, what I was hoping wouldn't happen did. Our friend began shaking slightly at first and then more and more violently as if she were about to go into serious convulsions. Marilynn and I glanced at each other, and without speaking, began working with Connie. We first placed a psychic shield around her and ourselves, and then began to cleanse Connie's magnetic field of energy. [23]

In no time, Marilynn was able to find where the tear was in Connie's energy body. I recognized that the curandero had plenty of power and that our task wouldn't be easy. We had several advantages, though. Our drawing in his awareness forced the issue, much like bringing a fever to a head. Also we were on our own turf, and the three of us had good energy together because of our close spiritual ties.

As often happens to me in times of spiritual emergency, rather than becoming hurried or apprehensive, I went into a state of deep calm. I am eternally grateful for this ability to change consciousness when it is most needed, as it allows me to be effective in crises. I noticed that Marilynn also had become extremely calm and alert. She had already begun to extract something from Connie's abdominal area.

Thankfully, within a couple of long minutes, the object that was attached to Connie's energy body suddenly came loose. It had the appearance of a sharp triangular stone. Instantly there was a dramatic transformation. As the convulsions ceased, Connie appeared serene, looking years younger, as I remembered her. Moments later she was sobbing, saying that it was the first time she had felt like herself since that terrible experience outside of Santa Fe. Now all she wished to do was to get on with her life, making up for the lost years.

But nothing is over till it's over. While reviewing the whole episode with us, Connie again made reference to the sorcerer by name. In our exuberance over her healing, neither Marilynn nor I had thought to warn Connie never to use the name of her formidable adversary. At the exact moment the name was spoken, my 200-year-old Blackfoot medicine pouch and pipe carrier flew off the wall where they had been hanging and landed near my feet. By this time we all should have been shockproof, but Connie began hyperventilating.

We were not out of the woods yet. Marilynn and I again attempted to strengthen the protective shield around Connie and to calm her down. Fear, if uncontrolled, will open one up to negativity more quickly than almost anything. Fortunately, the dark power of the curandero quickly dissipated and once more she was calm.

I will never forget the dramatic appearance of the elemental goddess as a powerful protectress, and the deadly struggle with the dark power of the curandero. It reconfirmed to me what I had seen many times before: that some problems faced by people are outside the realm of psychotherapy or conventional religious explanations.

The transformation of Connie was remarkable: from an almost dead old woman to a young and vivacious woman glowing with life. This was the real Connie, the one I knew in Austin, who had been so full of joy and spontaneity. I was grateful that Marilynn had been with me for this. It took the two of us. It amazed me how we became one mind in such trying situations.

What peculiar twists and turns my spiritual path had taken. Could I have anticipated doing this kind of healing when I first decided to become a priest? If someone had predicted it, I would not have believed a word of it. Perhaps it was a blessing that I was protected from knowing too much. I couldn't imagine anyone relishing this type of spiritual intervention.

And yet it had its own rewards. I knew that Connie had been saved from a psychological and physical deterioration that neither doctors nor therapists could have diagnosed, much less averted. My heart was very full.

ooo

When Connie departed, there was a lingering question that haunted me. Why did such a terrible tragedy happen to two highly evolved and positive people who wished only to serve their fellow humans? But even as I pondered the question, the answer was clear.

None of the great teachers ever promised that the spiritual path would be easy or even safe. Indeed the path could be deadly. No wonder the path of initiation had been described as the razor's edge or likened to the sword of Damocles, which hung by a thread over the initiate. There are casualties, sometimes even fatalities, as in the case of Connie and her associate. But for those on the positive path of service to others, there are fates worse than failure or death. It is far better to lose one's life than to lose ground spiritually or suffer irreparable damage to one's consciousness by causing great harm to another. I have never encountered anyone on a spiritual path who did not believe that the path was worth the effort and the risk.

ooo

THE POTTER'S PROTECTION
Nederland, Colorado: Late Winter

Laura, a young woman from a mining town in the mountains north of Denver, had come to ask my advice. She was a successful potter in her area, but for the past several weeks she had been having difficulty with the craft. Each time she had fired a new batch of pottery in the kiln, it came out ruined. Although she had the kiln checked out several times, nothing could be found to account for its malfunction. She explained to me that she couldn't afford to have more ruined pottery and hoped that I might be able to intuitively sense what the source of her problem might be.

While listening to her story, I became increasingly convinced that there was something more than met the eye. Through my inner vision I found my answer. I saw that Laura's problems were of a psychic nature and that she had been under the influence of something malevolent. She readily agreed with this, stating that recently some known drug dealers had rented the house next to her, and soon afterward she'd had a run-in with them. During that confrontation, they had become angry with her and had actually threatened her life.

In the days that followed, they continued to harass her, and the kiln had stopped working. In addition, she began to feel increasingly uncomfortable, often feeling a sinister presence in her once-peaceful home. Word was out in the local spiritual community that these men were into some dark rituals. This confirmed my own feelings, and I knew that Laura was in dire need of immediate protection. The following day I made the hour-and-a-half drive from Denver to her mountain home to attempt to assist her.

There were two areas of concern. First was the problem with the kiln. In the past, I had often observed a link between negative psychic energies in a home and mechanical or electrical failures. Far more serious, however, was the psychic and physical danger to this young woman herself. A death threat from drug dealers was nothing to be taken lightly under any circumstances. They had to be stopped right away. Laura had already been unable to get the local police to take her seriously, and she suspected that they might be paid off by the drug dealers to look the other way.

I was reluctant to tell Laura just how much danger I felt she was in, as fear would have impeded her ability to help with the strategy I was planning. It was not enough to restore the psychic balance to her kiln. On a powerful gut level, I was certain that her dangerous neighbors had to go.

To confront them would not only endanger me, but also further endanger Laura. My visit must be clandestine. Should any of them penetrate the purpose of my visit, there could be serious repercussions.

There was no time to waste. I set about at once cleansing Laura's home while placing a protective shield around both Laura and her kiln. Next I placed a psychic cloak around the drug dealer's home to contain their own negativity, preventing it from reaching us. With this containing cloak, they would have to eat their own negativity, since whatever they sent out would be immediately returned. Finally, I showed Laura how to continue each morning and each evening with the same methods I had used to reinforce the protection. I left her with some sage to smudge her home every day, and some simple prayers to use for protection.

I received a call from Laura ten days later, happily informing me that her kiln was working, and that the peaceful feeling had returned to her home. Then, a little smugly, the potter added that the drug dealers had also been taken care of and wouldn't be a problem anymore.

"What happened?" I asked, not really surprised, but knowing she had something extraordinary to tell me.

"Well," she said, "after you worked on my house, the negative energy totally disappeared. Since that time, my kiln mysteriously began to work again. That in itself was an immense relief. But still I was tense about these scary people living next to me.

"I didn't have to worry," she continued. "On the fourth day while I was doing my protection, the floor of the drug dealers' house collapsed—not just a small portion, but about three-fourths of the floor. Naturally they had to move. They are no longer in the area."

"Too bad," I said tongue in cheek, "the house was old. Must have been some rotten floor joists."

"Yes," she giggled, "a lot of very rotten joists."

Then I was on the floor in stitches, barely able to continue the conversation. Laura too erupted in laughter. Whether it was incredible poetic justice or the intense relief we felt, I couldn't tell, but we continued in convulsive laughter for some time.

OOO

Like so many other times of crisis in clients' lives, or my own, I succeeded with spiritual methods to rectify a problem where more physical methods had proven ineffective. And, in fact, by transforming the spiritual and psychic energies, a serious problem was alleviated in a way that was faster, more efficient, and safer than any physical confrontation would have been.

OOO

INTERLOPER

Ft. Lauderdale, Florida: Midwinter

A hushed silence had fallen over the entire group at a workshop I was conducting in Ft. Lauderdale. I was preparing to demonstrate healing on a 35-year-old woman with systemic lupus. Sandy was an attractive woman with long brown hair and hazel eyes. Her six-foot-tall frame and overall appearance made her a striking figure, and few who didn't know her would have sensed how much suffering she had been through.

In recent months, Sandy had taken a turn for the worse and had become increasingly concerned about whether she could continue to function in daily life. In addition to the pain, she had been suffering from extreme lethargy and depression, which her doctors attributed to the disease. It all seemed so unfair.

As always when conducting a healing, there was no certainty whether or not this person would respond. I had a gut level feeling about Sandy, and I was optimistic.

I had Sandy lie on a blanket in the center of our circle, and I made magnetic passes over her body with my hands. At first nothing happened, but then to my surprise, a shadow seemed to pass over her body. Her face appeared to grow distorted, and her eyes were hollow and sunken, giving the appearance of a cadaver. This was unexpected. I could hear the silent alarms going off inside me.

I saw sudden apprehension in the faces of those around me. I hoped the group was sufficiently protected. Still, I decided against stopping the healing because once a possessing spirit has been forced to the surface, the most difficult part has often already been accomplished. This, also, is the moment of greatest danger to all. From past experience, I knew that just about anything could happen.

"There's a very bad spirit here," I announced. Several of the more psychically perceptive members of the class nodded in agreement. I continued by requesting the assistance of all those present to help hold the energy. One could have heard a pin drop.

Sandy, too, must have felt the change. Later, I learned that she was experiencing the sensation of being a dead person lying in a coffin. I know now that she had enough knowledge to realize the seriousness of the situation and that she felt helpless in the netherworld power that held her in its grip. I was able to sense that Sandy's "persona" had become almost completely overshadowed by this interloper. How long, I wondered, had it been with her, and what was its relationship to Sandy's lupus?

Quickly, I assessed the situation. The negative entity had become attached to Sandy at some point in her life, and the magnetic force of the healing had driven it to the surface. I had seen this a number of times. Now it was hanging on to her energy field with a terrible tenacity. It had no intention of letting go.

After a few minutes, I realized that we had a psychic Mexican standoff. The entity, as powerful as it was negative, was determined not to give up its holdings. I requested that the group begin drumming to build up the energy while I continued what now had become an exorcism. I ardently prayed that the force of the drumming combined with our focused intent would tilt the balance of power enough in our favor.

After what seemed like an interminable amount of time, but in reality was only a few minutes, I sensed a change. With my inner vision, I saw the entity, a dark, formless mass, finally emerge. The standoff had broken. Now we were approaching the most dangerous time for all of us there. I prepared everyone.

In what should go down as one of my more memorable understatements, I warned, "Here goes!" No sooner had the words escaped my lips, then we all just about went through the ceiling.

A four-by-six-foot piece of lattice board that was leaning against the east wall of the room flew off, landing in the center of the hardwood floor with the sharp report of a gunshot.

At this moment, I recalled Rolling Thunder's warning to always leave open a door or window when attempting to get rid of evil spirits because they need a way to get out. It seems that some spirits built up such density from draining their hosts that they could no longer easily pass though solid surfaces. Once, when Rolling Thunder forgot to do this, an attic trap door in the ceiling flew open and closed with a bang; it was the only exit available at the time.

Not wishing to take any chances, I quickly had a student open a window. It may be difficult for some to understand, but our compassion must include the spirit as well as its human victim. The spirit may feel lost or terrified. In the Bible, Christ himself showed compassion for the demons inhabiting a man he healed by sending them into some nearby pigs. While the pigs went racing over the cliff to their deaths, nevertheless, some kind of law or obligation was fulfilled.

The flying lattice was the most dramatic finale of a healing I'd ever witnessed. No trumpet fanfare could have equaled this. Sandy was now sitting upright, and a radiant, beatific expression replaced her former cadaver face. She said she felt wonderful and was in awe.

In the weeks that followed, Sandy's lupus went into remission, and for the first time in years she had her old energy back, along with renewed hope and interest in life. Sandy's health held up during the next two years that I was in touch with her.

What really did happen in the seminar at Ft. Lauderdale? I'll probably never know for sure. Was Sandy's disease caused by the possessing spirit? Or was the spirit attracted to her as a result of her debilitated condition, thereby compounding the problem? Undoubtedly this was a question not for medical, but for spiritual, science. Did the spirit actually collide with the lattice? The energy of unconditional love and light, while uplifting to us, is actually painful to one whose polarity is largely negative. Most likely the entity, finally defeated in a contest of wills, simply wanted to vacate its host as quickly as possible.

* * ❂ * *

CHAPTER 11

FROM THE EDGE OF THE ABYSS TO THE THRESHOLD OF INFINITY

*N*ow I found myself standing at the edge of an abyss. I had come face-to-face with debilitating health and personal issues for which there seemed no solution. I wondered how I could have been allowed to live such an extraordinary and blessed life and then have it all come down to such pain and dissolution.

Perhaps, as one of my peers suggested, my struggle was the tax the universe extracted from me for having been given certain gifts. After all, there are no free lunches—especially on one's spiritual journey. Twice, I was unknowingly heading toward certain death, which I had only been able to avert at the last minute through information I received from my inner vision. I had also come back from death on two different occasions, but was it all worth it? Would I be able to continue with my life and journey in the face of such adversity I was experiencing?

THE WOUNDED HEALER

Santa Fe, New Mexico

Something happened to me in the early fall of 1980 that rang out like a clock striking midnight. It tolled the end of an era and the beginning of a new one. My life changed so drastically, that I was never quite the same afterward. It became a point of reference for me separating everything that happened before from everything after.

My former partner, Marilynn, and I had just moved from the mountains outside of Taos to Santa Fe, New Mexico. We had rented a small adobe house on Palace Street, a block off the famous Town Square where the local Hispanics and Anglos ran their classy boutiques and art galleries, and the Native Americans displayed their wares each day on blankets spread out on the sidewalks.

For the last year and a half, we had been part of a failed attempt to develop a holistic health center. Now past the disappointment, we were excited by the new directions opening to us. Marilynn was enrolled in the Santa Fe School of Massage, which she would be attending for the next year. I would begin traveling on the lecture circuit. From the onset of our move, however, I was stricken with a serious movement disorder of unknown origin. Each night when I attempted to retire, I discovered that I had to continually move my legs in bed, or worse yet, get up and walk.

I tried sitting in a chair to read to no avail. Furthermore, willing myself to not move my legs was equally impossible. I had to walk! In fact, I had to walk throughout the night, without reprieve. Even a few moments of sleep seemed impossible. Sleep eluded me. One time, years later, I walked a mile-long horse pasture all throughout the night, figuring later that I had covered more than eight miles.

The devastating result was that I was sleepless in Santa Fe for the next full year. I was even sleepless during my out-of-state travels. The continual walking and the sleeplessness began to take its toll, but I was able to take several catnaps throughout the day, which allowed me to barely survive.

During this early stage of my disorder, my morale was high. I felt that it would be a passing thing, or I would eventually find some medical explanation and a treatment. As peculiar as it sounds, it all seemed so unreal. "This just can't be happening to me!" I kept saying to myself. I could not fit my bizarre nightmarish problem into the terrain of my known world.

Unfortunately, it was unlike anything the medical profession had heard of before. The different doctors I consulted listened to me, often with raised eyebrows, and usually concluded that my problems were either psychological or an odd consequence of tension.

It was only after the symptoms continued for months that I began to grow desperate. Finally, after nearly a year of sleeplessness, I began having chest pains. They weren't extreme, considering the stress I'd been under, but my wife and I were concerned. When I checked with a cardiologist, however, I learned that my heart was in excellent condition. We weren't convinced. Common sense dictated that something eventually had to give.

Some of our psychically sensitive friends began calling from around the country to inquire if I was well. Each had experienced a dream, a vision, or premonition of me having a heart attack. One person dreamed that I had died.

Finally, early one morning while lying in bed, I had a spontaneous out-of-body experience. I found myself suspended in a glowing mist. I could sense other presences close by but was unable to discern anything. I sensed that there was a message for me. I was correct, but the news was not good.

The unseen presences began explaining to me that I needed

to make a choice. The medical specialists would be unable to diagnose or treat my health problem. My affliction would bring instability into my life, they explained, not just physically as it already had, but emotionally and mentally as well. To prevent this from happening, it was their recommendation that I break my connection from my physical body. It was only a recommendation, they clarified, and the choice must be mine.

I was stunned. I knew that my condition had to be serious. I knew each morning that I felt I could not bear another walking marathon throughout the night, but I also felt that sooner or later I would find someone that could help me. Now I was being told that help was not forthcoming. I could exit this world now or face a future of personal chaos.

I was greatly alarmed. The advice was not my idea of guidance from a higher spiritual realm. It was radical but had the ring of truth. I wondered if I could trust it. I did not want to leave this world. I asked for more information: *Why had this happened? What specifically could I anticipate in the future? Was there any way out of this other than death?* The presences told me that this was all they were allowed to say without interfering with my free will. The choice had to be mine. The answer must come from my heart.

For a long moment, I hesitated. What was I to do? Could I even believe this message? The unseen presences seemed benign and to have my best interests in their hearts. Furthermore, they seemed very familiar, like close friends, but not friends I'd known in my world. I sensed that they were of my spiritual family of another world, where I also belonged but could not quite remember.

Looking down, I could see a silvery cord extending from me into the mist. I knew that at the other end of the cord, in a separate dimension, was my physical body. I knew also that, ordinarily, that lifeline, which our consciousness has to the physical body, could not be broken except at the point of death. Its sturdy connection was a safeguard against whimsical deaths.

I also knew that there was a specific manipulation that would override the safeguard. A Tibetan lama told me of the existence of this method; however, he never told me how to actually do it.

I was surprised, therefore, that in my altered state I knew exactly how to break the cord. And I knew that it would work.

I didn't know what to do. I still hoped to find relief from my affliction. That hope had enabled me to go on in the face of great duress.

I'd been warned. Using the methodology that would separate me permanently from my body, I prepared to make the leap into the unknown. Hoping to see what lay beyond, I peered again into the glowing mist. I braced myself, desperately hoping, like Abraham preparing to sacrifice his son Isaac, that I'd be prevented from going through with this awful and irreversible deed.

At the very last moment, I chose not to do it. With that choice, I found myself instantly back in my body, wide awake.

My friends of the mist were right; the years that followed were exactly as they predicted. They were worse, and in other ways better, than I could possibly have imagined. For the next ten years, I lived on sheer willpower and the hope of a cure. I sought out medical specialists, natural-health practitioners, a psychic surgeon, Chinese acupuncturists, a Native American medicine person, and even the personal physician to the Dalai Lama. In later years, I made numerous trips to two of the leading medical clinics in the country.

I was almost continually on the lecture circuit during the cool months, and I led wilderness retreats during the warm ones. I continued my practice of intuitive counseling and managed to carry on with no sleep at night. With normal insomnia, sheer exhaustion eventually takes over and sleep occurs. With my syndrome, fatigue only intensified the problem.

I was not able to sleep a single night before my busy days of seminars and intuitive counseling. During my frequent flights, I would have to stand in the back of the airplane for the entire flight. On most of my long-distance drives, I had to stop every 15 minutes to jog in place in order to provide temporary relief to my legs. I carried on because I felt driven, fueled only by the power of my will. I suspected that I was running out of time. In retrospect, I cannot imagine how I was able to continue for so long.

I wondered whether, by turning down the recommendation from the invisible world, I had challenged the gods themselves. My life was becoming even more disrupted, if that were possible. I had devised a complete physical-fitness program to compensate for the stress, yet as had been forecast, my body was beginning to wear down. In time, my immune system began to deteriorate. I had allergic reactions to various foods, household products, and environmental pollutants. It seemed as if I were becoming allergic to life itself.

I survived by taking several short catnaps during the day, and by bringing the kundalini energy up my spine. In this way, I could feel regenerated and refreshed for several hours at a time.

My work flourished, against all odds, and my spiritual abilities continued to unfold. Perhaps it was the enormous challenge of a health crisis that provided the acceleration for my development. During most of these agonizing years, I knew little of the traditions of the "wounded healer" that spoke of a physical and psychological disintegration through which the shaman-healer must go. Nor did I know that in these traditions, shamans can never use their gifts to heal themselves. It was this very '"dismemberment," as it is called in shamanic tradition, that is believed to be the source of the shaman-healer's powers.

However, I hardly believed that I was living out an archetype. I felt alone in the world, caught hopelessly in a seesaw duality between the spiritual ecstasy I was experiencing more and more in my life as a modern shaman and the physical torment I went through in the evenings.

There were spans of time that I seemed to be witnessing almost daily miracles, many of which are described in these pages. The knowledge and abilities I possessed were useless to me, though, as far as my healing went. I was following my vision, and I felt I was living out my vision. I was able to help others, but I could not help myself. My biological clock was running down.

My symptoms spread from my legs to include my left arm and left side of my chest. The previously nocturnal problem began to occur more and more throughout the day, making it all but impossible to recuperate from my sleepless nights.

After years of dealing with my illness, I had no tolerance for any additional stress. I began making bad personal decisions across the board. My behavior had grown more and more bizarre. I was no longer myself and was beginning to lose my balance.

Finally, I could not continue my vocation on even a limited basis. And so after ten years of battling my debilitating illness, I discontinued my public work altogether. I knew then that my life was over. I was sobered by the realization that the information communicated to me in the out-of-body experience ten years ago in Santa Fe was good advice. The warning that I would lose my balance had been fulfilled. As predicted, the medical profession had been no help. I was broken. I wanted to die! I'd been a fool to believe that I could override my fate. Was it arrogance or plain stupidity that caused me to go against the gods themselves? Whatever the case, I began praying nightly to be allowed to die.

It was during this time period that around two in the morning I had a massive heart attack. Marilynn and I had been separated for several years by this time. Alone in my Highlands home, I decided not to call for help. In spite of the excruciating pain, I welcomed the blessed release that death would bring.

For five hours, I endured extreme pain, waiting to die. Then at last I began to leave my body. I was enormously relieved. I was free at last. I found myself surrounded by a diffused light. No tunnel with a light at the end for me. Instead, I was looking into a space filled with incandescent light that was truly indescribable. I knew that I wanted to go there. No angelic beings blocked my passage, nor instructed me that I had to go back. Instead, to my amazement, I saw a dear friend who was very much alive and was there in her subtle body.

How could she have known? I wondered. She caught me completely by surprise.

Before I had time to react, she said, "Peter, you can't leave! You have to go back. You're needed here on Earth."

Without any questions or a moment's hesitation, I went back into my body. The shock was enormous! Overwhelmed by the pain, I crawled across the floor to the telephone and dialed 911.

◊◊◊

AN AIRLINER CRASHES

Boulder, Colorado: Winter

Four years before my return from death brought on by a massive heart attack, I was told in a dream that I would not be able to go on living unless I had fully understood the lessons of the previous life cycle of 49 years. By this I understood there to be something akin to a countdown on my life and that the clock was rapidly ticking away. In case I'd had any doubt about the meaning of this lucid dream, I narrowly and miraculously averted certain death three times. In retrospect, this time period in which I was standing on the edge of an abyss was the most dangerous and yet most transformative period of my life.

I had always assumed that the "Grim Reaper" was just a colorful metaphor for our collective fears and our wild fantasies about death. If anyone had told me that death had an actual presence, I would have assumed that he or she was joking or was swayed by superstition. But that assumption changed in an instant one crystal clear day in Boulder, Colorado. Whatever it was that began to shadow me by the foothills of the Rocky Mountains that day certainly was no metaphor. It was as real as it was terrifying.

I first felt it when I was in the backyard of our rented home on Pine Street. One moment everything was normal; the next, without any warning, a presence was hovering directly behind me. It was opaque and mysterious, ominous and foreboding. My response was visceral: My knees began shaking and then buckled. I sat down quickly to avoid falling, and I tried to get a grip on myself.

From that moment on, the mysterious presence continued to stalk me. I could find no way to elude it. I could not run from it, and there was no place to hide. I could feel it read my every thought and anticipate my every move. It was not physical death itself that I feared. I had lived a full life, I had seen many of my own past lives and deaths, and the fear of death had long ago lost its hold over me. My fear was of the presence itself and of the strange power I knew it had over me.

To say that I was badly shaken was an obvious understatement. I was almost paralyzed, barely able to control my fear and struggling to think and act prudently. In spite of everything I did, I could not make the presence leave. It had become my constant companion, day and night, as one frightening moment ran into the next, and the days themselves blended mindlessly into each other.

It seemed totally abstract, impersonal, and sublimely indifferent to my existence, and yet to me, as if it was my life at risk; it felt intensely personal, up front, and in my face. On a primal level, I knew that the Angel of Death was stalking me, and that no other force in the world could be mistaken for it.

Death could not have been any more real to me than if the Grim Reaper were standing next to me in all its spectral horror. By our usual meaning of the word, this dark presence was indeed the Reaper itself. It was not until years later that I heard that the Mexican brujos, or sorcerers, see death as an actual entity that stalks each human being until the final confrontation. The brujos see death as a peerless advisor and an ally, to be respected and to learn from.

But I was not ready to leave this world. I loved my life and the vocation to which I had been called, and I felt I had so much to share. In desperation, as if it were some kind of magical incantation that would ward off an evil spirit, I began reciting the 23rd Psalm of the Bible, over and over again: ". . . And yea, though I walk through the valley of the shadow of death, I shall fear no evil, for Thou art with me."

As I prayed, it occurred to me that I knew exactly how the shepherd who wrote the Psalm must have felt. I imagined him out alone with his flock in the wilderness, shadowed by that very same presence that was shadowing me. I imagined his initial terror, his attempts to elude the Angel of Death, and his utter despair when it refused to go away. Finally, I knew his panic when he realized that this thing, so frightening and incomprehensible, was so much stronger than he and that he had no choice but to turn to God.

I knew that I was but one of a long procession of men and women throughout the ages who have taken refuge in the 23rd Psalm in time of need. From that time on, those words have always had special meaning to me, as if they were written especially for me in my hours of greatest peril. I clung to the words of the Psalm, as if my life depended upon the strength within them.

The Angel of Death had indeed cast its long shadow over me, closing over me like a heavy pall. Perhaps the awesomeness of my situation was merely for the purpose of getting my attention. If so, it worked!

At last, after 12 terrifying days and 12 sleepless nights, I had a breakthrough in this spiritual stalemate. It came to me on the 12th night, in a lucid dream.

I am under a brilliant night sky, and I see constellations in the form of dragons. A voice says to me, "Unless you understand the lessons of the seven dragons, you will not be able to go forward on your path through life." I feel grave concern over my immediate future, although I do not know why I am so concerned.

The next morning, as I awoke, I felt the imprint of the vision of dragons on my consciousness. I knew that it was the key to my survival. Yet it was so cryptic! What could it have meant by "seven dragons"? I had been given an important riddle, but I was unable to fathom its meaning. My life seemed to depend upon finding the right answer.

Desperately foraging through my library, I happened upon a

book on symbology. I discovered that dragons sometimes represent spans of years or cycles in a lifetime. According to the information in the book, with my 49th birthday, I had completed seven cycles of seven years each. I knew that in some tribal societies, at 49 or 50 years, one was considered to have completed a full life experience. One must reach that age to sit on a council or be considered an elder or wise person.

Suddenly the meaning was irrefutably clear. I had not fully understood the soul lessons of my first 49 years, and, unless I did, I would not be allowed to go on with my life.

This came as a total shock to me. I felt that I was standing before the Almighty on Judgment Day and was being told that I had failed. My life had been weighed in the balance and found wanting! But what had I missed? What had I misunderstood? I was leading groups of seekers, and, at least by my own standards, I was reasonably successful. I had committed my whole adult life to the path of spiritual understanding. And now I was being told that my understanding was flawed and insufficient.

Needing spiritual direction as never before, I turned to my most trusted companion and spiritual advisor. I quieted my mind, and called upon the Spirit of Wisdom that has been watching over me since I began my spiritual journey. I humbly requested guidance.

From the silence I heard Spirit's voice. I was told to do a complete and thorough review of my entire life. I was shown that this was the only way I could understand the soul lessons that I had not yet fully completed.

Beginning with the present moment and working backward to my birth, I sought to understand the choices I'd made at the various junctures, the lessons learned through my choices, and the opportunities I'd missed as well. I willingly forgave myself for my mistakes and for my transgressions, and forgave those who had transgressed against me. I also followed the pathways not taken, to the next choice and the choice that would have followed, looking at what might have been gained or lost along the roads not traveled. I felt I could leave no stone unturned lest I miss something of vital importance. I set about my task with the fervor of a fanatic and the desperation of a death-row prisoner hoping for a stay of execution.

As I completed my review, I was able to see more clearly the larger patterns of my life. I saw the impact of earlier actions on the later ones. I looked at my unresolved issues and tracked their subtle sway over my feelings and actions.

The review was perhaps unremarkable in its overall findings. I experienced no heartwrenching release of pain, no repressed childhood memories, no moment of truth, no startling revelation. It resulted in no change in my approach to living. Yet, the outcome of the exercise was fantastic. To my immense relief, the mysterious presence of Death left. That very night, I had another lucid dream.

I am on a commercial airliner, preparing to leave the Denver Stapleton International Airport for Boise, Idaho, where I am scheduled to lecture and consult. While waiting for takeoff, I chat with a flight attendant, and we establish a connection.

Abruptly, my perception shifts. Although my surroundings have not changed, I sense that some terrible catastrophe has befallen us. But what? I remember that our plane took off just a few minutes ago. So why are we back here on the runway, awaiting takeoff? Why do things seem so terribly wrong? I feel it is vitally important that I remember. I reach into the recesses of my mind and struggle to bring some lost fragment of memory back into my conscious awareness. Then, finally, though dimly at first, the reality comes back to me.

Our plane sped down the runway in an icy snowstorm and then crashed on takeoff. I died in that crash, along with those I see around me. We are all dead! And yet, strangely, no one else seems to have the sense that anything is wrong at all.

For a few frantic moments, I attempt to piece together the final minutes of my life. Focus! I have to focus! I fear that I will forget again, as I had a moment ago, unless I can lock it firmly in my memory.

I now look at those around me, who are waiting patiently to continue their journey. I know my companions are dead as well, but are sharing the collective illusion that we are all alive and all is as it should be. I also know that they are stuck in their comfortable illusion and cannot move on into the afterlife until they too can understand and acknowledge what has just happened to them.

I speak to the passenger on my right, insisting that we have just crashed. He looks at me for a moment, then glances ahead again, ignoring me, as if I didn't even exist. I try speaking to a young couple behind me. They too dismiss me. "Why don't you just be quiet," the woman says. "You're going to get everybody alarmed."

I'm stunned. Everybody is so complacent, and nobody wants to hear about being dead. I feel that the passengers are irritated with me for what I am trying to tell them. Surely others also know that they are dead, on some level, but are denying it to themselves. I feel it is urgent that we all recognize our situation so that we can move on past this illusion.

I see the captain, apparently overwhelmed with guilt and mumbling to himself; and the first officer, who must have also died in the crash. I can imagine the responsibility they must feel for whatever mistakes they might have made on takeoff.

My best chance to get through to someone might be the flight attendant with whom I had chatted before takeoff. I push through the passengers, now wandering aimlessly through the aisles, until I find her. Surely, she must know something is wrong!

I tell her we've crashed and that I need her help to convince the passengers. She is startled at first and then confused, as if she is trying to remember a dream of her own. I provide the particulars, patiently filling in the gaps in her own memory. Finally, she understands. She agrees that we crashed upon takeoff and that we are dead. We both realize now that our surroundings are but an illusion, created out of our collective memories and our yearning for what is familiar.

Together, we talk to the other flight attendants, who finally understand, and then together, we are able to convince the rest of the passengers. I feel a sense of accomplishment as I realize that my task here is complete. We have freed the passengers from their comfortable illusions so that they can continue on their journey into the afterlife.

As I awoke, the dream continued to feel as real as physical reality itself. I could hardly shake the feeling that my airplane had actually crashed. It took several minutes to orient to my surroundings as I realized that I had been dreaming.

I was scheduled to fly out of Stapleton International that morning, for Boise, Idaho, and again that following November, where I would give lectures and workshops along with private consultations. I needed to make a decision. Marilynn and Rick encouraged me to cancel my flight and drive to Boise. These two had seen enough to know that my dreams and visions are often prophetic. How could I do otherwise? I knew inside that my airplane was indeed doomed and that, if I chose to fly, I would pay for it with my life.

It was a brisk winter morning in January of 1987, and a snowstorm was coming in from the west. I loaded my luggage into my car, and set out on what would be a strenuous 14-hour drive along the snowy interstates to Boise.

I had time along the way to reflect on my actions. I had canceled a comfortable two-and-a-half-hour plane trip to set out through a blizzard because of a dream? I had a nagging suspicion that all of this was crazy and that I had lost some marbles somewhere and was now short a few.

Once I reached Boise, I found out that all the airliners had been grounded at Stapleton because of the snowstorm and that nobody had crashed. Perhaps my dream was a false alarm and was never meant to be taken literally. I wasn't convinced. Too many of my lucid dreams had been precise. I had publicly predicted the eruption of Mount St. Helens based on a lucid dream. Before he had announced his candidacy, I predicted the election and attempted assassination of President Reagan to a group of about 50 people at a summer-solstice ceremony.

The days and weeks turned into months. Spring came and went, summer passed, and fall came to the front range of the Rockies. For a brief moment, the world exploded in a blaze of colors, and then, all too soon, the trees were bare.

I was scheduled to return to Boise on November 15th of that year to begin personal consultations about midafternoon that day. Even with the images of the Grim Reaper and the airplane crash still fresh in my memory, I was hesitant to undertake another exhausting drive to Idaho. No snow had appeared yet on the upper elevations of the nearby Rockies, and the days were balmy. A major snowstorm seemed highly improbable so early in the year, and commercial airlines are vastly safer than automobile travel.

I had to trust my intuition. Reluctantly, my partner and I set out on the drive together on November 14th so that I would have the next morning to rest before my work would begin. Ironically, in our attempt to avoid an improbable plane crash, we risked our necks and ended up nearly freezing to death. Around nightfall, we ran into an unexpected snowstorm on the back roads of Idaho. We had a four-wheel-drive vehicle, but the radiator froze, and we were stranded for several hours without heat before a sheriff found us, half frozen, and had us towed into a nearby town. It was a veritable nightmare. In my attempt to avoid an imaginary catastrophe, I had almost gotten us both killed.

It was the next night, on the evening news, that we learned that a Continental flight out of Stapleton International had crashed upon takeoff during an unseasonable snowstorm. Even before it was announced, I knew that the plane was headed to Boise, and that ice had somehow contributed to the crash. The morning of the 15th was indeed when I would have flown, to arrive for my afternoon meetings. I knew for certain that this was the flight I was on in my dream, and, but for the dream, I would have been in that crash.

The same snowstorm we had encountered in Idaho the night before had continued east and had hit Denver early that morning. The airplane was properly deiced, but then sat on the runway, with ice accumulating on its wings, and was not deiced again as regulations would have required. The airplane stalled after takeoff, dipped a wing, and turned over, crashing on its back.

The captain and first officer were killed, along with 26 of its passengers. Miraculously, given the severity of the crash, 54 passengers survived. If I had been on board, I know that I would not have been one of the survivors.

Conflicting thoughts and emotions flooded through my mind. My heart went out to the families of those who had died. I also felt tremendous relief that the danger was finally over, and I could fly again like normal people do. My relief was mixed with gnawing feelings of guilt and knowing that I had no way to warn airport officials of an upcoming crash. Even if someone had believed me, no mechanical malfunction would have been found on the flight headed out for Idaho that morning.

In some unfathomable way, I felt that I actually knew those who had died on the flight. I could still remember some of the faces, especially those of the flight attendants. I knew these people, from my time travel into the future, and we had shared the most profound experience imaginable—that of our own deaths. I grieved for those friends whom I had never met in this physical world.

Paradoxically, after I watched the news of the crash that evening, I hardly thought about the airplane again. Everything in my life was much the same as before the crash. Looking back, I think I know why. I had already experienced the crash the previous winter in my dreamtime, and it was as much a part of my reality as it was for everyone else nine months later in mid-November. The actual crash was merely the completion in this ordinary world of what was already true for me in the reality of my time travel into the future.

Months later, I had another archetypal dream that I felt must have been related to the totality of this whole experience, especially to the warning in the vision of the seven dragons.

I see a Great Wheel before me that begins slowly turning for perhaps a quarter of a revolution before coming to a grinding halt. I marvel that I can actually hear it creaking and settling into place. It feels very ancient. Then I hear the voice of my visions saying, "The Great Wheel turns and yet another cycle begins!" The voice then states what the lessons of the new cycle are. There are three main lessons, all of which I feel are worthy pursuits, and I know that they will be challenging in the years ahead. I think to myself, How often does one have the privilege of knowing the exact lesson one must learn? It seems a little like getting to know the test questions before taking an exam.

I occasionally remind myself that by all odds, I should no longer be alive. Whether I am living on borrowed time, or whether that time was somehow earned or bequeathed to me, I cannot say. Never in my wildest dreams could I have imagined that the fabric of reality, which we assume to be so immutable, could be altered so that I would be allowed to change my future. Nor could I have known that it would be altered twice more in the next four years. I know only that each day that goes by is a precious gift, and that it was a mystical intervention on my life path that is allowing me to share these magical stories with you.

OOO

A LOVE TWICE LOST

Boulder, Colorado, Spring Equinox

Shortly before midnight on the eve of the spring equinox, Marilynn and I were returning to Boulder on the turnpike. A light snow on the plains had just melted, but the temperatures were still falling and it was freezing again. I was ready for spring, and I hoped it would be the last snow of the season. I was wide awake.

A few miles outside of Boulder, our Toyota Forerunner lost its grip on the road, and the back end began skidding to the left. We both instantly knew that we had hit black ice, which is so dangerous because it's almost impossible to see—especially at night—as car lights do not reflect off of it.

I turned the wheels to the left in the direction of our skid and managed to control the skid and straighten the car. My quick reactions, it seemed, had saved us. Yet I had barely regained control when we hit another span of black ice, and I had no time to react.

The car skidded to the left, and an instant later we catapulted off an embankment at nearly 50 miles an hour. Although it was dark, I could see enough to know that it was a long way down. I felt a wall of protection around me, like a womb, and knew beyond any doubt that I would survive. But would Marilynn?

In a microsecond I realized that neither of us had our seat belts fastened. A seat belt could be fastened in but a few seconds, but those seconds were gone, and the opportunity had vanished in that brief span before the accident. How stupid of us to not have taken this simple precaution and belted ourselves in! In spite of my intuition, my mind told me there was no way for anyone to survive this fall.

Our vehicle turned over as it fell through the night air—finally landing on the edge of its roof and then toppling over onto the driver's side. We learned later that we had dropped about 30 feet off a bridge.

It took me only a moment to realize that I was unhurt, but I was equally certain that Marilynn had been killed. In an instant, I was trying to find her, asking her if she was okay. In the darkness, I could sense that she wasn't moving at all.

At that very moment, I recalled a dream I'd had some weeks earlier about losing Marilynn in a previous lifetime. I instantly saw the striking parallels to what had just happened. Was I destined to relive that heartwrenching anguish?

It is perhaps the 18th century, in England, and I am a well-known composer, 31 years old and deeply in love with a much younger student. I am engaged to marry Marilynn, who is my keyboard student and a prodigy at only 16.

I see myself speaking with her uncle, saying, "She has such enormous natural talent. I give her my most complex compositions, and she plays them perfectly."

On the day before our wedding, we go riding in the country, as we often did. Tragically, the stable boy had neglected to fasten her saddle properly, and it slips, causing her to lose her balance and fall from her horse. The accident is fatal, and the love of my life is no more.

I blame myself. I am so brokenhearted that I am unable to compose any more music. I am never able to reconcile myself with her death, and nothing else matters to me. I just give up. Years later, I die with a sense of desolation and emptiness in my heart.

I have recalled more than one hundred past lives, but none so heartwrenching as that lifetime when I lost the one I loved most in the whole world and gave up on everything else.

I had shared the beginning of the dream with Marilynn. Before I told her how it turned out, she said that she knew that she had fallen from her horse and died in that lifetime.

Through the blackness, I heard groans from her side of the

car. I knew that she was at least alive. Soon we heard the rescue vehicles, and help was on its way. Neither the police nor the rescue squad could understand how anyone could have survived the fall, even with seat belts fastened.

The hospital staff determined that Marilynn had broken bones in her head and later that she had a severe concussion. As impossible as it seems, I had walked away from the fall without even a scratch or a bruise.

Marilynn's broken bones healed quickly, while residual problems from her concussion lingered. For months she had frequent memory lapses, bouts of confusion, and panic attacks. In addition, she experienced periods of disassociation from everything with which she had been familiar. What did not heal and never healed was our relationship.

Although the accident did not actually "cause" the separation, it had the effect of bringing to the surface and greatly magnifying underlying problems we had not dealt with at a time in our lives when neither of us had any tolerance for such an upheaval. Consequently, our relationship unraveled very quickly in the months that followed. In retrospect, I can see that we may have been caught up in living out our shared vision that we spent too little time nurturing the personal aspects of our relationship and healing some of the emotional scarring that was the legacy of our dysfunctional childhoods.

The parallels between the past life of losing Marilynn and the present situation were obvious. We had a professional and a romantic relationship in each instance and were also best friends. We had a fateful ride together, in each lifetime, with the saddle improperly secured and the seat belt unfastened, and a tragic fall, resulting in a head injury to Marilynn, and my loss of a love that gave joy and meaning to my life.

I feel a deep sense of gratitude for having had the opportunity of being in partnership with such a remarkable woman. Marilynn was with me when I first set out on my spiritual journey, and for years we shared a common quest. It was a time of discovery and enormous growth for both of us. It was also the opportunity for us to be of service to our fellow human beings, but at a certain point we could no longer function as earthly partners.

I certainly cannot speak for my former partner, but in hindsight I perceive our relationship not as "failed" but as "completed." In a very tangible way, we accomplished many of the things we set to do during our 18 years together, including the founding of metaphysical and healing centers, an apprenticeship program, and taking groups on sacred journeys in wilderness areas. These accomplishments in and of themselves were of little importance; however, they were vehicles through which we were able to bring light and healing to a number of people, and, hopefully, to our marvelous earth as well.

OOO

REBIRTH AND RENEWAL

Highlands, North Carolina

After I had recovered from my heart attack and heart surgery, according to some strange sense of logic, I believed that I had paid my dues and that my health problems would disappear. I could not have been more mistaken. No sooner had I withdrawn from the painkillers did my symptoms return more acutely than ever.

How could I have fallen into such a personal hell? Instead of being immobilized, like a paraplegic, I was faced with a life of almost constant motion throughout the night and parts of the day. Now my left arm, as well as my legs, needed to move. Were it not so hellacious, my dilemma could have seemed comical.

I discovered that the concept of being sentenced to a life of constant motion was incomprehensible to people—including medical professionals who continued to wonder if I was having psychological problems. I had neither sympathy nor support for my peculiar ailment.

I was trapped in a nightmare. As a last resort, I tried numerous prescription drugs and combinations of drugs to bring myself relief from my symptoms. Sleeping pills and sedatives proved useless. My symptoms overrode all medications. Barbiturates gave me partial relief. Unfortunately, it took so many pills each night to have any effect at all, that frequently by the time I finally calmed down to sleep, I was totally out of it. Since I was a nondrinker and had seldom used prescription drugs in my adult life, I was horrified. Never in a million years could I have envisioned this scenario of taking large amounts of drugs to stay alive. I had substituted one kind of hell for another, and I could see no way out of this double bind.

I wondered if the gifts that I had been given had come with a price. Had the Divine Order extracted a heavy tax from me by permanently impacting my life in a way that I would never have consciously chosen?

I also wondered if my health condition was some kind of evolutionary pressure to transform my consciousness. A diamond is only formed under enormous pressure. It begins humbly as an ordinary piece of carbon. Was this principle operating in my life? Was mine the destiny of the diamond?

I had stepped off the lecture circuit, stopped my shamanic counseling and healing, and discontinued my wilderness retreats. The next five years were lost ones for me in which I was just trying to stay alive. The tribal peoples of our land believe that each person, to be fulfilled, must have a vision. To not have a vision, they say, is the same as death. I could no longer follow my vision. For me, it was worse than death. Beyond my survival mentality was a despair that continually haunted me.

Finally, after seven years, I could no longer continue down that destructive path. One morning I felt so overwhelmed that I prayed with great intensity that I might be healed. I had done this many times before but never with such passion. In the midst of my prayer, I felt a familiar presence. It was none other than the Earth Mother herself, who had come to me in dreamtime numerous times and twice in my waking state.[24] With great feeling, I said to her, "I'm glad you're back! Where have you been?"

"I'm glad *you're* back!" she replied, even before I finished my thought. "Where have *you* been?"

I was momentarily speechless. After my initial shock, I realized that she was right. I was the one who had been gone.

"Why have I not been able to find healing for my afflictions?" I asked.

Her response completely disarmed me. "I've given you so much! Look at the countless miracles in your life. Look at the many spiritual gifts I've given you. Look at how many of my children I have healed through you!"

There was a pause, as if I were being given time for all of this to sink in. Then she spoke again. "Is all this not enough? Do you still ask for more?"

Her words cut though me like a sword. I was completely undone. Never would I have looked at things this way. It was a totally holistic point of view that stretched my imagination to the limit. This exalted being, with whom I had developed such an intimate connection, was making no distinction between healing someone else and healing me. Her gift of healing to me was to heal those I had worked with for *their* healing. Suddenly and unexpectedly, I was reduced to tears.

It was a gentle and loving chastisement. I felt humbled by the truth of her words. I had given up my life of service and, with it, my vision, just as I had in my life as a composer. The Divine Mother anticipated my next question, which I had been wrestling with for years: "Why am I having to go through such suffering? I was told years ago that it was not the result of bad karma from past lives."

She said that my affliction was something to slow me down. "You are always in a hurry. You are overzealous, trying to accomplish too much too quickly! You've been too driven throughout your life." The Earth Mother paused, allowing me time to have all of this to sink in. "It is not up to you to save the world. I asked you to serve me, not to sacrifice your health and well-being."

The Divine Mother then referred to my college years, when I was a star athlete of the track team. "You were asked to be a servant of the Divine Mother, not a racehorse. Racing through life (even with a sacred mission) as in your case, can lead to disaster. You asked that we intercept you, before an even worse disaster struck you. As the saying goes, you need to 'stop and smell the roses.'"

I found this revelation staggering. Undeniably, I had been in a hurry most of my life. I never felt that I had enough time. I was always feeling rushed. I'd failed to see this pattern as a flaw. So in time, it had resulted in the extreme imbalance in my body.

I recalled something that the Shoshone shaman, Rolling

Thunder, once said to me at Rock Eagle, an ancient megalithic structure in the shape of a giant eagle. "When your personal power is awakened, then every thought, feeling, and action is magnified by that power. If, therefore, there is an imbalance within you, no matter how inconsequential it might seem, it has within it the seeds of chaos, which sooner or later will disrupt your life."

Always being in a hurry now manifested in a nightmarish parallel. I had to continually move my legs. I recalled a warning given in an ancient book of spiritual law: "Man becomes in a hurry, becomes awed at his own potential. He runs so fast that he stumbles over his own feet."

This could literally be applied to my own life. My legs and feet no longer served me and had become huge stumbling blocks. It had been so obvious that I failed to see it. Our physical bodies are our greatest teachers in life because they impeccably mirror the state of our inner beings. In spite of that knowledge, I had been searching into increasingly obscure areas in my life to such an extent that I'd missed what now seemed obvious.

That night I had a lucid dream, which perfectly reflected my situation and the way I needed to deal with it.

A teacher hands me a bottle with a goose sealed up inside of it. He says to me, "The goose is in the bottle. You have got to get it out!" The teacher leaves.

I understand this to be a test that I must pass to move into another level of awareness. Even in the dream, I remember that this is an old Zen riddle given by the master to his student to solve. I'd never known of anyone who knew the correct answer, although I'd heard preposterous guesses. As I gaze at the bottle, I feel compassion for the goose as if it were an old friend. The bottle has a long narrow neck, so a little grease on the goose would not help. I seem to know that breaking the bottle is not allowed.

But then the solution appears, and I just seem to know it. The master reappears. "I am the goose," I tell him, "because I've allowed myself to become all bottled up by my thinking. I've become trapped in the prison of the mind. When I change the way I perceive myself, then the prison walls dissolve and I'm out of the bottle."

No sooner have I finished speaking then the goose is free and the bottle has disappeared.

When I woke up, I had no idea whether or not this was the answer required of students in the Zen tradition, but I knew that it was the answer for me. I had become trapped in a prison because of the way I had always perceived my health issue. My attempts to resolve it had been linear and analytical. In so doing, I had become caught up in the dualities of health and sickness, life and death.

The dream was showing me that from a linear point of view there was not an answer. Breaking out of my prison was a material impossibility, and yet I had to do it in order to be free. That was the paradox. None of my choices were correct. All were dead ends. This then was the riddle. I could not take the normal avenues for my healing. I had to achieve the impossible. To transcend the law of cause and effect, I had to square the circle, so to speak, if I were ever going to be free.

Finally, I surrendered to the impossibility of my situation. I no longer had any investment in its outcome. Something had to happen, but it was beyond my comprehension. All I could do was wait. I did not realize, at first, that at long last I had learned the difference between "giving up" and *surrendering.* This time I had surrendered completely, totally, unequivocally.

It was a result of my surrender that I spontaneously entered a profound sense of emptiness. I felt as if some dark energy had run out of me. Somehow I stepped out of years of a survival mentality. The emptiness remained during the following months, unaffected by the vicissitudes of my daily life. At that time I didn't realize that I had made a quantum leap in consciousness.

A young, living East Indian master says that when one is on the verge of achieving an awakened mind, the forces of negativity rush in as if to prevent its accomplishment. When we make a bid for freedom, bliss, or enlightenment, something out there seems to come forth and challenges us and works to stop us. When this happens, we usually believe that we must be doing something wrong. So often when we are so close to achieving our goal, we give up. I had become brother to the wild creatures, the plant spirits, the fire, the wind, and the storm. I had merged with the Spirit of the Planet and even the Allness of the Infinite Creation.

Massive health problems were my formidable challenge.[25] I was trapped in the duality of suffering and not suffering, sleep and sleeplessness. I had failed to comprehend what was happening to me and that I had been going through some kind of final purging. Now, I understood that total surrender was the great lesson of my previous cycle—the "lessons of the seven dragons." Emptiness was its reward. I sensed that the previous cycle might have encompassed many lifetimes, rather than a single lifetime. The Dalai Lama has said that emptiness is "the ultimate expression of reality." Ironically, when I am "empty," I lack nothing; when I am "full," I always seem to want more.

It slowly dawned on me that after years of suffering, I was being given back my life. Had it all been worth it? Perhaps only the future would provide this answer.

In the months that followed, I returned to an active life. Gradually, I could see that I was a different person. I no longer had an agenda. I was no longer striving. I seemed to exist much more in the present moment. Although I did not always approve of the strange and sometimes difficult twists and turns my life had taken, I felt total acceptance.

But how could anything be the same after all that had happened? In Santa Fe, I'd come back from the brink of death. In Boulder, I'd miraculously survived a 30-foot plunge in an automobile without seat belts. I was destined to die in a plane crash and later in a desert storm, and was able, through inner vision, to intervene in my fate. And that night in the Highlands, I actually did die and then chose to come back. A few people close to me joked about my having nine lives like a cat.

What more could happen to me? What could I fear now? I had already perceived the world through the eyes of a dead man . . . and had made the decision to continue with my life.

I sensed that there was more ahead because the Journey never ends. I'd seldom had the luxury of basking in the laurels of past achievement or wallowing in my regrets.

In spite of the new freedom I felt, I began to be haunted by the mandate, from the Divine Mother who appeared to me years ago as Artemis Huntress,[26] "You are the servant of the goddess. You will help bring many back to the Earth Mother . . ."

Our planet is in jeopardy so the need now is greater than ever. More of my visions about the earth had come to pass. There were things that did not bode well for our future.

For years, I had shared my experiences and Earth visions on lecture tours and in classes. The response was overwhelmingly enthusiastic, but now they had become a burden for me. At first, I could not understand how anything so powerful and transformative could affect me in such a way.

Finally, I realized that they had become excess baggage for me. Just as I had once grown beyond organized religion, so now I had grown beyond my own experiences. I had embraced shamanism as I had once embraced Christianity, yet now it seemed I had moved beyond that, also. My visions and experiences were so interwoven into my consciousness that I could no longer separate myself from them.

To be free, I would have to release my experiences. I read over my tattered journal notes realizing, finally, that the way to be free would be to write them out as stories. I took about four years to complete *Soul on Fire*. As I finished each story, my burden became progressively lighter, until, finally, I felt free. It was at this point that I had another profound realization. I saw parallels between my personal health and the health of the earth herself. Like me, the earth's own nervous system has been thrown into such imbalance that physical methods alone can no longer save her. It has become necessary to find spiritual solutions to achieve the impossible.

Several decades ago I had visions of how the forces of chaos were likely to be unleashed.[27] I remembered my vision of the present world dying while the new earth was being born. I was no longer identified with the dying earth, but with the new world that was coming into being—a world with all the hope, promise, and potential of a newborn child. I wanted to be a part of ushering in that new world.

ooo

TWIN FLAME

Knoxville, Tennessee: November

It was during my long agonizing struggle with health issues that a woman I had known and loved for 15 years only in my dreams unexpectedly walked into my waking life. I was shocked. It was as if an apparition had materialized before my eyes. The mystery woman from my dreamtime suddenly appeared to me in the flesh. She had first come to me on the dreamscape a decade and a half ago. The memories of this event are as vivid today as they were from the beginning.

At first I believe that I am experiencing a physical phenomenon. Things seem unusually lucid. I can smell the recently painted walls as well as the faint odor of household cleaning fluid drifting in from an adjacent lavatory.

I am in Tucson in the home of my good friend and raconteur, Monica. When not keeping me riveted with laughter at her latest stories, she supplies me with clientele for intuitive counseling and seminars, and she has scheduled a seminar for me in a couple of days.

While I am lying in bed in a basement apartment trying to recharge from a morning of consultations, a man appears at the threshold of the door. I am caught off guard and wonder how he got here unnoticed. He has a short beard, olive skin, and black piercing eyes.[28]

"I have someone here to see you," he says simply, and quickly vanishes before I have time to respond. There had been a smirk on his face and a sparkle in his eyes as if to say he were privy to some kind of private joke of which I was the brunt.

He immediately disappears, and in his place stood a lovely young woman. She is tall, blonde, and probably no more than 18 years old.

I'm surprised when she greets me by name because, although she seems strangely familiar, I am certain that we have never met. Nevertheless, powerful emotions well up inside of me. I am complete and happy in her presence.

"I feel we know each other," I say with unexpected passion.

"We do," she replies with certitude, "but not on this plane!"

"Yes, that must be it," I say, realizing for the first time that I'm no longer in my physical body.

"I'm so happy to see you!" I continue, reaching out to take both of her hands.

"I am, also!" she says.

I embrace her, quite caught up in her magnetism. At the moment of our embrace, I feel a powerful electrical force surging through me. It has the effect of sending me hurling back into my physical body, and bringing me out of an altered state.

When I opened my eyes, I was aware of two powerful emotions. First, there was a feeling of profound loss. I had not wanted her to leave. Second, I realized that at the exact moment of our embrace, I went into a state of total balance and well-being. I felt complete.

This unforgettable out-of-body encounter was the first of many successive ones that occurred once or twice a year over the next 15 years. Each time when we touched hands or embraced, I would experience the same electricity emanating from her, which always put me in a state of completeness and balance. Nevertheless, I would be frustrated by her abrupt disappearance. I even began trying to think of ways to prolong our next encounter, such as not embracing or joining hands right away.

I was haunted by several questions: Who was this mystery woman with whom I felt such magnetism and who, like Cinderella, would always leave so abruptly? For what purpose were we brought together? Why did I feel so complete in her presence? Did she experience the same thing with me?

During the years following our first encounter on the dreamscape, I had the experience of watching her mature. At our last encounter, around 1994, she appeared to be in her early 30s. This meeting occurred late one night while I was sleeping.

I am in an underground cave listening to a haunting flute melody that is reverberating through its passageways. The melody has a striking resemblance to Bach's "Badinerie," but I cannot say for certain that it is the same melody.

Feeling compelled to go toward the source of the music, I discover that the musician is both officiating a wedding and playing the flute. He is a being who seems to radiate immense power. He is wearing a dark cape that represents some kind of authority.[29] This same being, in fact, had appeared several other times in my inner plane encounters.

Even though the enormous power of this being makes me uneasy, I am determined to find out who the couple is. When I walk around in front of them to get a better view, I am met with a huge surprise. The bride is none other than the mystery woman of my dreamtime, and the groom is me!

I had no idea what all this meant, and yet this strange experience left me deeply moved. It was less than two years later, in mid-November, 1996, that I drove to Knoxville to give a lecture and workshop. My plan was to remain there for a week of intuitive counseling sessions. As a result of my health problems, I had taken a nearly seven-year leave of absence from the work I had loved so much. However, on this occasion, I felt mysteriously compelled to accept this invitation.

I had just walked into the building where I would be speaking when I abruptly turned my head to look straight at a woman in her mid-30s who was speaking with a friend. Although there were perhaps 50 people milling around the room, my eyes had locked on this particular person. I knew that never before had I seen such radiant beauty. It felt as if her essence was somehow reflected in her physical body.

The woman's friend, August, who was sitting next to her, leaned over and whispered, "Did you see how he looked at you?" The woman, Astrid, slowly nodded. She had not failed to notice.

When Astrid first heard about my lecture in Knoxville, she knew that she would make the three-hour drive from her home in middle Tennessee to attend. It was not the lecture topic, but my name, which evoked some kind of inner response within her. Even though she had never heard of me, she felt mysteriously drawn to attend.

During my presentation, Astrid had a peculiar sense that she would be involved with me in some way. Perhaps she would study with me or maybe do promotional work for me. It was during my lecture that Astrid experienced something that had never happened to her before. Whenever I spoke, my voice seemed to resonate inside of her (a phenomenon that continues to this day). She became determined to get in touch with me after the lecture.

Upon returning to her home, Astrid continued to be haunted by the experience she had had with me. "What did this mean?" she repeatedly asked herself. Finally at August's insistence, she decided to call me. This marked the beginning of frequent phone conversations that continued over the next several months. Whenever we talked, I felt as if we had known each other forever.

However, whenever Astrid suggested we get together, I balked and made excuses. After all, I had already had a serious heart attack and, because of the impossibility of any effective treatment of my acute neurological condition, I felt that there was no way I could live very long. A person simply cannot continue indefinitely without sleep. Under these conditions, I certainly was not looking for another relationship. It would not be fair to either of us, I kept telling myself.

Still, I had felt such unprecedented closeness to this mystery woman. I felt an inexplicable attraction to her, although I had no idea that she was the same woman for whom I did a double take on the night of the lecture. I began to realize that she possessed wisdom beyond her years.

The time came, however, when Astrid no longer called me. Because of my reluctance, she had begun to doubt her own intuitive feelings about us. It was the fact that her intuitive feelings seemed to be inaccurate that led her to back off. The days and nights passed by, and still I had not heard from her. It was during this period that I realized how dependent I had become on our frequent, lengthy phone conversations.

I felt profound loss. What was wrong with me? I wondered. Had I fallen in love with a faceless woman?

Astrid had decided that the next move had to be mine or it was over. It would seem that the destiny of two people was reduced to a single phone call. I made that phone call! It had been several months since my lecture. Astrid was in the process of completing a divorce, and it had been a difficult time for her.

When we finally got together, I immediately recognized her as the stunningly beautiful woman who caused me to do a double take in the entrance of the auditorium on the night of my lecture. The most powerful emotion for both of us was the sense that we had always known each other; and yet, paradoxically, when we shared our backgrounds with each other we realized that there as no way we could have met. Thus, for me the question lingered, "How could I be so absolutely certain that we *had* met?" This question continued to haunt me.

It was decided that Astrid would do promotional work for me. The first item on the agenda was for me to do a few days of consultations in her area, which Astrid herself would arrange. I felt that this schedule would provide an easy reentry into the life that I once loved so much.

On the other hand, I realized that there were health risks involved if I returned to my life as a modern shaman. Something was happening to me. I had begun to have hope again for the first time. Since Astrid had two young children, it seemed best for me to move to her home in Tennessee so that we could work together. I rented a small apartment, and our relationship quickly deepened.

During this time, I continued to be haunted by the question of who this woman was that seemed so utterly familiar. Then, at last, late one evening I had my answer. I awoke, startled with the realization that this woman, who was now doing promotional work for me, was none other than the mystery woman who had been coming to me for years on the dreamscape.

Why, I wondered, had I not known this right away? It was

the same face! The same vibration! Even Astrid's age and that of the mystery woman of my dreamtime would have corresponded exactly over the last 15-year period. I was overwhelmed by this realization. I wondered what the ramifications of all this could be.

Mark Twain once wrote a story entitled "My Platonic Sweetheart," which was based on his actual "dreamtime" encounters throughout his life with the same unknown woman. The time period, setting, and circumstances would change, but he always felt the same deep love for this person of his dreams. Once he dreamed of her dying a horrible death, and the dream left him more shaken than any waking experience.

Mark Twain never had the opportunity to meet the woman of his dreams that he had come to believe was his soul mate. In my case, however, I did meet the woman of my dreams, literally, after years of knowing her only in my dreamtime.[30]

And what a 15 years it had been! So much had happened during this time. I knew that this mystery woman had first come to me the very year I was stricken with my strange affliction that had ultimately disrupted my life. Paradoxically, since our first encounter, it seemed as if I had been through lifetimes of experience, and yet it was as if it had happened only the day before.

As I pondered the mysterious twists of fate (or more likely, destiny) that had brought us together, it seemed truly impossible that we had found each other after all of those years. I decided that for a time I would not share this information with Astrid. I thought it would be better to let our relationship unfold naturally. I also knew that she needed to focus on her divorce, which was only weeks away, and to make the necessary adjustments that are always required of someone undergoing a major life change.

One day, however, Astrid called to ask me if I would attempt to communicate with the wood bees that had been boring inside her home for nearly a year as well as the honeybees that had built hives in the threshold of several doors and windows to her home and were beginning to work their way inside. My attempt was a phenomenal success in that they were gone within the hour, much to the elation of both Astrid and her four-year-old son.

The irony of what happened did not occur to me until months later. Although I had been successful in getting the bees to move out of Astrid's home, I ended up moving into her home in their place.[31] All in all, it was the kind of trade-off that I like.

Five years later, Astrid and I were married by a close friend who was a minister of a Methodist Church near our home in east Tennessee. The wedding I had witnessed on the inner planes had become a reality on the physical plane.

In retrospect, it seemed truly miraculous that we had some-how found each other in the physical world. How, I asked myself, could it have been known that we would not only meet on the physical plane but also end up in an unlikely partnership? Was there nothing that happened by chance? Soon after our coming together, I had suspected that Astrid was my "twin flame." Much more has been written about what have been called soul mates than twin flames or twin souls, as they are sometimes called.[32]

I have been told that unlike soul mates, twin flames seldom incarnate at the same time. Apparently there is the need for one to remain on the subtle planes, while the other is in an incarnation in order to provide a kind of balance. However, there are times when the commitments of one are such that the other's presence is needed on the physical plane. I assume that this is the case with Astrid and me at this time in our lives.

As energetic counterparts, Astrid and I always experience a kind of effortless compatibility. We find balance in each other, experiencing such completeness in the other's presence that it has the effect of our being in an almost continual state of elation.

This extraordinary closeness is not without its challenges, however. It is the fact that we so perfectly reflect each other that sometimes we feel as if we are watching movies of our own behavior in the other. The effect of this phenomenon is that at times we are forced to face in ourselves those things that we see reflected in the other—things that we may not always like.

Sometimes this phenomenon has its humorous moments. For example, for years I would discover that I had misplaced my car keys when I was in a hurry to leave for an appointment. This always resulted in a minicrisis. Today, I am forced to be involved in Astrid's minicrises when she does the very same thing once or twice a week. One thing we both have learned from being together is that one must truly love oneself a great deal to have such a mirror continually held up to oneself.

We were also caught completely by surprise at the phenomenon of dreaming together without any attempts to do so. From the time we began living together, we have been in each other's dreams nearly every night. Comparing notes on our dreams each morning has become a daily ritual for us.

Another phenomenon we experience is a sophisticated level of telepathy that has spontaneously emerged in our relationship. Although I have been somewhat telepathic for years, I have never experienced anything remotely like what we have. Throughout the day we are continually anticipating and finishing each other's thoughts, even when these thoughts have been obscure and quite unpredictable, and it is difficult to know who came up with a thought first. When this first started happening Astrid good-naturedly complained about my eavesdropping on her, but now she gets into my mind as often as I do hers.

It was when my health had deteriorated so much that I had nearly given up when my twin flame came into my life. On some level, she must have known that I was in trouble.

Since then, Astrid has been an immeasurable part of my healing. For apart from this healing and her continued encouragement, I probably would never have completed this book or made the decision to return to my work.

There are moments in which I pause to reflect on the storybook way we came together. I am rendered speechless in awe of how my twin somehow, against all odds, managed to reach across the dimensions and distance, and not only find me, but also assist me in pulling out of a downward spiral. Then, perhaps this is something that only one's twin is able to do.

OOO

Early one morning, shortly after I had submitted this story to my editor, I awoke hearing a voice speaking words that seemed as if they belonged to a poem. I wrote down the words and was amazed at what I read because they described the essential nature of the relationship between Astrid and myself as twin flames:

Two kinds of light
Joined to the flame
Serving each other
As one and the same.

❁ ❁ ✴ ❁ ❁

EPILOGUE

Toward a Conscious and Ecstatic Union with All That Is

In the preceding pages, I have shared a number of experiences and epiphanies that have been part of my spiritual journey. Ultimately, they revealed to me both a personal destiny and one that has been forgotten by the whole of humankind. Throughout my spiritual quest, whether I searched in world religions, in traditional and esoteric philosophies, or in shamanism, I continually found a hidden theme running like a golden thread throughout all of these systems of knowledge. This golden thread is the theme of ecstatic union with all life. Hidden behind the outer trappings of all religions and all systems of knowledge, this forgotten path of humanity can be found.

Whenever I read about the lives of saints and seers, of mystics, and medicine healers of every spiritual tradition, I discovered that, although their visions and messages differed, they shared one thing in common: the experience of a conscious and ecstatic union with the world around them. Amazingly, even though many of these people were aware of the pathos of the human condition, their state of being was one of ecstasy that grew out of a unity with the whole of Creation.

In the biblical accounts of the Last Supper and Calgary, Jesus has been depicted as sorrowfully carrying the burdens of the world. But this kind of mood would have been impossible for anyone who is in perfect union with the Divine. Jesus was most likely in a state of ecstatic joy during this time because he was in the process of completing his mission and fulfilling his destiny as the avatar for that age.

Perhaps it was my unconscious yearning for the ecstasy of being in union with something greater than myself that led me into the priesthood. However, after ten years of total absorption in that life, I realized that organized religion would not get me where I longed to be spiritually. What ecstasy there was within the evangelical faiths and charismatic movements seemed always to be focused through the very narrow lens of biblical literalism or church doctrine.

I felt that this created a shaky foundation for spiritual growth, at best, because if one truly is united with the Whole, then one must validate and honor the infinite diversity of All That Is. The expressions of ecstasy do not yield attitudes of elitism or of being part of an "elect" or of being "chosen."

It was not by poring through volumes of moldy old books that I became aware of this awesome truth about our true destiny as a people. Instead, as I have described, I discovered it etched into the hieroglyphics of the natural world around me. It happened as a result of my many excursions into the eastern and western mountains, as well as the remote canyons and deserts of the American Southwest. Sometimes these treks were for personal quests, and at other times they were to help prepare groups for sacred wilderness journeys.

As I shared in "Return to Eden," through the solitude of the natural world and the magic of Creation, I became connected to the world around me in the deepest, most intimate way I could have imagined. I became one with the rugged canyons, the misty mountains and the empty desert, one with the flowing waters, the cooling breezes and the blazing council fires. I became brother to the plant spirits, the silent forest, the deer and the coyote. And finally, I began to experience an ecstatic oneness with many of the people with whom I had become so deeply involved. These are not metaphors to express a reality—they *are* my reality!

The culmination of all of these experiences for me was merging with a great feminine deity who identified herself as Gaia, our own Earth Mother. I was taken out into the Infinite Creation and from there into the Measureless Void where I felt the all-pervading presence of the Great Mother herself.

All of these experiences had one thing in common: *They were ecstatic!*

My initial purpose in writing this book was to share the valuable life lessons in the stories, and share the very different perspective of the world from that of our consensus view of reality that these stories reflect. The deeper truth in all of this, however, eluded me for nearly three decades.

Then, one day, a realization came as an epiphany. I realized that, while seeking to understand the many lessons that came from my spiritual quest, I had failed to perceive what was happening to me personally: the growing experience of a union with the world around me that was both conscious and filled with ecstatic joy. Ecstasy cannot be experienced alone. It has to be shared. For me that ecstasy did not happen until I was in relationship with the world around me.

The pathos of our time is that we have all but forgotten that such connections are possible and, consequently, we have no idea who we really are. We cannot know ourselves in a vacuum. True understanding comes only when we see ourselves in relationship to the Greater Whole. Beyond our illusion of separateness lies the truth that we are all fragments of one Single Being. Our wondrous earth and all life on her is the manifestation of a Single Unified Consciousness.

Each of us carries locked up in our DNA an ancestral memory of a time in which we were not separated from the Creation. This original state is described metaphorically in the biblical Garden of Eden and other Creation stories. In one of my early visions, I saw that we all have been a part of many worlds. We move from world to world on a great cosmic journey, but, here on Earth, our journey has become interrupted. We have become caught in some kind of tidal backwash or eddy in which we have the illusion of moving forward when in reality we are standing still. We are in an endless cycle of recurrence where we tend to make the same choices, repeating the same patterns, and make the same errors lifetime after lifetime.

This is much like the movie *Groundhog Day,* in which we have the vague sense of familiarity that we have done all this many times before. We just do not know how to break the cycle. We have fallen asleep in the time-stream of physical existence and do not know how to wake up. This book is my *wake-up call!*

Once while on a vision quest in a remote wilderness area in Utah, I encountered a hiker who was wandering aimlessly about in a state of total amnesia. Since it was only an hour before dark, I took him back to his campsite and stayed with him throughout the night, looking after him until he could be lifted out by helicopter the next day.

Throughout the night he kept asking me the same three questions: "How did I get here? Why did I come? Where am I going?" Within seconds after my answering these questions, he would not only have forgotten my answers but also that he had asked the questions, and he would begin asking all over again. If I ignored his constant questions in hopes of catching a little sleep, he began wandering off, and I had to retrieve him. It was a frustrating, sleepless night for me in the wilderness.

While all this was happening, I began to get the peculiar feeling that things were not as they seemed. It was not until later that I realized that the larger, subtler drama being played out in the Utah outback was that of the human condition. We come into this world over and over again believing that we are here for the first time, and like that poor confused hiker, we do not know where we came from, why we are here, or where we are going.

I saw that deep down we know the answers to these questions, but we have to find that place within us that remembers. That place is deeper than the ordinary mind can penetrate. When we do remember, we are able to rediscover our connections to the world around us as well as our place in the greater scheme of things.

It is my hope that these stories will provide evidence that such connections are possible for everyone, and that they are the key to a truly ecstatic life that emerges when we begin to rediscover our original unity with the Creation. True wisdom comes out of personal experience—as opposed to mere knowledge that is gleaned from books, lectures, or through the media.When something is experienced . . . when there are witnesses . . . when the same things bring similar results again and again . . . this is science, a science of the soul, rather than another religion based on "belief." The world does not need more religions!

There have been many books written about teachings from a wise teacher or master. Unfortunately, the good that these teachings offer is often offset by our tendency to perceive these beings as separate from and superior to the rest of us. We conclude that this is about these special beings, that we cannot possibly have such wisdom or spiritual powers.

I hope that the stories in this book will prove otherwise. Years ago I longed to have a "teacher". I had many people who were teachers for me, but I could never find a "teacher," as such, back then. Finally, at the height of my frustration, I was told that in this lifetime, my task was to remember all that I have been and awaken my own abilities gained in other ages. I eventually was able to accomplish this. It is my fervent hope and prayer that these stories will point the way for others to accomplish the same things and more.

It is time for us to challenge one of the dominant paradigms of world religions and secular philosophy: the paradigm that teaches us that we are weak and limited and dependent and that only a few privileged persons can act with any real power and wisdom in our world.

The promises of all religions pale against the real experience of ecstatic union, which is sublime beyond imagining. Ecstatic union is the true and forgotten path of the whole of humankind.

These experiences, as well as the magical stories in this book, I share to offer hope for my sisters and brothers on a spiritual path as well as for the large number of people who do not have a path and are beginning to search for meaning today. I know how easy it is to give up, as I did for seven years when I was deluged with extreme health issues. I also know that often when we are closest to attaining our spiritual goals, our path can become most difficult as we undergo some sort of final purging or testing.

Each of you with whom I have shared so much of my own spiritual journey is a magical being living in a magical world. I hope that these stories have helped you rediscover that magic, along with the realization that there can be a different way of living, feeling, knowing, and being. Finally, I hope that these stories have helped to awaken your memories of what we once had as a people and can reclaim for ourselves in the present age.

— **Peter Calhoun (Snow Eagle)**

PRACTICAL
GUIDELINES

APPENDIX A

Principles for Conducting Sacred Ceremonies
to Heal and Protect Our Earth

1. *The power of a sacred ceremony increases exponentially with each additional person who joins the ceremony.* Thus, the power of two people is more than double, and three people have a combined power far greater than triple the sum of their individual powers and so forth.

2. *When ceremonies are performed at power spots, the power is amplified almost beyond conception.* Many of the major power spots are well known; however, there are thousands of much smaller magnetic vortices throughout the planet. It takes only a little bit of sensitivity to locate one. In addition, you can create a power spot by having repeated sacred ceremonies and rituals in a specific place. Any place, such as a garden, that becomes infused with the consciousness of love and joy becomes its own power spot.

3. *Solstices and equinoxes are "windows" into the annual natural cycles.* These windows provide channels to the invisible world through which we can draw in more power for our ceremonial requests. Sunrise and sunset are windows into the diurnal cycle. At noon the sun is at its zenith and there is a special outpouring of energies. The most powerful time in the diurnal cycle is the darkness before dawn because the energies at this time most resemble the moment just before the dawning of Creation.

4. *An alliance between the human and the elemental world is unbeatable.* Directly requesting the assistance

of the Nature Elementals will empower a ritual. Just as we have become alienated from the natural world, so have we also become alienated from these special beings. It is important that we restore our lost alliance between the worlds.

5. *A ceremony or ritual is a means of bypassing the conscious mind and nudging our "second attention," which is our magical consciousness.* Ceremonial movements, gestures, ritual objects, songs, and chants might seem silly to the ordinary mind, but they powerfully affect your unconscious mind as well as the subtle realms.

6. *There is a language of nature: This language is sometimes spoken of as the "Gaia Codes."* More and more people today are intuitively tapping into these codes, the understanding of which may be essential to our future survival. Many older tribal shamans of each continent still remember some of these codes, but unless we earn their trust, this knowledge will die with them. The language of the Gaia Codes is mathematical, but a higher mathematics is involved. Perhaps the key to understanding how this could be possible might be found in quantum physics theory of entangled protons, superposition, and indeterminacy instead of Newtonian physics.

7. *There is a consciousness in nature.* If you walk into a forest, the forest is aware of you. If you reach out in love to an aged oak or evergreen tree, for example, the tree is aware of your presence. The next time you visit this spot, the tree will recognize you and will energetically reach out to you. Sacred mountains, rivers, canyons, or forests are all individual entities every bit as much as we are. Their consciousness is comprised of every life form existing within their sphere of

influence, just as the consciousness of each one of us includes the awareness of every cell and organ of our bodies.

8. **Animals, including our more wild sisters and brothers, understand most of what we say.** Animals read our thoughts and perceive the pictures in our heads. They also send us pictures and feelings to communicate their needs, feelings, and concerns for us. Our lack of response to their messages is a source of frustration for them.

9. **A sacred ceremony or ritual is an energetic gift from us to the elemental kingdom or spirit world.** A sacred ceremony is not only a way to attract the elemental kingdom or spirit world's attention, but it is also seen as part of an exchange. There is a universal law of exchange that says that when we ask for something we must offer something in return, and a ceremony can be part of an offering.

10. **We must learn to listen.** The spirits, as well as the second-dimensional Nature Elementals, will tell you what is required of you to receive their assistance. For example, Nature Elementals are ready and willing to work with you in growing a bountiful garden. They will also share with you what is needed to restore balance in your environment. I have known some people who have had to promise to offset damage they caused to the land before they could get water in their wells or healing for their home or property.

11. **Always give thanks!** Giving thanks is an energetic offering to the invisible world. It has nothing to do with morality or worthiness. Remember that your positive energy and love is like money in these realms. *It is highly valued!* Your promises must be backed up with action, however, or they are meaningless to the invisible world.

12. *Always show respect!* It is best to approach our friends in other dimensions humbly and respectfully. Remember that they have been "burned" too often by humans acting as if they are laws unto themselves. No one should not lord over the rest of life on this planet. You are meant to be caregiver, not taker of their care. You need to have the consciousness of the good gardener who loves and is in relationship with the plants and animals, the waters, and the land herself.

13. *There is a spiritual law that states that each plane controls the plane just below it.* In ceremony we are tapping into the fourth dimension, archetypical realm. It is through your movements, gestures, imaging, feeling, mantras, and words of power that you can exert a direct effect on the third-dimensional, human kingdom. This is why the ceremonies described in this book have had such a powerful effect on such things as the weather.

14. *If you surrender to the earth, she will surrender to you and give you spiritual gifts beyond your imagination.* Be humble, open, and loving and always let your cup be empty and not full of self-importance or egoist needs. In time, with practice, you will develop a command over the elemental forces and their counterpart within yourself.

❂ ❂ ❂ ❂ ❂

APPENDIX B

Steps for Conducting a
Sacred Ceremony for Our Earth

1. ***Select a Location.*** A suitable site for performing your ceremony for the earth is a place with a strong magnetic field occurring naturally in nature. These fields can be identified by your bodily response of feeling immediate relaxation, calm, drowsiness, and/or a sense of letting go when you're there. Avoid places that make you feel energized, restless, or nervous. Although places that evoke these feelings are sometimes mistaken for power spots, they are *not* places of power.

    You may also make your own power spot by charging a location with your own energies of love and positivity. Once you have selected a site, whether in a naturally occurring power spot or one you have created, make an altar for your ceremony out of stones, wood, or any combination of natural materials. Your organic garden is an excellent place to perform a ceremony for the earth since it is already charged with your consciousness and love, and it is a habitat for the nature elementals.

2. ***Establish Protection.*** Facing the east, make a clockwise circle around your altar with cornmeal for which you have asked a blessing. With the cornmeal, you are setting a boundary or "ring-pass-not" for your ceremony. This sacred circle provides the dual function of containing the positive power within the circumscribed space and serving as a ring of protection against outside invasive negative energies.

3. ***Purify Yourself and the Location.*** Smudge the area within your circle, including yourself and any power objects, with sage, copal (a resin from South America), or incense with a strong, heavy scent such as frankincense or cedar. These are the best methods for purifying your energy field and protecting against negativity. After smudging, burn some sweetgrass, sandalwood, nag champa, or any light fragrance as an offering to bring in positive energies and spirits.

These fragrances and other sacred fragrances have more power than most people realize. They penetrate the subtle ethers and attract not only the nature elementals of the subtle regions of Earth's physical plane, but also the higher spiritual forces as well. They also serve to break up disharmonious energies in your energy field and help focus your attention.

4. ***Invoke Sacred Space.*** Now it is time to call in what is known as Sacred Space, by inviting and honoring the powers of the Directional Forces. Beginning with the east and moving clockwise to the south, west, and then the north, ask the power of each direction to be with you. Touching the ground, invoke Mother Earth, and finally call in Father Sky and Grandmother Moon above.

Each of the directional forces represents a fundamental principle of the Infinite Creation (see Chapter 5: "Commanding the Elements" for more detail). Specific goddesses and the archangelic powers rule these directions. The east is ruled by the Rainbow Goddess and Raphael. The south is ruled by the full-breasted Mother Goddess and Michael. The west is ruled by the Serpent Goddess and Gabriel, and the north is ruled by the Crone and Ariel.

These goddesses are more than just symbols, impersonal forces of creation, or archetypes, as many believe. Like the Earth Mother herself, who is an aspect of the Divine Mother, these are specific beings. It is important to remember that these great beings that assist us with our evolution are not abstractions. If we think of these beings too abstractly, we weaken the power connection with them that is possible. It is like calling on the assistance of the Christ Principle, the Buddhist Principle, or the Krishna Principle rather than remembering that Christ, Buddha, and Krishna are great souls who, like us, have lived on this earth and continue to exist in our timeless universe.

Finally, after calling in the directions, ask the blessing of the One Infinite Spirit, God, or the Great Spirit, however you identify our Creator. In addition, you might invite the Nature Elementals, members of the Fairy Kingdom, as well as your guides, teachers, and allies to be with you in your Sacred Space. You could also invoke specific deities if you wish to honor and ask for a blessing in a specific deity's area of power.

By creating a Sacred Space, you open a window to the powers of the invisible world. Within your ring-pass-not, linear time and space cease to exist. It is a place for your magical workings, because ordinary limitations are dissolved. This is also a place where you take yourself out of the picture, allowing yourself to be an instrument for the will of the higher world.

5. *State Your Intent.* When requesting something, it is proper to explain the purpose of your request as well as how you plan to use what is sought. In order to honor the Universal Law of Exchange, state what you wish to give back in return for your request. This exchange

is of great importance when working with our allies from other realms. Results are bound to follow your ceremony if you focus your attention and have pure intentions while in your Sacred Space.

6. *Make an Offering.* The giving of an offering naturally follows your statement of intent. As mentioned, there is a Universal Law of Exchange: When we ask for something, we must give something of equal or greater value back in return. The value of what you give is not measured in monetary terms, but in terms of what you value. What is given can vary greatly. For example, you may offer food to animals, give your time, or give of or re-commit your physical or mental energy to activities that serve the earth. Other examples of offerings are commitments to restore land that has been abused and work toward protecting endangered species, old-growth forests, rain forests, or fighting against clear cutting; or caring for elderly in your community or for abused and homeless animals.

You could also make offerings that are particularly favored by the aspects of the invisible world whose help you most need. For example, offerings of cornmeal and untreated tobacco may be used in seeking the help of the Nature Elementals. Flowers and ghee (reconstituted butter) are effective in seeking the help of the Fire Spirits.

It is absolutely essential to back up your promises with action. And, by the way, the Nature Elementals and spirits can read your thoughts—they know your true intent. With your statement of intent, you may choose to incorporate chants, sacred dances, songs, and sounds from flutes, drums, and other instruments into your ceremony. Generally speaking, the ceremony itself is an energetic offering from you to the invisible world. *Remember, it is greatly valued!*

7. ***Release the Sacred Space.*** The energy of your ceremony needs to be released into the world to fulfill its purpose. This may be done simply by saying, "I now release the Sacred Space." As you open up your circle, you may say something like, "My highest energies, thoughts, and love go out into the heart of hearts, the soul of souls, and the center of the Universe, from where blessings, love, and wisdom come forth." You can also combine this with the physical motion of raising your hand above your head and turning your hand counterclockwise (the reverse of how you created your ring-pass-not) to release the sacred space.

Remember that releasing means just that. If you repeatedly go back over your petitions throughout the day, you are actually pulling energy away from the force field you created with your ceremony instead of reinforcing your ritual. Likewise, maintaining doubts in your mind will also pull energy away from the force field you created.

❋ ❋ ❋ ❋ ❋

OTHER IMPORTANT COMPONENTS IN CONDUCTING SACRED CEREMONIES

Empowerment Through Thoughts and Feelings

The most important element left out of most books and articles about any form of manifestation or ceremonial procedure is *emotion*. Emotion is energy in motion. An intensity of feeling empowers the thought-forms you create through your affirmations and visualizations. Your thoughts and visualizations create a vehicle, and your impersonal feelings of love and prosperity provide the high-octane fuel that propels that vehicle. Do not worry about whether or not you are "connected." Remember the rule, "Energy follows thought!" Whatsoever or whoever you visualize and hold in your consciousness is certain to be the recipient of your energetic offering. Also, for manifestation and in sacred ceremonies and rituals, stating your intentions, requests, and offerings out loud is usually more effective than doing so with your thoughts alone.

Simplicity

Remember to keep your ceremony simple and to be natural. It is best to avoid making a formal speech in your ceremonies unless doing so is natural for you. Your ceremonial conversations (and any conversation) with your friends from the invisible world should flow as if you were talking with a trusted friend.

Thanksgiving

Always give thanks! It is important to express appreciation in *all* worlds! Sacred ceremonies can be performed as celebrations, not only for requests when something is needed. There is great empowerment for all when a ceremony is performed as a celebration of thanksgiving to the Earth Mother, the Four Directions, or Grandmother Moon, and, most important, to God, or however you identify your Creator.

ACKNOWLEDGMENTS

Anything of value that is achieved is never the result of one person. There are always a number of people behind the scenes whose selfless service and generous offerings make it possible. My heartfelt thanks to the following people:

Dr. Kimberly Naujock, words are insufficient for me to express my gratitude and appreciation for all of your contributions to this book and your detailed and skillful editing. You have been instrumental in assisting me and providing guidance for this project every step of the way. Kim, you truly are a kindred spirit with Astrid and me. Remarkably, you always seem to know my mind, and from the beginning have been connected to the "soul" of this book. I cannot thank you enough.

Dr. Richard Driscoll, who took the raw material of my journal notes and helped me weave some great stories and even become a pretty decent writer in the process. You were the first to give me hope, the first to see the potential of this book, and threw yourself into the project of making it happen as if it were your own.

To my former earthly and spiritual partner for two decades, thank you for sharing an incredible journey and a common quest with me.

Katy Koontz, who knows the territory of the literary world. Thanks, Katy for giving so much of your time and invaluable suggestions.

Susan Ripatti, thank you for your generous support, your copy editing, boundless enthusiasm, and the plethora of ideas from your fertile mind, which you so freely shared with me.

Pat Bradley, without your generous support, this book would not have been birthed. Thank you, Pat, for believing in me and that I had some stories worth telling.

Jill Burton, thank you for your copy edits and helpful suggestions.

Christopher Driscoll, your editorial remarks and many helpful suggestions made my work easier.

Chris Hargrove, thank you for your critical eyes and input.

Marylyn Dobson, thanks for lending your eyes as well.

Julie Costner, thank you for your wonderful cover design.

Tony Myers, thank you for your photographic work.

Jane, thank you for lending me a typewriter when I could no longer find a ribbon for mine.

Kim and Susan, I appreciate your attempts to bring me into the "terrifying" world of computers.

To the many people who have had a part in the evolution of this book who I have not named here, I thank you.

In addition to the people above, I cannot fail to mention all those who accompanied me on numerous sacred wilderness journeys, who witnessed some of the magic described in these stories, and from whom I have learned so much about myself.

Nor can I fail to mention another group of companions, participants and teachers for me. These were the marvelous wild creatures, the wondrous plants, the incredible elemental spirits of Earth, Water, Fire, and Air. Also among these were the Mountain Spirits and Storm Spirits, and the Powers of the great canyons and desert places. Most especially there was our own Earth Mother, who played such an indispensable role in getting me on my "Earth" path and has been a source of comfort and guidance on my journey.

To the magnificent being, Artemis Huntress, who came to me both in dreamtime and in real time and foretold my destiny to "bring many people back to the Earth Mother" and accurately predicted many things that have come to pass.

To Rolling Thunder, a great teacher and shaman-healer during his last earthwalk, who is often with Astrid and me in our healing work and ceremonies. In the power of your *silence*, you taught me more than any other human being and helped me to remember who I am.

To my wonderful family, I wish to express my deepest thanks, especially to:

My daughter, Rebekah, who is still the apple of my eye, for her love and understanding.

My granddaughter, Charlotte, who is such a delight and bright spirit.

Rhiannon, what can I say!? It has been quite a journey with you, watching you blossom and transform into such a talented and beautiful being.

Aidan, truly a shining spirit, for your love and patience with me through the writing of this book when I should have been out jumping on the trampoline with you or playing video games with you and getting clobbered.

Rick, though our paths have diverged, I cherish the memories of all the great times we had together. They are an important part of my past.

Lauren and Heather, you are two special ladies! I value the friendships and love you have always extended to me.

❖ ❖ ✹ ❖ ❖

ENDNOTES

1 Holy Bible: King James Version, John 14:12.

2 For example, at the Second Council at Constantinople in A.D. 553, reincarnation and the preexistence of the soul were tenets that were voted out of the church doctrine by a very narrow margin, indicating that reincarnation was widely accepted by Christians in the first five centuries. Another example is that the Empress Theodora pressured the Emperor, her husband, Justinian, to have these doctrines taken out of the Bible because as a former prostitute, she feared she might have to come back as one again in a future life.

3 Holy Bible: King James Version, Exodus 13:21–22.

4 Holy Bible: King James Version, Acts 2:2–3.

5 Burnham, Sophy (1997). *The Ecstatic Journey.* New York: Ballantine Books, p. 198.

6 Holy Bible: King James Version, John 14:12.

7 Excerpted from T. S. Eliot's *Ash-Wednesday* (1930).

8 Fortunately we had our camera with us and were able to capture this magical moment on film.

9 Holy Bible, Genesis 1:26.

10 In Native American traditions, it is said that when medicine persons (shamans) move into an area, their animal allies will soon appear, even if they were not already living in that area.

[11] Stanza from *Dzhan,* an East Indian manuscript of unknown origin reputed to be over 5,000 years old.

[12] See the story "The Goddess's Promise."

[13] Holy Bible, John 10:7.

[14] William Shakespeare, *Julius Caesar* (1599).

[15] Within a year we had our western site at the foothill of the Rockies. The prophecy was complete.

[16] A full account of the visions I received of possible futures for the earth will be included in their entirety in a forthcoming book. For a summary of these visions, please see "Visions of the Future" in Chapter 3.

[17] Doug Boyd. *Rolling Thunder* (1976).

[18] Holy Bible, John 13:34.

[19] In esoteric traditions in both the East and West, it is said that animals are under the protective canopy of "collective" or group soul until individuality is achieved.

[20] This story is shared in Chapter 5: "A Fiery Lesson."

[21] The Apostles' Creed of the Christian church.

[22] Holy Bible, Corinthians 15:54–55.

[23] In spiritual traditions throughout the world, the aura is believed to be the electromagnetic emanations of the body, mind, and spirit. Each color, shade, and hue becomes an energetic signature of a specific attribute.

24   Theses experiences are described in Chapter 3: "The Glow and Luminous Threads of the World" and "The Goddess's Promise."

25   New holistic medical information along with medical breakthroughs have enabled me to control my multiple syndromes. Medication is now available to me that relieves the worst of my symptoms without harmful side effects. I still have nights when I am unable to sleep, but it no longer has much effect on the quality of my life.

    I suffer from extreme restless legs syndrome, adult-onset diabetes, degenerative heart disease, candida, and multiple food allergies. It is always a juggling act because something that will help one syndrome often aggravates another. Somehow I am able to find a balance, and my health has improved enormously.

26   Excerpted from Chapter 3: "The Goddess's Promise."

27   A full account of the visions I received of possible futures for the earth will be included in their entirety in a forthcoming book. For a summary of these visions, please see "Visions of the Future" in Chapter 3.

28   I also had another realization. The olive-skinned bearded man was Sri Yukteswar, mentor and master for the late Paramahansa Yogananda, who is credited with bringing the teachings of the Vedas to America. Yogananda had been commissioned by Sri Yukteswar to show the West the close similarity between the Vedas and Christianity.

29   Later it reminded me of Carl Jung's "dark lord," who appeared in his dreams and possibly served as the source of inspiration for his work.

30 Later I learned from Astrid that she had no recall of our dreamtime encounters. Instead, her remembrance came through a visceral response to hearing my name and the way my voice seemed to resonate through her total being. This is a different kind of remembering, but one that is equally as powerful.

31 The full account of this experience is in Chapter 2: "Wood Bees and Honeybees."

32 It is my understanding that a soul mate is one's energetic opposite and a twin flame is one's energetic counterpart. A relationship with a soul mate involves the tensions of opposites that can be either highly creative or can be stormy because soul mates usually come from opposite points of view. It is said that one can have more than one soul mate.

❀ ❀ ✸ ❀ ❀

ABOUT THE AUTHOR

Peter Calhoun is a former Episcopal priest who has followed the path of modern shamanism for nearly four decades. He has taught an accredited course in shamanism at Boulder School of Psychology and in a number of community colleges and is currently traveling throughout the United States for book signings, lectures, and workshops on the subjects of shamanism, healing, and personal empowerment.

In addition, Peter offers an apprenticeship program for in-depth studies of modern shamanisn. He and his partner, Astrid, are cofounders of an international Alliance for Spiritual Ecology. During the warm seasons, they take groups of adults out into wilderness areas for vision questing. For more information, please visit Peter's Website: **www. petercalhoun.com**.

○○○

Vision Quests

If you are interested in participating in a Vision Quest with Peter and Astrid, please send an e-mail to **visionquest@petercalhoun.com** and you will be added to their mailing list about upcoming Quests. In your message, please include: your name, city & state, and phone number(s).

Seminars & Lectures

If you would like to sponsor a seminar or lecture by Peter in your area, please send an e-mail to **info@petercalhoun.com**. In your message, please include any ideas you have about location, dates, and times, and topics you might like addressed.

To Learn More about Peter Calhoun

Readers wishing to know more about Peter's healing, intuitive counseling, and practices for spiritual growth and personal transformation may also visit his Website at: **www.petercalhoun.com**.

Course in Shamanistic Training

An online course in Shamanistic Training is now available on Peter's Website: **www.petercalhoun.com.**

Alliance for Spiritual Ecology

If you're interested in conducting monthly ceremonies for healing our earth in your area, check out Peter's Website and learn how to join the Alliance for Spiritual Ecology.

NOTES

NOTES

NOTES

NOTES

NOTES

NOTES

○○○

We hope you enjoyed this Hay House book.
If you'd like to receive a free catalog featuring additional
Hay House books and products, or if you'd like information about the
Hay Foundation, please contact:

Hay House, Inc.
P.O. Box 5100
Carlsbad, CA 92018-5100

(760) 431-7695 or **(800) 654-5126**
(760) 431-6948 (fax) or **(800) 650-5115 (fax)**
www.hayhouse.com® • **www.hayfoundation.org**

○○○

Published and distributed in Australia by:
Hay House Australia Pty. Ltd., 18/36 Ralph St., Alexandria NSW 2015
Phone: 612-9669-4299 • *Fax:* 612-9669-4144 • www.hayhouse.com.au

Published and distributed in the United Kingdom by:
Hay House UK, Ltd., 292B Kensal Rd., London W10 5BE
Phone: 44-20-8962-1230 • *Fax:* 44-20-8962-1239 • www.hayhouse.co.uk

Published and distributed in the Republic of South Africa by:
Hay House SA (Pty), Ltd., P.O. Box 990, Witkoppen 2068
Phone/Fax: 27-11-706-6612 • orders@psdprom.co.za

Published in India by:
Hay House Publishers India, Muskaan Complex, Plot No. 3, B-2, Vasant Kunj,
New Delhi 110 070 • *Phone:* 91-11-4176-1620
Fax: 91-11-4176-1630 • www.hayhouseindia.co.in

Distributed in Canada by:
Raincoast, 9050 Shaughnessy St., Vancouver, B.C. V6P 6E5
Phone: (604) 323-7100 • *Fax:* (604) 323-2600 • www.raincoast.com

○○○

Tune in to **HayHouseRadio.com®**
for the best in inspirational talk radio featuring top Hay House authors!
And, sign up via the Hay House USA Website to receive the Hay House online
newsletter and stay informed about what's going on with your favorite authors.
You'll receive bimonthly announcements about Discounts and Offers,
Special Events, Product Highlights, Free Excerpts, Giveaways, and more!
www.hayhouse.com®